TWAIN, ALCOTT, AND THE BIRTH OF THE

ADOLESCENT REFORM NOVEL

Twain, Alcott,
and the Birth of the
Adolescent Reform Novel

Roberta Seelinger Trites

• • •

University of Iowa Press

Iowa City

University of Iowa Press, Iowa City 52242

Excerpts from the Louisa May Alcott papers, the Alcott Family papers,
and the Roberts Brothers papers are used by permission of the Houghton
Library, Harvard University, Cambridge, Massachusetts.

Portions of chapter 6 appeared, in Danish, in "Autorer og autoritet: Mark
Twain og Louisa May Alcott [Authors and Authority: Mark Twain and
Louisa May Alcott]," trans. Nina Christiansen. *Nedslag i børnelitteratur-
forskningen 6* [*New Research in Children's Literature*, vol. 6], 73–86.

Portions of chapter 7 appeared in "Hope, Despair, and Reform:
Adolescent Novels of Social Hope," *Changing Concepts of Childhood
and Children's Literature*, ed. Vanessa Joosen and Katrien Vloeberghs.
Newcastle, UK: Cambridge Scholars Press, 2006. 3–16. Published with
the permission of Cambridge Scholars Publishing.

Cataloging data on file at the Library of Congress
ISBN-13: 978-1-58729-622-2 cloth
ISBN-10: 1-58729-622-5 cloth
LCCN: 2007924057

07 08 09 10 11 C 5 4 3 2 1

CONTENTS

INTRODUCTION

What do Caddie Woodlawn and Laura Ingalls and Holden Caulfield and Ponyboy Curtis all have in common? Obviously, they are all adolescent protagonists—and independent rebels who refuse to adhere to social conventions. Furthermore, for the purposes of literary history, their nonconformity can be read as a shared form of cultural critique in that their rebelliousness results from negatively portrayed societal pressures. Caddie Woodlawn chafes against gender conventions, as does Laura Ingalls— whose story also serves as blatant libertarian propaganda.[1] Holden Caulfield's criticism of "phonies" is a well-known commentary on the shallowness of postwar conformity in the United States. Ponyboy Curtis—who runs away with a boy of color in hopes of finding freedom from the law—criticizes the rigidity of social class in his community and, by extension, in the rest of the United States, too.

American adolescent literature is replete with adolescents whose rebellions are linked to social critique. Perhaps this is no surprise, and the genre is simply reflecting the ongoing social consciousness of a country founded on concepts of civil liberty. But European traditions of adolescent literature grew out of a romantic emphasis on the maturation of the individual's creative spirit. Thomas Hughes's *Tom Brown's Schooldays* (1857), for example, equates a boy's growth with becoming more spiritual. Tom never rejects his culture; he just learns to love God more. American adolescent literature, however, even in the nineteenth century, often equates maturation with the type of rebellion that indicates the author's underlying intent to criticize the culture's values. Teenagers in more recent American literature grow to maturity, as the *bildungsroman* tradition dictates, but they often do so in a trajectory that includes rebellion as a form of social criticism. For example, Virginia Hamilton's *Planet of Junior Brown* (1971) is about two runaway boys for whom race and homelessness intersect. Cynthia Voigt's Tillerman family saga describes four orphans who face class discrimination that is exacerbated by their ages. M. T. Anderson's

Feed (2002) and Janet Tashjian's *The Gospel According to Larry* (2001) are as critical of consumer culture as is *The Catcher in the Rye* (1951). These award-winning novels are representative of an entire class of adolescent literature that assumes adolescent readers want to read—and will buy—narratives that contain social criticism. In fact, so many American novels for youth are steeped in social criticism that the phenomenon often goes unremarked. I can't help wondering why this is so.

My first impulse in noticing the strain of social criticism that permeates adolescent literature in the United States (and, to be fair, in Canada, too, although that country's literature lies largely outside the scope of my project) is to look at the two authors in the nineteenth century who wrote the most enduring novels about adolescence: Mark Twain and Louisa May Alcott. Myriad authors wrote for or about adolescence in that century, although most of them would have referred to adolescents as "youth" or "children" or "young people" since the term "adolescent" did not come into popular usage until the twentieth century. In writing for this audience, many authors included social critiques of the culture. Susan B. Warner's *The Wide, Wide World* (1850) and Harriet Beecher Stowe's *Uncle Tom's Cabin* (1852) come to mind, as do Mary Mapes Dodge's *Hans Brinker; or The Silver Skates* (1865) and Thomas Bailey Aldrich's *The Story of a Bad Boy* (1869). But only *Uncle Tom's Cabin* outsold Twain's and Alcott's work in the authors' lifetimes, and none of those works has been as widely read in the twentieth and twenty-first centuries as *Adventures of Huckleberry Finn* (1885) and *Little Women* (1868, 1869).

Two schools of thought seem to typify the received wisdom about Twain's and Alcott's endurance as authors of adolescent literature. Most traditional histories of adolescent literature segregate them by gender, assigning Twain's writing for children to a category called "adventure stories," which are assumed to be written for boys, and Alcott's writing to a category called "domestic stories," presumably for female audiences. Beverly Lyon Clark, for example, refers to Alcott as the "quintessential writer of girls' books" and to Twain as the "quintessential writer for boys" (103). Clark is, however, unusual in being willing to analyze why Alcott's and Twain's texts have experienced this type of gender separation when they are being studied in the academy (103).[2] Most critics superficially attribute the books' popularity with young readers to their ability to appeal to one gender or the other.[3] Another group of critics—largely people who teach Alcott and Twain together or who are critics of social culture—perceive the two as writing within the same traditions of American Victorianism within which other reform-oriented writers such as Harriet Beecher Stowe and

William Dean Howells and Henry James wrote. But none of those authors wrote as extensively about adolescence as Twain and Alcott did.

Moreover, critics who evaluate Twain's and Alcott's *bildungsromane* as social criticism often themselves fall into what seems to be a type of inadvertent sexism that segregates Alcott with women writers and Twain with male writers, contrasting the two because of their genders rather than comparing them because of their similar social agendas. Glenn Hendler, for example, analyzes separately how Alcott and Twain rely on "readerly identification" to evoke gendered sentimentality (113–46, 184–97), concluding that "like the sentimental novel, which registers nineteenth-century limits of female individuality in its recurrent images of death and self-effacement, the bad-boy book's model of theatricalized masculine individuality is predicated on self-negation" (194). Hendler describes Tom Sawyer's self-negation and Christie Devon's self-negation in *Work: A Story of Experience* (1873) as attempts to situate the reader in a mode of sentimentality that flourished in post–Civil War America. But both analyses are still formulated entirely around gender: Alcott's work is "women's sentimental fiction," while Twain's is "masculine public performance" (114). Feminist Lynda Zwinger believes that Huck Finn escapes sentimentality "successfully, easily, even automatically" (47) because he can escape from his father, but Jo March is forced to reenact the "plot . . . of heterosexual desire . . . constructed by and for the father" (75). Zwinger identifies this plot as the predominant pattern of sentimental fiction for female readers. Richard Brodhead acknowledges that Alcott was among the first group of public woman writers who "chose to situate [themselves] in a historical field of writerly possibilities" (86)—as Mark Twain also did, albeit more flamboyantly than any other author of the age, male or female. But Brodhead analyzes Twain's work separately from Alcott's, exploring Twain's development as a writer of regionalism, while ignoring how Alcott is herself an early regionalist. Brodhead acknowledges the early import of Alcott's publishing in the *Atlantic Monthly*—the magazine whose editor encouraged Twain throughout his career—but Brodhead cannot seem to equate the similarities in the way the two authors constructed themselves as public figures. Marxist critic Peter Stoneley argues convincingly that Twain and Alcott were mightily influenced by the emerging culture of consumerism that created a "feminine aesthetic" during the Gilded Age. Interestingly, Stoneley analyzes the two authors in different books and never connects how they both created adolescent protagonists as a response to the commodification of femininity that occurred during the era in which they were writing.[4] As critics, we seem to know intuitively that the authors who created Huck Finn and Jo March are connected, but we have not yet grappled fully with those connections. The gender division that has long separated *Adventures of Huckleberry Finn* and *Little Women* in the study of adolescent literature fails to take into account how similarly intertwined both novels—and both novelists—were in the cultural milieu from which they emerged.

What was it that made Twain and Alcott write major novels about adolescence that assumed social criticism was appropriate reading material for youth?[5] Though I've looked extensively, I have not yet found anyone who has investigated the factors that led both Twain and Alcott to write about adolescence in ways that are informed by their reform impulses.[6] Nor have I found anyone who has investigated the net effect of both authors writing such novels. Literary critics and teachers in the twenty-first century take as a given that adolescent readers will respond positively to such works as Harper Lee's *To Kill a Mockingbird* (1960) and Betty Smith's *A Tree Grows in Brooklyn* (1943) that show adolescent protagonists questioning cultural practices like racism or classism that affect their daily lives. I argue that we do so because of the marked influence Twain's and Alcott's popularity has had with the reading public for generations. My goal in this text, then, is to investigate what caused Twain and Alcott to write so similarly and to then analyze some of the effects of that similarity on American adolescent literature as a genre.

Certainly, these two writers' lives ran on parallel trajectories. Some of the parallels were coincidental, and some of them could be said of virtually any author in nineteenth-century America. But when we start comparing the coincidental similarities between Twain and Alcott, a pattern emerges in their development as writers. They both served for only a month or so in the American Civil War, though on opposite sides. Eventually, both were advocates for the rights of African Americans—Alcott early in her career, Twain by mid-career. They both chose to become writers because that profession seemed the most feasible way to support their families, yet they were both left feeling sullied as artists because of their endless need to write for profit. They both wrote for children, but only because editors or publishers they respected strongly encouraged them to do so. And both, understanding the potential for profit, accepted the challenge of writing for youth again and again—but they later denigrated that writing, even though their juveniles were among the most respected classics of the nineteenth century. They interacted with some of the greatest names of their age—Frederick Douglass, Harriet Beecher Stowe, Ralph Waldo Emerson, Oliver Wendell Holmes—but rarely interacted with each other. They lived eighty-five miles from one another but rarely met. They had little respect for one another. Heretofore, they have been only superficially compared by literary critics and historians, even though they were among the best-selling authors of their day and shared in the creation of the adolescent reform novel, a genre of American literature so ubiquitous that its heritage has effectively remained unstudied as unique.

Many of the similarities between Twain and Alcott are transparent: their best novels were both influenced by the politics of the Civil War, and both authors returned nostalgically to writing about their own childhoods when they crafted their first commercially successful novels for youth, *The Adventures of Tom Sawyer* (1876) and *Little Women*. But other similarities between the two may be equally compelling. For example, neither writer had a particularly pleasant adolescence. As adults, both continued to write for children because of financial pressures exerted upon them by their increasingly ill and needy families. Both also reflected in those novels the *zeitgeist* of romantic evangelism that shaped their intellectual growth: Ralph Waldo Emerson influenced both of them in significant ways. Twain and Alcott achieved national prominence in the same year, 1869, and adopted public personae as a result of their fame that differed from their self-perceptions, Twain becoming the flamboyant humorist whose white-clad image has become iconic, Alcott assuming a public posture as a protector of children's morality that she occasionally found distasteful. Finally, Twain and Alcott were products of the Victorian repression of sexuality that led them to seem to have, from a post-Freudian perspective, social tensions caused by their sexuality that may also have influenced their interest in writing about the young.

Twain was a controversial writer in his own day, largely for creating evocative antiestablishment characters such as Huck Finn and Pap. But Alcott was also criticized for failing to write in terms Christian enough to please the religious right of her day.[7] Especially later in her life, she was bitter about having been pigeonholed for writing nothing but "moral pap for the young" (*Journals* 204; *Jo's Boys* 50). Her publisher wanted her to write a compelling novel for adults that would command as much critical attention as *Little Women* did, but Alcott's most famous work was her "pap" for youth—just as one of Twain's notorious literary accomplishments was creating a character as psychologically dark as Pap and making him palatable to a youth audience.[8] Both Mark Twain and Louisa May Alcott, then, created "Pap" for the young, and they both had their share of ambivalencies about the matter.

In fewer than three decades, Twain and Alcott published fifteen novels for youth between them. Alcott wrote *Little Women, or Meg, Jo, Beth and Amy* (1868,

1869), *An Old-Fashioned Girl* (1870), *Little Men: Life at Plumfield with Jo's Boys* (1871), *Eight Cousins; or, the Aunt-Hill* (1875), *Rose in Bloom: A Sequel to "Eight Cousins"* (1876), *Under the Lilacs* (1878), *Jack and Jill: A Village Story* (1880), and *Jo's Boys, and How They Turned Out: A Sequel to "Little Men"* (1886). Twain wrote *The Adventures of Tom Sawyer* (1876), *The Prince and the Pauper* (1882), *Adventures of Huckleberry Finn* (1885), *A Connecticut Yankee in King Arthur's Court* (1889), *Personal Recollections of Joan of Arc* (1896), *Tom Sawyer Abroad* (1896), and *Tom Sawyer, Detective* (1896).[9] The intellectual intersections of these novels include a range of ideological issues and assumptions about adolescence. As a corpus, they have a number of often unconsidered similarities.

Thus, *Twain, Alcott, and the Birth of the Adolescent Reform Novel* explores the biographical and historical influences on Twain's and Alcott's novels for youth, while also providing an exploration of the genre-defining intellectual trends that emerged from their novels—in terms of the works that Twain and Alcott wrote for the young and in terms of the many novels in the literary legacy that Twain and Alcott solidified in the United States. Both authors relied on adolescents as metaphors for reform; that is, for both of them, the young represented the capacity for change that is necessary for a culture itself to change. Whether these two novelists were writing about race or gender or education or any other aspect of Victorian progressivism, their youthful protagonists provided them with a site for the potential to change that is a prerequisite of reform.

This book relies on the methodologies of American Studies, pulling together biographical studies, the history of ideas, publishing history, and literary criticism. Chapter 1, "The Fantasy of Self-Reliance: An Introductory Biography," lays out the biographical aspects of Twain's and Alcott's lives that are pertinent to an analysis of their writing for children. As early as 1961, Albert E. Stone, Jr., lamented that writing about Twain is "now so voluminous that few writers today can hope to be wholly original" (135n22). While that was not then true of Alcott's biography, it certainly is now, more than forty years later. My goal in this biographical first chapter, then, is to elucidate those factors that influenced both authors to write for a youth audience. I am particularly interested in how they struggled with the impossibility of leading independent lives, given their families' dependence on them. (Readers already intimately familiar with Twain's and Alcott's biographies might find more to interest them in the later chapters of historical interlude that provide contextualized analyses of the factors that influenced both authors to write for youth.) Chapter 2 is a chapter of literary criticism. Entitled "The Metaphor of the Adolescent Reformer: *Adventures of Huckleberry Finn* and *Little Women*," the chapter demonstrates how Huckleberry Finn and

Jo March function in remarkably similar ways to model for contemporary Americans the need for social reform.

Chapter 3, "Historical Interlude: *Vita Religiosa* and Romantic Evangelism," continues the historical work of this project by assessing the intellectual history of the era in which Twain and Alcott wrote, particularly in terms of the religious history of romantic evangelism that influenced them to write as reformers. The next two chapters of literary analysis rely on the history of ideas that that interlude has described. Chapter 4, "Education and Reform: Victorian Progressivism in Youth Literature," examines Twain's and Alcott's educational ideologies in *An Old-Fashioned Girl*, *The Prince and the Pauper*, *A Connecticut Yankee in King Arthur's Court*, and *Little Men* as they are influenced by romantic evangelism. Chapter 5, "Gender and Reform: New Women and True Womanhood," continues the same work as chapter 4 but focuses instead on gender ideologies in such novels as *Eight Cousins*, *Rose in Bloom*, *Jo's Boys*, and *Joan of Arc*. The goal of these three chapters is to trace how social engagement came to saturate adolescent literature as a genre in the United States.

Chapters 6 and 7 continue the historical project of examining the causes and effects of Twain's and Alcott's writing for youth. Chapter 6, "Historical Interlude: Authors, Authority, and Publication," examines both authors' attitudes toward publishing, especially publishing juveniles. William Dean Howells of the *Atlantic Monthly* and Thomas Niles of Roberts Brothers emerge as especially influential on Twain's and Alcott's careers as writers of juveniles. Undeniably, publishing for youth proved lucrative—especially to authors like Twain and Alcott who learned to capitalize on the American demand for novels about adolescents engaged in social change. Chapter 7, "Adolescent Reform Novels: The Legacy of Twain and Alcott," traces the influence that Twain's and Alcott's reform-minded adolescent protagonists have had on adolescent literature in the United States. The vast majority of novelists who write consciously about social change in adolescent literature have been in some way affected by either Twain or Alcott or both. The influence of these authors on the genre is significant, and connecting the ideological patterns in contemporary fiction to the progenitors of this pattern seems long overdue.

I have chosen to write about novels in *Twain, Alcott, and the Birth of the Adolescent Reform Novel*, rather than the many short stories and sketches available by both authors, for two reasons. First, Twain's and Alcott's novels have been far more widely read and available to audiences throughout the world—and are thus more influential—than much of the ephemera the authors published in periodicals. Second, the novels are inclusive enough to make the points that I hope to make. Indeed, I have not included for in-depth analysis in this book two of Alcott's children's novels, *Jack and Jill* and *Under the Lilacs*, because I believe that her other novels make the case I am trying to make thoroughly enough without their inclusion.

The problem of what to call Mark Twain/Samuel Clemens also besets my work, as it has the work of numerous other critics. When I write about him as a historical figure—in chapter 1 and the historical interludes, chapters 3 and 6—I tend to refer to him as "Samuel Clemens." In the chapters in which I am writing about him as an author or a public persona—chapters 2, 4, 5, and 7—I tend to refer to him as Mark Twain. There seems to be no elegant solution to this dilemma, as Forrest Robinson aptly points out (14–18), so I apologize for the times that my usage seems inconsistent.[10]

I would also like to note that the material I quote herein reflects the authors' original punctuation, italicization, and—especially in Alcott's case—occasional bad grammar. (Her works frequently include a space in a contraction: "should n't," and she often fails in her letters to include the apostrophe in a contraction: "dont.") Rather than littering so many quotations with "italics in the original" and "[*sic*]," I have chosen to quote material as it was written in its original source, unless otherwise noted.

Twain and Alcott participated in a cultural dynamic that marked the changing nature of adolescence in America. Their novels for youth, published in the twenty-eight years between 1868 and 1896, reflected the increasing cultural attention being paid to the potentiality of youth. Victorians recognized that young people have the potential to be educated (for better or for worse), they have the potential to participate in a culture as reformers or as people in need of reform, and they have the potential to participate in a consumer economy. The extension of adolescence as a stage of life in which people should be segregated into high schools, where they interact largely with their peers, did not become institutionalized in the United States until the twentieth century (Mintz 185–99). But the evolution of adolescence as an educational and psychological concept could only emerge in a culture that believed a transitional stage between childhood and adulthood existed. Twain and Alcott were two of the voices that contributed to that belief. The factors that led them to write for youth and the effects of their decisions about how and what to write for that audience involve the literary and intellectual history of two people—and the nation in which they lived.

The scholars who worked with me to shape this manuscript deserve much of the credit for inspiring me. Mike Cadden has been endlessly supportive, reading the full manuscript and managing to make me laugh in the process. Anita Tarr also read the full manuscript, writing her own wry comments as she went. J. D. Stahl and Mark West kindly shared their comments with me as well. Susan Stewart read early drafts and provided encouragement when I needed it most; Karen Coats provided many hours of the type of brainstorming and laughter that makes being an academic worthwhile.

Other scholars have provided venues in which I have been able to garner public feedback about Twain and Alcott. I am grateful to Kara Keeling and Scott Pollard for hosting my presentation on this material at Christopher Newport University. Kenneth Lindblom and Patricia Dunn were equally gracious in hosting me at the State University of New York at Stony Brook. Nina Christensen made it possible for me to share my work with the Center for Børnelitteratur in Copenhagen, and she translated portions of chapter 6 into Danish for their publication, *Nedslag i børnelitteraturforskningen* (*New Research in Children's Literature*). Betsy Hearne and the members of the Youth Literature Interest Group provided insightful comments at the University of Illinois at Urbana-Champaign. Cindy Christiansen of Boston University hosted me during the glorious week I spent in 2004 researching the Alcott family materials at the Houghton Library at Harvard University by day and watching the BoSox beat the Yankees to win the pennant by night. I thank all of these friends for their intelligent commentary and kind-hearted encouragement—and for their willingness to make merry whenever possible.

The graduate students in my Twain and Alcott seminar in the spring of 2006 at Illinois State University deserve much credit for helping me refine the existing manuscript into its present state. Jennifer Gyursin, Heidi Oldenburger, Mindy Mahannah, Ben Smallwood, and Melissa Smith suffered through my enthusiasms with amazing good cheer and even more amazing scholarly acuity. A similar seminar in 1995 included Sally Parry, Denise Anton Wright, Michelle Martin, Linda Benson, Christie Lau, and Candy Jendro. Their ideas influenced the early stages of this work.

As far as I can tell, librarians make all things scholarly possible. The librarians at Harvard University's Houghton Library, the University of Illinois at Urbana-Champaign's Rare Book and Manuscript Library, and the Concord Free Public Library provided me with both new materials and new insights. Moreover, the librarians at Illinois State University's Milner Library have supported this project for many years. Pat Meckstroth, Vanette Schwartz, and Kathe Conley deserve special note for their dedication to serving others in the name of scholarship.

As for the publishing process, I could describe the University of Iowa Press staff in the same terms that one of Alcott's characters describes her publisher: Holly Carver is "generous, kind, and the soul of honor" (*Jo's* 188), as are Joe Parsons (who accepts and forgives how obsessive-compulsive I am) and Charlotte Wright and Alayna Cohen (who are ever-patient in the face of said OCD).

The two advisors during my academic career who were most influential in teaching me how to be a scholar are Lilian R. Furst, who directed my master's thesis on Alcott, and J. R. LeMaster, who directed my dissertation on Twain. Were it not for them, I would never have conducted the original studies that culminated in this book, nor would I have had the self-confidence to try.

Because this work began during a difficult time in my administrative career, I wish to thank those people who gave me the reassurance it took for me to sit down and write another book. For supporting my sabbatical, inspiring chapter 6, and helping to secure funding for this book's publication, my department chair, Tim Hunt, deserves special commendation, as does another department chair who gently refuses to let my spirits flag, Rick Martin. I am blessed with many friends who have been willing to listen to and laugh with me: Susan Burt, Pam Riney-Kehrberg, Sally Parry and Bob McLaughlin, Peggy Haycraft, the 10's (Susan Sprecher, Barb Heyl, and Judi Sevel), Sarah Diel-Hunt, Jonathan and Lisa Rosenthal, Barb Blake, Pat Witzig, Kathy Kiessling, Karen Khusro, Lisa Choate, Norma Huber, and Laura Pedrick, who helped me outline this work during an intellectually rejuvenating camping trip with our families one summer in Michigan. Diane Smith has helped me keep things running while I write, for which I am deeply grateful. And Peter Hunt continues, as he always has, to challenge my thinking in numerous ways.

I must conclude, as many acknowledgments do, with recognition and respect for my loving and supportive family. My husband, George F. Seelinger, and our children, George H., John, and Katharine Seelinger, have been enthusiastic during trips to Hannibal and Boston, forbearing during my many absences, patient while I've been obsessing, and genuinely willing to celebrate Alcott's birthday every year on November 29 and Twain's on November 30. (We eat plummy cakes on the 29th and devil's food cake on the 30th, of course.) I am blessed to have a family with whom I can share Twain's and Alcott's reform novels for youth.

ABBREVIATIONS

LthP   Twain, Mark. *Mark Twain's Letters to his Publishers,
                      1867–1894.* Ed. Hamlin Hill. Berkeley: U of California
                      P, 1967.

MT&EB   Twain, Mark. *Mark Twain and Elisha Bliss,* by Hamlin
                      Hill. Columbia: U of Missouri P, 1964.

MT-Howells Letters Twain, Mark. *Mark Twain-Howells Letters: The
                      Correspondence of Samuel L. Clemens and William D.
                      Howells, 1872–1910.* Eds. Henry Nash Smith and
                      William M. Gibson. Cambridge, MA: Belknap, 1960.

TWAIN, ALCOTT, AND THE BIRTH OF THE

ADOLESCENT REFORM NOVEL

CHAPTER ONE

The Fantasy of Self-Reliance
An Introductory Biography

"I have paddled my own canoe since I was thirteen."
—MARK TWAIN

"I'd rather be a free spinster and paddle my own canoe."
—LOUISA MAY ALCOTT

The central irony of the relationship between Samuel Clemens and Louisa May Alcott lies not in the authors' differences, but in their frequently ignored similarities. Of specific interest are the social, economic, and psychological factors that led both of them to use adolescence as a platform from which to write about reform. With *Adventures of Huckleberry Finn* and *Little Women*, these two authors established literary patterns that are still being replicated by novelists in the twenty-first century. Although their interactions with each other were few and not particularly kind-spirited, Clemens and Alcott nonetheless shared some values and biographical similarities that establish a context for comparing their novels for youth.

My analysis of their literary influence must, perforce, start with brief biographies of each author. Examining their lives side by side clarifies some of the ways in which they were and were not alike. Their family backgrounds, their psychological profiles, their troubled youths, their involvement in the Civil War, their attitudes toward their families and financial success, their communities, and their apparently conflicted sexualities mark multiple aspects of their biographies that significantly influenced their writing for youth. Moreover, both authors experienced their first major literary success in 1869, and in those writings, both rely on parallel rhetorical tropes that demonstrate some of the similarities in their writing styles. Their shared intellectual heritage—which I discuss at greater length in the historical interlude that follows as chapter 3—may well be the sine qua non that made it possible for them to become authors of adolescent literature. And their shared attitudes toward publishing—which I assess in another historical interlude, chapter 6—provide a context for the publication of juveniles, both theirs and those of the authors they influenced. The many connections between Clemens's and Alcott's lives establish a strong basis from which to understand why they both employed adolescent reformers as characters in their most famous novels.

Mutual Disregard

Although Clemens and Alcott were influential figures in American literary history, they seem to have had little respect for each other. A poem parodic of Alcott's writing that is attributed to Clemens was published in the *Buffalo Express* on September 25, 1869, months after the second volume of *Little Women* was published. The poem assumes the self-righteous tone of a group of pious young women, but turns into gender comedy in the final couplet. The poem was signed "Some of the Little Women" and reads, in its entirety:

> Mr Twain:
> Honored Sir—We have seen, from your pen,
> An article headed, "Last Words of Great Men."
> O, thank you, sir! Bless you! You've started a doubt;
> That shall grow till it puts our maligners to rout;
> For these great men were married, or some of them were,
> That's certain; and we, sir, shall beg to infer,
> Hence, the probable end of a charge we have heard,
> That a man with a wife never has the last word.
> Yours truly,
> Some of the Little Women (Scott 70)

Twain's column to which the poem refers, "Last Words of Great Men," is a comic sketch about the inadequacy of most people's dying words. The "Great Men" include, by the way, Queen Elizabeth, Joan of Arc, and Empress Josephine, who Twain claims said on her deathbed, "'Not for Jo—' and could get no further" (*MT at the* Buffalo Express 46). While it seems unlikely that Twain is connecting Jo March and Empress Josephine in "Last Words of Great Men," he is certainly parodying Jo and her sisters in the poem he himself wrote pretending to protest his own column.

Another intersection between the two authors occurred when both were present at a lecture by Charles Kingsley, author of the British children's novel *The Water-Babies* (1863), in Boston on February 17, 1874. Alcott, who kept a detailed journal for much of her life, noted that she attended the lecture. She described how pleasant Kingsley was, but did not mention in her journal entry about the event that Twain had introduced the speaker.

The most notable tension that is alleged to have occurred between the two happened in 1885, with the release of *Adventures of Huckleberry Finn*. On March 2, 1885, the *New York World* described the book as "cheap and pernicious stuff" (Budd, *Contemporary Reviews* 265); on March 5, the *Boston Evening Traveller* called it "singularly flat, stale and unprofitable" (267). On March 12, the *Boston Advertiser* expressed regret that "the author laid himself open to the charge of coarseness and bad taste" (268). On March 17, following all this bad press, the *Boston Transcript* reported that the Concord Public Library in Massachusetts had banned the book from the library:

> One member of the committee says that, while he does not wish to call it immoral, he thinks it contains but little humor, and that of a very coarse type. He regards it as the veriest trash. The librarian and the other members of the committee entertain similar views, characterizing it as rough, coarse, and inelegant, dealing with a series of experiences not elevating, the whole book being more suited to the slums than to intelligent, respectable people. (Kesterson 17)

Alcott did not sit on the library committee that banned the book, but her close friend Edward Emerson—Ralph Waldo Emerson's son—did ("Town Officers" 5).[1]

Later that month, Clemens responded with characteristic wit in a letter to the Concord Free Trade Club that the library's action had doubled the sales of the book and would prompt those who had bought it "to read it, out of curiosity, instead of merely intending to do so" (*MT-Howells Letters* 2.876–79). Frank Luther Mott claims that Alcott responded to the letter by saying, "If Mr. Clemens cannot think of something better to tell our pure-minded lads and lasses, he had best stop writing for them" (249).[2] Even if Mott's assertion of Alcott's comment is apocryphal, the incident illustrates the public roles that both Twain and Alcott played in 1880s New England. Twain was a bad boy, but the lovable type, like Tom Sawyer, who could be forgiven because of his good heart. Alcott was a bluestocking—a literary spinster and suffragette—who was known for her moralistic children's fiction. Both were best-selling authors at the time, Twain because of his fictionalized travel writing and *The Adventures of Tom Sawyer*, Alcott because the seven successful children's novels she had published by 1885 made her the best-selling author of novels for youth in the U.S. Moreover, Alcott was consciously a strong-minded reformer who believed passionately in women's rights, especially the right to vote. During Alcott's lifetime, however, Clemens was publicly ambivalent about women's suffrage, although he reversed his position later in life.[3]

A well-documented episode in Clemens's public life marks particularly well how his occasionally inappropriate behavior created tension between his roots as a Western humorist and the East Coast intelligentsia that he aspired to be part of and to which Alcott belonged. On December 17, 1877, Clemens was invited to speak in Boston at the seventieth birthday celebration of American poet John Greenleaf Whittier. The birthday party was sponsored by the *Atlantic Monthly*, so Clemens's close friend, William Dean Howells—editor of the *Atlantic Monthly*—served as toastmaster for the event. After Howells introduced Twain to the group of fifty-eight distinguished literary men, the humorist regaled them with a burlesque he had written about three scoundrels he once met in a mining town in the California Sierras. The three rapscallions in the sketch dub themselves "Ralph Waldo Emerson," "Oliver Wendell Holmes," and "Henry Wadsworth Longfellow." All three of those literary giants were in the room, and none of them—nor Whittier—laughed at Twain's recounting of how these three characters drank whiskey, cheated at cards, and misquoted the authors they purported to be. The speech anticipates much of the king's and the duke's comic pretentiousness in *Adventures of Huckleberry Finn*, so it is important as a literary precursor to Twain's greatest novel. But it also puts into perspective how Clemens regarded himself as an imposter in the literary scene of the day. On December 23, Clemens wrote to Howells:

> My sense of disgrace does not abate. It grows. I see that it is going to add itself to my list of permanencies—a list of humiliations that extends back to when I was seven years old, & which keep on persecuting me regardless of my repentancies.
>
> I feel that my misfortune has injured me all over the country; therefore it will be best that I retire from before the public at the present. It will hurt the Atlantic for me to appear in its pages, now. So it is my opinion & my wife's, that the telephone story had better be suppressed. . . .
>
> It seems as if I must have been insane when I wrote that speech & saw no harm in it, no disrespect toward those men whom I reverenced so much. And what shame I brought upon *you*, after what you said in introducing me! It burns me like fire to think of it.
>
> The whole matter is a dreadful subject—let me drop it here—at least on paper.
>
> Penitently yrs
>
> Mark (*MT-Howells Letters* 212)

Clemens's sense of shame in the face of having potentially hurt men he "reverenced" was profound, even though Howells and Whittier later tried to reassure him that no one had been as offended as he imagined.

Louisa May Alcott also reverenced the men who were the butts of Clemens's joke at the *Atlantic* dinner. She was especially fond of Emerson, about whom she wrote: "He is the god of my idolatry, and has been for years" (*Journals* 99), although his son, Edward, noted that when Alcott was twenty-five, she had fun gently parodying his father in a performance during which she referred to him playfully as "Rolf Walden Emerboy" (Shealy, *Alcott* 95). When Ralph Waldo Emerson died, she described him as "our best & greatest American" and an "illustrious & beloved friend" (*Journals* 234). She could not possibly have found humor in the situation of the Whittier dinner if it was ever recounted to her, and it seems possible that it might well have been. The *Springfield Republican*—a newspaper Alcott read and had been published in—reminded its readers in 1885 of the Whittier dinner when it was excoriating *Huckleberry Finn* for being "trashy and vicious": "The trouble with Mr. Clemens is that he has no reliable sense of propriety. His notorious speech at an Atlantic dinner, marshalling Longfellow and Emerson and Whittier in vulgar parodies in a Western miner's cabin illustrates this, but not in much more relief than the 'Adventures of Tom Sawyer' did, or these Huckleberry Finn stories do" (qtd. in Vogelback 270). Alcott might have agreed with the *Springfield Republican*'s assessment that the Whittier dinner lacked propriety; Clemens certainly did.

Psychological Tension

The causes of Clemens's and Alcott's apparent disregard for one another could easily be explained as a function of their backgrounds. Through her mother, Alcott descended from the Boston upper class, including the only judge of the Salem witchcraft trials, Samuel Sewall, to recant his decisions after the trial. Through Alcott's father, the family participated in the grandest philosophical movement of antebellum America, transcendentalism. Clemens, on the other hand, a westerner, descended from a family that had lost its money and land well before the Civil War. He moved permanently to the East Coast after he married into money, and his entrée into literature was as a humorist rather than as a novelist. It seems entirely possible that Alcott would have regarded Clemens as vulgar and déclassé, while Clemens likely considered her a snob and a prig. It is almost certain that both would have been partly right in their opinions.

They would have also been partly wrong, however, because both of them were much more complex people than these putative stereotypes of their personae allow, as a multitude of their biographies has shown. Like many nineteenth-century writers, including Charles Dickens and Harriet Beecher Stowe, Twain and Alcott struggled with anxieties and self-doubts that led them to write in multiple genres as they sought to earn their fortunes. Their family lives were complicated by finances, poor health, and depression—yet they were both sustained throughout their careers by their families' confidence in them and their writing. Both were entangled in various political agendas, sometimes even taking apparently self-contradictory political stances. Many biographers and critics have been obsessed with pointing out the internal conflicts that created their psychological tension. For example, critics from Justin Kaplan to Fred Kaplan have debated whether Samuel Clemens and Mark Twain represent opposing sides of one man's nature.[4] While Justin thinks so and Fred thinks not, both critics explore the interior dichotomies that motivated the writer's public persona.[5] Regardless of what anyone considers the cause of Clemens's at times contradictory personality, his biographers often assume that his personality had both public and private manifestations in which optimism competed with cynicism. For my purposes, another reading of the Twain/Clemens duality might be to observe that his adolescent faith in the Romantic potential of mankind warred with his more adult cynicism. When Clemens writes for children, his cynicism is more veiled than it is when he writes for adults in such texts as *The Innocents Abroad* (1869), *The Tragedy of Pudd'nhead Wilson* (1894), *What Is Man?* (1898), or *The Mysterious Stranger* (1916)—but neither the optimism nor the cynicism ever disappears entirely from his writing for any audience.

Alcott, on the other hand, has had her darker side attributed to everything from repressed sexuality to emerging feminist anger. Madelon Bedell identifies Alcott's Freudian struggle with her father as the source of her sexually repressed imagination.[6] Indeed, Alcott's father believed that Louisa's temper came with the dark complexion she had inherited from her mother, while he and Anna, Louisa's sister, were more peaceful because of their fair complexions (Bedell, *Alcotts* 74; Strickland 30).[7] Like Bedell, Sarah Elbert assumes sexual repression is the source of the psychological darkness that led Alcott to write sensational psychodramas in her youth and to depression in later life (e.g., *Hunger* 110). Martha Saxton notes how much guilt motivated Alcott, which Robinson also notes of Clemens (e.g., Saxton 354; Robinson 19).[8] Their feelings of guilt were exacerbated by their perceptions—and their families'—that they were socially maladroit. As with Clemens's, Alcott's biographers have tended to depict her as a psychologically complex figure whose imagination was stimulated by repressed emotions. And as with Clemens, the depression she appears to have experienced may well have involved the relationship between her frustrated youth and her inability to reach what she perceived as her own adult potential.

Additionally, both Alcott and Clemens felt burdened by the public pressures placed on them by their fame. Clemens intentionally cultivated the well-known public personality "Mark Twain" by manifesting a public sense of humorous irascibility and wearing showy white suits as he grew older. But fame intruded into his family life, and his self-created image must have been a hard one to live up to, especially in his later life. For Alcott, on the other hand, her public persona required that she be a wholesome protector of childhood's purity, a role that she did not always enjoy. She especially resented people who lionized her, expecting her to look and act like Jo March. She detested autograph hounds and fan letters that required her attention; she did not want to define herself always in terms of her writing for the young. In chapter 3 of *Jo's Boys*, Alcott parodies the persona of the "literary nursery-maid"; Jo March complains about "lion-hunters in search of their prey" and then laughs about her fans' naïveté when they expect a woman of her age to look like her adolescent characters (50). Alcott did not enjoy her fame as much as Clemens seems to have, but they both, nonetheless, found their lives changed radically by the excessive enthusiasm of their admiring public.

Perhaps every great writer can be described as psychologically tormented, sometimes by fame, sometimes by troubled youths and family lives, but Clemens's and Alcott's biographers have made an industry of pointing out those facts about both of them. And since angst is such an omnipresent condition in adolescent literature, that particular parallel between the two authors' lives seems worth noting. It is likely that the same psychological phenomena that keep intriguing their biographers led Clemens and Alcott to create believable adolescents, such as Huck and Jo, who are morally conflicted and occasionally angst-ridden.

Pressured Youths

Like virtually every American in the nineteenth century, Clemens and Alcott had youths that were truncated by family tragedy. Both of them, however, experienced some of the same traumas: premature deaths of siblings and downward social mobility from their fathers' financial irresponsibility that caused their families to move multiple times. One of Alcott's childhood neighbors in Concord, Lydia Hosmer Wood, reported that the Alcott family was reputed to have moved "twenty-one times within twenty-two years" (qtd. in Shealy, *Alcott* 163). Clemens moved well over a dozen times before he was twenty-one: in addition to moving from Florida, Missouri, to Hannibal, Missouri, his family moved five times within the town of Hannibal (Powers 32–45), and between

1853 and 1856, Clemens moved eight more times (LeMaster and Wilson xiii). While death, disease, poverty, and mobility were not uncommon for many families in the antebellum U.S., Clemens and Alcott seemed to develop in their youths an inflated sense of responsibility for supporting their families financially because of their fathers' impecuniousness and their families' itinerant tendencies.

Clemens's life story is so well-known that it bears little need for re-biographizing. He was born in Florida, Missouri, the sixth of seven children born to John Marshall Clemens and Jane Lampton Clemens. His birthday was November 30, 1835, which was, incidentally, the day after Louisa May Alcott's third birthday. His father was a lawyer whose family fortune was lost following the premature death of his own father in 1805. The Clemenses moved from Tennessee in 1835 to Florida, Missouri, and to Hannibal in 1839. Samuel's sister Margaret died that year, and his brother Benjamin died in 1842. Seeking to reverse the family's failing fortunes, John Clemens opened a law office and a general store in Hannibal. When his father died in 1847, young Sam quit school and began work, eventually becoming apprenticed as a printer's devil to Joseph Ament, who was the publisher of the Hannibal *Courier*. Clemens's mother remained dependent on him and his brother and sister for the rest of her life, just as Alcott's father would be dependent on her financially for her entire late adolescence and adult life. In 1853, Clemens moved to St. Louis and then to New York City to work as a typesetter, returning to work as a journalist and printer at various towns along the Mississippi from 1854 to 1857. In 1857, Horace Bixby agreed to teach him steamboat piloting, and he worked on the Mississippi River until the outbreak of the Civil War. In 1858, Sam's brother Henry died in a steamboat explosion. Only days earlier, Samuel had been sent to work on a different boat from the one on which Henry was clerking, so Samuel considered himself responsible for not being there to save Henry. His brother's death was one of many with which Clemens would continually torture himself into paroxysms of guilt. Clemens struggled financially until he was twenty-two, and his early letters to his family indicate how obligated he felt to support their needs. Although Clemens's childhood reminiscences provided the source material for some of his richest texts, *Life on the Mississippi* (1883), *The Adventures of Tom Sawyer*, and *Adventures of Huckleberry Finn*, those revisions of his youth on the river mask the concerns with finances and health that troubled his family when he was young.

Alcott also exploited a romanticized version of her childhood in her most successful novels, even though she had experienced the same downward social mobility and the same sense of obligation to support her family by the time she was in her twenties. Her mother's family defined Alcott's social class: Abigail May Alcott, known as "Abba," was descended from Judge Samuel Sewall and from John May, a London shipmaster who emigrated to Massachusetts in 1640. Abigail's brother, Samuel Joseph May, was a Harvard-trained Unitarian minister who introduced Abigail to Bronson Alcott because of their mutual interest in school reform. Bronson Alcott, however, grew up on a Connecticut farm that afforded the family little in the way of luxury. When he was eighteen, he moved to Virginia, hoping to teach, but he eventually became a peddler who spent most of his spare time reading philosophy, history, and literature. By 1823, he had returned to New England to teach.

By 1840, however, his most famous educational endeavor, the Temple School in Boston, had failed—and he and Abba had four children to support, Anna (1831–1893), Louisa (1832–1888), Elizabeth (1835–1858), and May (1840–1879). At least three factors seem to have led to the school's failure: Bronson's publication of *Conversations with Children on the Gospels* (1837), which was controversial for its discussion of the maternal body during birth; Bronson's association with abolitionists such as William Lloyd Garrison and the enrollment of an African American student, Susan Robinson, in the school; and the Panic of 1837 (Elbert, *Hunger* 36–37). Abba also blamed Harriet Martineau's public critique of the school for its failure (Shealy, *Alcott* 174). From 1840 until his death in 1888, Bronson Alcott was never once steadily employed, although in 1843, he established a utopian community, Fruitlands, the failure of which was predictable. As one of Louisa Alcott's childhood friends, Llewellyn Willis, put it, "The scheme of Fruitlands would have been impossible because it was eminently impractical of application to the simple principles of common sense" (Shealy, *Alcott* 175). After that experience, Bronson Alcott relied financially on the generosity and grace of his friends, many of whom were active transcendentalists. Ralph Waldo Emerson was Bronson Alcott's most important patron.

As a result, Louisa May Alcott's values were rooted in transcendentalism, even though she professed never to have understood her father's philosophy (*Selected Letters* 251). She revered nature; she was a social dissenter and reformer; she valued independence and presented herself as a nonconformist. Yet because her father's unprofitable philosophizing at times left the family destitute, she had little tolerance for it—though she could occasionally laugh about it. For example, her fictional persona Tribulation Periwinkle describes a mock hotel soon to be built in Concord, "where pilgrims to this modern Mecca can be entertained. . . . Walden water [and] aesthetic tea . . . will constantly be on tap for the refreshment of thirsty guests. . . . Wild apples by the bushel, orphic acorns by the peck, and Hawthorne's pumpkins, in the shape of pies, will be furnished at philosophic prices. . . . Telescopes will be provided for the gifted eyes which desire to watch the soarings of the Oversoul, when visible" (*Selected Letters* 127). According to one of her early biographers, Ednah Dow Cheney, Alcott gave as her definition of a philosopher, "a man up in a balloon, with his family and friends holding the ropes which confine him to earth and trying to haul him down" (263). The joke apparently made her father laugh hardest of all.[9]

Alcott was largely educated by her father and grew up with a belief that she was a misfit, undoubtedly because of his singling her out as such among his daughters. When she was thirteen, she wrote in her journal, "I am old for my age, and don't care much for girl's things. People think I'm wild and queer. . . . But I'm going to *be* good. I've made so many resolutions, and written sad notes, and cried over my sins, and it does n't seem to do any good!" (59). Four years later, she wrote:

> In looking over our journals, Father says, "Anna's is about other people, Louisa's about herself." That is true, for I don't *talk* about myself; yet must always think of the wilful, moody girl I try to manage, and in my journal I write of her to see how she gets on. Anna is so good she need not take care of herself, and can enjoy other people. If I look in my glass, I try to keep down vanity about my long hair, my well-shaped head, and my good nose. In the street I try not to covet fine things. My quick tongue is always getting me into trouble, and my moodiness makes it hard to be cheerful when I think how poor we are, how much worry it is to live, and how many things I long to do I never can. (61)

Perhaps Alcott's ability to write convincingly for adolescents stemmed from her own self-consciousness as a teenager. Her father practically ensured that she was incapable of confidence in her adolescent—or her adult—self.

In 1848, the Alcotts moved from their family home in Concord, which had been largely subsidized by Emerson, to Boston, where Alcott's mother found work as a social worker. Alcott herself worked as a teacher, a governess, a tutor, and a servant over the following years, and in 1852, the *Olive Branch* published her first story, "The Rival Painters." From 1855 to 1857, the family lived rent-free in a house Alcott's uncle owned in Walpole, New Hampshire, but they moved back to Concord in 1858. That was the same year that Alcott's sister Elizabeth died of complications following the scarlet fever she and May had contracted in 1856. Alcott tortured herself with grief about Lizzie's death throughout her life, much as Clemens tortured himself about his brother Henry's death in 1858. By 1859, Alcott had moved back to Boston to teach and write. The *Atlantic Monthly*, then edited by James Russell Lowell, published her story "Love and Self-Love" fifteen years before Clemens was able to publish anything in the journal so respected it conferred some degree of literary status on its authors.[10] Alcott's reputation during her lifetime as a writer of domestic and children's fiction was kept intact by the pseudonyms she used to publish sensation fiction during the 1850s and 1860s, but she published those pseudonymous thrillers primarily to support her family. Alcott, like Clemens, felt unduly responsible for supporting her family financially at a very young age.

The Civil War

The trauma of the Civil War inevitably affected virtually all Americans, but its initial effect on Clemens was a pragmatic one: because of the closing of the Mississippi River, he could no longer serve as a riverboat pilot. Thus, according to his own fictionalized account in "The Private History of a Campaign That Failed" (1885), in July 1861, he joined a small troop of fifteen Confederate irregulars responding to the governor's call to defend the state. They called themselves the Marion Rangers, and Clemens enlisted, motivated more by peer pressure than political conviction. He claimed to have been elected second lieutenant, though the group had a captain but no first lieutenant ("The Private History" 650–51). Several factors alienated him from the group: its disorganization, poor food, and seeming lack of purpose. In the account Twain wrote twenty-odd years later, he describes a gruesome death when the Rangers fired as a group on a solitary Union soldier: "He was lying on his back, with his arms abroad; his mouth was open and his chest heaving with long gasps, and his white shirt-front was all splashed with blood. The thought shot through me that I was a murderer; that I had killed a man—a man who had never done me any harm. That was the coldest sensation that ever went through my marrow" (665).

In *Mark Twain: A Life*, Ron Powers distinguishes the facts from the embellishments in Twain's account of his Civil War service: the Rangers shot at each other and at wildflowers and at their own horses, but they never killed a Yankee while Clemens was enlisted with them (98–100). What is significant in Clemens's version of his Civil War story, however, is his identification of his own sense of guilt and responsibility for having served the Confederacy. His fictional account of his month as a Rebel was published—not insignificantly—in the same year that *Adventures of Huckleberry Finn* was published. On July 18, 1861, Samuel Clemens deserted from the Marion Rangers and, like Huck, "lit out to the territory" with his brother Orion, who had just been appointed secretary of the Nevada Territory. More than twenty years after the end of the Civil War, Clemens still felt compelled to justify his actions as a deserter, and the narrative he wrote about himself was one that Northern readers could forgive twenty years after the Battle of Appomattox: youthful Mark Twain did not have the stomach to kill staunch defenders of the Union.

Twain's "The Private History of a Campaign That Failed" is not his only piece of writing that rationalizes his actions in July of 1861. *Adventures of Huckleberry Finn* also contains within it Clemens's justification for deserting the Confederacy. Huck is revulsed by Southern conflict throughout the novel: by the violence of the Shepherdsons and Grangerfords; by the inhumanity of the men aboard the sinking *Walter Scott*; by Sherburn's cold-blooded murder of Boggs; and by the duke's and the king's ill-treatment of Jim. On one level, all of these aspects of the plot serve to justify the reader's contempt for ante-bellum Southern culture, even though the book was published twenty years after the war was over. Perhaps Clemens's guilt was two-fold: he had served on the "wrong" side of the war, and he was a deserter. Regardless of what might have been motivating him, however, the fact remains that Clemens wrote a novel about a youthful deserter who rejects Southern culture, both in running away from St. Petersburg and in running away from Aunt Sally at the end of the novel. He runs away from everything that has anything to do with Southern violence and is considered heroic for doing so. The Civil War changed Clemens's economic life—he could never again support himself as a riverboat pilot, so he became a writer. But the Civil War may also have given him a sense of culpability that inspired him to write about a guilt-laden adolescent running away from his past.

As with Clemens's, the Civil War changed Alcott's life dramatically. Hailing from a long line of abolitionists, most notably her uncle, Samuel Joseph May, Alcott burned to serve in the war. Thus, Alcott's was not the patriotism of many Northern sympathizers who fought to preserve the Union; hers was based in a conviction that slavery was evil. She published a number of anti-slavery stories, including "M. L." (1863), "My Contraband" (1863), and "An Hour" (1864), all of which included interracial rivalries and/or romances.[11] After the raid on Harper's Ferry in November 1859, she referred to John Brown as "St. John the Just" (*Journals* 95), and her family boarded his daughters in 1861. Preserving the Union was secondary to freeing the slaves in her economy.

Alcott wanted to put her political convictions into physical action. On May 19, 1861, she wrote to her dear friend, Alf Whitman, "Are you going to have a dab at the saucy Southerners? I long to fly at some body & free my mind on several points, but there is no opening for me at present so I study Dr Home on 'Gun shot wounds,' & get my highly connected self ready to go as a nurse when the slow coaches at Washington begin to lay about them & get their fellow men into a comfortably smashed position" (*Selected Letters* 65). As she put it in her journal in April 1861, "I've often longed to see a war, and now I have my wish. I long to be a man; but as I can't fight, I will content myself with working for those who can" (105). In 1862, she added, "I like the stir in the air, and long for battle like a warhorse when he smells powder" (109). Later that year, she asked her paternal grandmother, "Have any of our people gone to the War? Four or five Mays have gone & if I was only a boy I'd march off tomorrow" (*Selected Letters* 80). Her desire to fight parallels Clemens's before he actually enlisted.

In December, Alcott got her wish to go to war. She went to Washington, D.C., and served as a nurse for six weeks at the Union Hotel Hospital, until she was sent home with typhoid pneumonia. Although she had longed to go to war, the reality of the hospital was very different for her than she'd anticipated prior to nursing, when she wrote her friends from Concord who were fighting in the war, "Now boys, if you intend to be smashed in any way just put it off till I get to Washington to mend you up, for I have enlisted & am only waiting for my commission to appear as nurse at the 'Armory' Something Hospital so be sure you are taken there, if your arms or legs fly away, some day (which the Lord forbid!) & we will have good times in spite of breakages & come out jolly under creditable circumstances like Dickens 'Mark Taply'"[12] (*Selected Letters* 82).

While she admired the stoicism of many of her patients and appreciated when they called her "motherly" (*Journals* 111), Alcott also found herself frustrated by the conditions in her life as a nurse:

> After unwelcome progress through my stifling ward I go to breakfast with what appetite I may; find the inevitable fried beef, salt butter, husky bread & washy coffee; listen to the clack of eight women & a dozen men; the first silly, stupid or possessed of but one idea, the last absorbed in their breakfast & themselves to a degree that is both ludicrous and provoking, for all the dishes are ordered down the table *full* & returned *empty*, the conversation is entirely among themselves & each announces his opinion with an air of importance that frequently causes me to choke in my cup or bolt my meals with undignified speed lest a laugh betray to these pompous beings that a "child's among them takin notes." Till noon I trot, trot, giving out rations, cutting up food for helpless "boys", washing faces,

teaching my attendants how beds are made or floors swept, dressing wounds, taking Dr. Fitz Patrick's orders, (privately wishing all the time that he would be more gentle with my big babies,) dusting tables, sewing bandages, keeping my tray tidy, rushing up & down after pillows, bed linen, sponges, books & directions, till it seems as if I would joyfully pay down all I possess for fifteen minutes rest. (*Journals* 114)

Given how financially conscious Alcott was in her adult life, her willingness to "pay down all I possess" to rest seems significant. But instead of paying all her money, Alcott "paid down" all her health to get her wish to rest—and for quite a bit longer than fifteen minutes. After six weeks as a nurse, Alcott was sent home ill. She was an invalid for most of the spring and experienced intense nightmares: about being molested and threatened by a Spaniard to whom she was married; going to heaven and finding it "all very busy & dismal & ordinary"; being attacked by a Baltimore mob; "being hung for a witch, burned, stoned & otherwise maltreated"; worshiping the devil; and "tending millions of sick men who never died or got well" (*Journals* 116–17). Her biographers have speculated about the violent and dark nature of her dreams—both that she had them and that she recorded them (Elbert, *Hunger* 156–64; Strickland 108).[13] The dreams illustrate her identification with alterity—she perceives herself as a witch, for example—but she is also terrified by otherness, as she is by the menacing Spaniard and the devil.

Two long-term consequences of Alcott's war experiences changed her life. For one thing, she published her first book, *Hospital Sketches* (1863), a sanitized version of her nursing experience that mixes humor with a good dose of abolitionist sentiment. The favorable notices and sales it received inspired her to write a novel, *Moods* (1864), which was far less successful but helped establish her reputation as a novelist. But the illness Alcott suffered affected her health for the rest of her life. Typhoid patients were generally treated with calomel—as was she. Those who survived the heroic doses of calomel, or mercurous chloride, given to them as a purgative eventually died from mercury poisoning as a result. Alcott also casually used laudanum—which is derived from opium—to alleviate the degenerative pain of the mercury poisoning that was slowly killing her (Saxton 258, 368).[14] She died March 6, 1888, two days after the death of her father, with symptoms that are indicative of long-term mercury poisoning (Elbert, *Hunger* 282; Saxton 252–58). Her illness was a direct result of her service in the Civil War, but as with Clemens, the Civil War changed the direction of her career and inspired her as a writer.

The Fantasy of Self-Reliance

The rest of Clemens's life was also affected by his participation in the Civil War, for after fleeing the conflict, he ended up finding a career as a journalist, learning skills that shaped much of his writing career and establishing himself as an emerging humorist. In 1867, the *Daily Alta California*, a newspaper for which Clemens worked, commissioned him to write letters about a 163-day voyage he took to Europe. Upon his return, Elisha Bliss approached him about issuing an expanded version in book form. Mark Twain's *The Innocents Abroad* was soon published, and his literary reputation as a noted humorist was firmly established on the East Coast. While he was aboard the cruise ship that took him to Europe, Clemens met Charles Langdon, who showed him a picture of his beautiful sister, Olivia Langdon. The Langdons were a prominent family in Elmira, New York, as their fortune had been made in the coal industry. They were also abolitionists who very likely worked on the Underground Railroad and who hosted Frederick Douglass when he was lecturing in the Elmira area (Harris, *Courtship* 2; Phipps 90). Mrs. Langdon—Olivia Lewis Langdon—was friends with abolitionists and suffragettes, including Anna Dickinson, Julia Beecher, and Isabella Hooker (Harris, *Courtship* 27). In other words, Olivia "Livy" Langdon was raised in a political environment not unlike the one in which Louisa May Alcott was raised. After a two-year courtship, Olivia and Clemens were married on February 2, 1870, and settled in Buffalo, New York. Within a year, they had moved to Hartford, Connecticut, where they lived until 1891 when they were not living abroad or summering in Elmira. Their son, Langdon, was born in 1870, but died in 1872; their daughters were Susy (1872–1896), Clara (1874–1962), and Jean (1880–1909).

Various critics make a strong case for how influential these women were on Clemens. Susan K. Harris describes Livy's intellectual influence on Clemens (*Courtship* 8–9), and Shelley Fisher Fishkin describes Clemens's daughters and Livy as vital to his "creative process" ("MT and Women" 54).[15] Clemens reviewed his manuscripts with his family, especially Livy, and his wife and daughters served as critics, censors, and inspiration to him. Clemens was particularly vulnerable to Livy's criticism and sometimes curtailed what he wrote at her behest.

Thus, both because of and despite his family's involvement in his writing, Mark Twain's literary reputation grew as exponentially as his business endeavors failed. By 1894, he had published the bulk of his major works, including *Roughing It* (1872), *The Gilded Age* with Charles Dudley Warner (1873), *The Adventures of Tom Sawyer*, *The Prince and the Pauper*, *Life on the Mississippi*,

Adventures of Huckleberry Finn, A Connecticut Yankee in King Arthur's Court, and *The Tragedy of Pudd'nhead Wilson.* Most of the profits from his lucrative writing career, however, he sank into business enterprises that eventually failed, including a publishing firm (Charles L. Webster & Company), an illustrating process called "Kaolatype," the Paige Typesetting Machine, and even a health food called "plasmon" that was made from dry milk (Lauber 286). In addition to his daughters and wife, Twain also supported financially his mother, his brother, Orion, his sister and her family, and a retinue of servants and secretaries. Although Mark Twain was one of the most prolific literary sensations of late nineteenth-century America, by 1894, Clemens had entered voluntary bankruptcy. Eventually, he repaid all of his creditors, even though they had agreed to accept a fifty-percent settlement (Leary 16).

Following the bankruptcy, much of Clemens's life was as tragic as the end of Alcott's life was. His family had been a continual source of both inspiration and frustration to him, and his wife and daughters grew increasingly ill. Throughout their marriage, Olivia guarded his public image from the vulgarity of which he was capable (Hill, *MT: God's Fool* 95; F. Kaplan 415–16; Cardwell 98–99). But she was often an invalid and suffered from a range of maladies that included partial paralysis as a youth to a heart condition later in her life. Clemens's daughters were also often unwell: following a round of scarlet fever she contracted in 1896, Jean suffered epilepsy and apparent depression; Clara also appeared to have been depressed. Both spent time in rest homes and sanitariums, especially after the death of their sister, Susy, who died unexpectedly of spinal meningitis in 1896, the year Jean's epilepsy began. Early in the twentieth century, Clemens was such a strong and disturbing presence in his family members' lives that he was often not permitted to visit them when they were ill (Hill, *MT: God's Fool* 47, 51, 55, 61, 106, 114, 198–99; Willis 269–70). After Olivia died in 1904, Jean's and Clara's conditions worsened. Jean drowned in the bathtub on Christmas Eve of 1909, four months before Clemens's death. He blamed himself for not having been with Susy when she died and for Jean's death (Hill, *MT: God's Fool* 6, 253–55). Clemens memorialized his love to his wife when he fictionalized Adam's eulogy for Eve: "Wheresoever she was, *there* was Eden" ("Eve's Diary" 709). He had been inspired to write much of his children's fiction for his daughters, most notably *The Prince and the Pauper,* which was Susy's favorite (J. Kaplan 239), and *Joan of Arc,* which was Clemens's (Cooley xxiv). He died April 21, 1910.

While Clemens's life was marked by periods of dramatic swings in his family's income, Alcott never achieved the level of wealth that Clemens at times sustained, even though she attained a higher level of financial success because of her writing than she might have dreamed possible early on. The disparity between their incomes in 1880 demonstrates the difference succinctly. Clemens's total income that year was approximately $250,000 (Powers 450), while Alcott's publisher reported her total income from her book sales as $4,065 (Shealy, "Author-Publisher," Diss. 249). Alcott's earnings from her book publications would not have been the entirety of her income that year, but she certainly never had a year with a six-figure income. The difference between their financial successes may be explained, in part, by gender, and it may also be explained by Clemens's involvement in publishing and the lecture circuit. Despite these financial disparities, Alcott's adult life was marked by a familial dependence similar to the one that Clemens's family placed on him.

Moreover, the deaths in Alcott's family contributed both to her financial responsibilities and to her increasing sense of bereavement. She grieved her mother's and her sisters' deaths profoundly, just as Clemens grieved his brother's, his wife's, and his daughters' deaths continually. Alcott's sister Lizzie died when Louisa was twenty-five; Clemens was twenty-one when Henry died. Alcott was also filled with despair when her brother-in-law died in 1870, when her mother died in 1877, and when her sister May died in 1879. Throughout her adult life, she supported her parents, and she supported her sisters and two nephews for long periods of time, the latter following her brother-in-law's death. Eventually, she adopted and raised her youngest sister's daughter, Lulu, after May died. Because of Alcott's ongoing mercury poisoning, but also perhaps because she was never able to fulfill her fantasy of self-reliance, she suffered depression and a variety of intestinal disorders that were particularly disabling and that were similar to the various neuralgias experienced by the women in Clemens's family. Yet *Little Women* and its sequels would never have been written without Alcott's family to inspire her, both by providing material for the plot and by supporting her while she wrote. She was especially tireless in her praise of her mother, whom she referred to as "a very brave, good woman" (*Journals* 63) and to whom she expressed gratitude for her many notes of encouragement (e.g., *Journals* 55, 63).

Alcott and Clemens both took pride in their independence, even using the same metaphor to describe their Emersonian self-reliance. When Clemens was courting his wife, he wrote to his future mother-in-law in 1869, "I have paddled my own canoe since I was thirteen; *wholly* without encouragement or assistance from any one" (*Selected Letters* 3.91). He would have been thirty-four at the time. Nine years earlier, Alcott had written about her sister's wedding in her journal: "I'd rather be a free spinster and paddle my own canoe" (*Journals* 99). She was then twenty-seven. It is not so unusual for both authors to use the same metaphor—paddling one's own canoe was a common figure of speech in the 1860s—but the shared metaphor does emphasize the value both placed on self-reliance.[16] The idea of a budding writer paddling his own way downstream seems especially apropos of Clemens, given how many of his books are set on the Mississippi River.

Ultimately, however, Clemens and Alcott ended up sharing their canoes with enough family members to sink a barge. Because they both coveted self-reliance, they at times resented those who kept them from achieving it. In truth, Emerson's use of the term has nothing to do with whether one is financially independent or supports dependents; it implies that greatness comes from determining one's values and the course of one's life from relying solely on one's self-knowledge. As Emerson puts it in "Self-Reliance" (1841): "To believe your own thought, to believe that what is true for you in your private heart is true for all men, —that is genius" (257). It was through Emerson that the term entered the popular consciousness of many Americans in the nineteenth century, and Emerson's influence on Clemens and Alcott has been well-established.[17] Both valued independence and the workings of their own minds. Yet for people with the clamoring families they had, it may well have felt at times impossible to hear only the inspiration of their private hearts.[18] Nonetheless, despite being independent people saddled with others' dependency—or perhaps even because of that dependency—both authors were motivated to write novels that would keep their families solvent. The tension between self-reliance and being depended on by others permeated their lives.

Communities of Writers

Both authors' choices to write about adolescence may also have been influenced by the fact that they lived in communities in which other notable authors published for the juvenile trade market before they did. For example, Harriet Beecher Stowe and Lilly Warner both lived in the Nook Farm community of Hartford in which Clemens also resided.[19] Clemens boasted to his publisher that Stowe had praised *The Prince and the Pauper*: "The other day Mrs. Stowe said 'I am reading your Prince and Pauper for the *fourth* time, and I *know* it's the best book for young people that was ever written'" (*LthP* 216). Thomas Bailey Aldrich was also a frequent and influential visitor to the Nook Farm area (Stone 3–5). Indeed, Aldrich's *Story of a Bad Boy* (1869) is a precursor of *Tom Sawyer* that may well have influenced how Clemens structured that novel

(Gribben, "I Did" 153–59).[20] As for Alcott, Nathaniel Hawthorne was her next-door neighbor in the early 1860s; by then, he had already published *A Wonder-Book for Girls and Boys* (1851) and *Tanglewood Tales* (1853).[21] Although Harriet Beecher Stowe did not live in Concord, she had close ties to the community because of its citizens' abolitionist activities. In 1871, Alcott's publisher told her that "Mrs. Stowe praised L[ittle] Women and [*Old-Fashioned Girl*] heartily" (Roberts Brothers, Jan. 13, 1871). Knowing that authors with the stature of Stowe and Hawthorne were publishing for youth—and in Stowe's case, encouraging Clemens and Alcott to continue doing so—may well have been an important legitimizing influence for both authors.

Both authors also grew up reading romanticism's greatest novelist of childhood, Charles Dickens, whose child characters in books from *Oliver Twist* (1837) to Pip in *Great Expectations* (1861) captured the Victorian imagination. Moreover, Stone argues that the transcendentalists' romantic interest in childhood dignified childhood as a topic for many American writers, and he traces how Emerson thus influenced Clemens, even noting the quotation from Emerson engraved over the Clemenses' fireplace in Hartford, "The ornament of a house is the friends who frequent it" (3). It follows logically that Emerson would have had even more impact on Alcott's willingness to publish for youth than he had had on Clemens, given that Emerson lived down the street from her. The communities in which Clemens and Alcott lived, then, sanctioned their nostalgic returns to their childhoods so they could redefine their own youths in more positive terms than what they actually experienced.

Sexuality

Accounts of Clemens's family's ill health and his frustration with their condition appear throughout his letters and notebooks and have led critics such as Hamlin Hill, Fred Kaplan, and Guy Cardwell to speculate that Clemens's ego was a "dominating pervasiveness" (F. Kaplan 417) so narcissistic and demanding that his family repressed their emotions and fell ill as a result (Hill xx; Cardwell 128). In 1906, Clemens's egoism began to manifest itself in an increased pursuit of young girls, or, as he put it, in his "worship of school girls—if worship be the right name, and I know it is" (qtd. Cooley xx). He claimed to "collect pets": girls between the ages of ten and sixteen "who are pretty and sweet and naïve and innocent," girls whose "degraded and willing slave I am" (qtd. Cooley xv, xx). In 1908, he referred to them as his "Angel Fish" and organized what he called the Aquarium Club. His correspondence with these girls eventually included over three hundred letters. For the most part, his interest in the girls seems relatively harmless. Perhaps he was seeking a surrogate for Susy, dead at the age of twenty-four, as John Cooley suggests (xxi); perhaps he was compensating for a loss of control over his daughter Clara, as Harris suggests ("MT and Gender" 184); perhaps he was seeking a surrogate for his first love, Laura Wright, a fourteen-year-old with whom he fell in love when he was a twenty-two-year-old cub pilot on the Mississippi, as Hamlin Hill suggests (*MT: God's Fool* 261); perhaps he was filling his life with grandchildren, as he himself suggested (qtd. Cooley xx); perhaps he was looking for the only substitute for sexual gratification available to an impotent moral masochist (Cardwell 144–57).[22] Or perhaps he was actually enjoying the titillation of "owning" and caressing youthful girls.

In only one incidence, in the final months of his life, did the parents of one of these girls seem to have concerns about the propriety of his attentions. Apparently, Clemens expressed an inappropriate amount of jealousy about a young man who was interested in fifteen-year-old Helen Allen, the daughter of William H. Allen, the U.S. consul in Bermuda at the time. In one letter, Clemens wrote of the young man, "If I catch him around these premises again, I will carve him up" (Cooley 278). Hill intimates that Clemens's actions might have motivated Allen and his wife to ask that the aging humorist be removed from Bermuda to the U.S. One employee described "something very terrible that happened in Bermuda shortly before M. T.'s death. . . . It is something unprintable" (qtd. in *MT: God's Fool* 261). In Clemens's last letter to Helen, he warned her to "be cautious, watchful, wary" and to protect against an ill-matched marriage (Cooley 281). Although it seems unlikely that Clemens was a full-blown pedophile, it is undeniable that he pursued the young girls in his Aquarium Club as if they were commodities he could collect. He commodified their innocence and in one sense wished to exploit that innocence by owning it. Very likely, he raised the expectations of these girls, if not romantically, then perhaps in terms of their hopes that something might come of associating with someone so famous. Even if the relationships were platonic, they still seem sexualized to the twenty-first-century eye by the very nature of a seventy-five-year-old man wishing to own part of a young girl, even if only her attention.

Alcott, on the other hand, rejected the compulsory heterosexuality of the Victorian era. Most notably, Alcott's family provided her with a sororal environment in which she could develop as what Lillian Faderman would call a "woman-identified woman." Faderman describes relationships Alcott had with sculptor Emma Stebbins and her lesbian partner, Charlotte Cushman (219). Alcott had to have known what a "Boston Marriage" was; the term was a nineteenth-century euphemism for lesbianism.[23] Faderman notes the passionate female friendships that Alcott depicts in various of her writings, including *Work*, "Happy Women" (1868), *An Old-Fashioned Girl*, and "Diana and Persis" (1978) (173–74, 187, 218–20). And Anna Ricketson, the daughter of an old friend of Alcott's father, was dear enough to Alcott that in 1884 she wrote a poem that includes these stanzas for Anna[24]:

Who when we've earthquakes in the head,
And humble flat upon our bed
Tho e're the vital spark is fled?
     Dear Anna . . .

Sweet spinster, fond as my wife,
Friend, loyal through all her wife [*sic*][25]
Woman free from petty strife,
     True Anna

What shall our Xmas wishes be?
Health, happiness, prosperity,
And loving hearts to cherish thee,
     Our Anna. (Alcott Family, Letters to Anna Ricketson, folder 1)

In 1887, Alcott celebrated their anniversary with a poem that concludes:

Heaven send the day soon!
  Or I shall get *curs*-ory
With longings for home
  And each dear Anna-versary.
     (Alcott Family, Letters to Anna Ricketson, folder 3)

It is impossible to determine the exact nature of the love that Alcott held for Anna Ricketson, but defining her as being "as fond as my wife" is certainly an indication that Alcott was a woman-identified woman.

At least three Alcott critics besides Faderman have defended the lesbian possibilities in Alcott's adult novel *Work*: Elizabeth Keyser (*Whispers* 109) and Angela M. Estes and Kathleen Lant ("Feminist" 245). Charles Strickland writes, "Although there is precious little evidence that she was a lesbian, it is undeniable that she felt strong erotic feelings toward her mother and toward other women." However, Strickland believes Alcott to have been more androgynous than lesbian (108–09). Like him, Elaine Showalter concludes that it is "impossible to say" whether or not Alcott was a lesbian (49). Alcott, however, left some indicators that she might well have been. In 1860, she wrote to her friend Alf Whitman, "I was born with a boys nature & always had more sympathy for & interest in them than in girls" (*Selected Letters* 51–52). In an 1883 interview with biographer Louise Chandler Moulton—who was also a correspondent of Clemens's—Alcott claimed, "I am more than half-persuaded that I am a man's soul put by some freak of nature into a woman's body . . . because I have fallen in love in my life with so many pretty girls and never once the least bit with any man" (qtd. in Showalter 48).[26]

Speculations about Alcott's sexual orientation—whether she was lesbian, heterosexual, bisexual, or asexual—are less significant to her relationship with Samuel Clemens than is the observation that she was a woman-centered woman who valued sorority. Given the hypermasculinity of Mark Twain's public personality, Alcott might well have found much about the man offensive. He wrote privately circulated essays about masturbation ("Some Thoughts" 722–24) and flatulence and sexual prowess in Queen Elizabeth's court ("Date 1601" 661–66), and he revised several times a short story about one of his maids getting pregnant by an intruder whom she claims has raped her—although the maid ultimately proves to be also a man (*Wapping Alice*). In Letter VIII of the posthumously published *Letters from the Earth*, Twain wrote this skewed description of human sexuality:

> During 27 days in every month (in the absence of pregnancy) from the time a woman is seven years old till she dies of old age, she is ready for action and *competent*. As competent as the candlestick to receive the candle. Competent every day, competent every night. Also, she *wants* that candle—yearns for it, longs for it, hankers after it, as commanded by the law of God in her heart.
>
> But man is only briefly competent; and only then in the moderate measure applicable to the word in *his* sex's case. He is competent from the age of sixteen or seventeen thenceforward for thirty-five years. After 50 his performance is of poor quality, the intervals between are wide, and its satisfactions of no great quality to either party; whereas his great-grandmother is as good as new. There is nothing the matter with her plant. Her candlestick is as firm as ever, whereas his candle is increasingly softened and weakened by the weather of age, as the years go by, until at last it can no longer stand, and is mournfully laid to rest in the hope of a blessed resurrection which is never to come. ("Letters from the Earth" 914–15)[27]

In the same essay, Twain criticizes women for letting men create adultery laws that limit their performance to only one man, which men have clearly done to protect their own interests. Moreover, Clemens was a prurient observer at

Henry Beecher's adultery trial (Phipps 114) and—of course—Clemens also had a life-long fascination with nubile girls.[28] Both Clemens and Alcott professed that they loved pretty girls. Perhaps that interest was yet one more factor that inspired both of them to write about adolescents who were pretty girls, like Joan of Arc and Rose Campbell. Both of them were fascinated with youth and its possibilities in ways that may well have been connected to their socially veiled sexual yearnings.

The Pilgrim's Progress in 1869

It is very unlikely that Alcott would have ever known the private details of Clemens's life or his unpublished writings—nor did she, of course, know of the events that occurred after her death. But she had to have known something about his reputation while she lived. She had certainly read *The Innocents Abroad*, with its depiction of can-can girls who "expose [themselves] as much as possible" (1.184) and "delightfully immoral" *grisettes* (1.202). In that narrative, Twain enjoys being "flattered out of [his] senses by every petticoat that chooses to take the trouble to do it" (1.110–11), and he recounts the story of Heloïse, impregnated out of wedlock by Abelard, who is in turn castrated by Heloïse's uncle. He describes slave girls being sold in Turkey as if they were livestock. Although Alcott's publisher, Thomas Niles, jocularly encouraged her to write "the Female Innocents Abroad" in 1870, Alcott would undoubtedly not have wanted to follow in Twain's masculinist footsteps (Roberts Brothers, July 7, 1870). She never even dignified Niles's suggestion with a response.

The Innocents Abroad and the first volume of *Little Women* were best sellers in 1869, so both authors' earliest major financial success were prominent in the public eye at the same time. The second volume of *Little Women* was published in April 1869, making the novel complete, and by the end of that year, total sales were 38,000 (Stern, *Louisa* 196). *The Innocents Abroad* appeared three months later, in July. In its first eighteen months, it sold over 82,000 copies (Powers 277).[29] The preparation of both manuscripts, however, differed in ways that exemplify how these writers approached their craft throughout their careers. Alcott wrote the first half of *Little Women* in about ten weeks between May and July 15, 1868, and it was published on October 1, 1868. She wrote the second half between November 1 and December 31 of the same year, and that half was published in April 1869. For all practical purposes, Alcott spent about twenty weeks writing the novel. While she revised some of it based on her publisher's suggestions, the majority of the revisions occurred when she was reading page proofs. Clemens, however, wrote *The Innocents Abroad* in multiple stages. He wrote some of the letters on which the book was based during his travels in Europe and the Middle East in the summer of 1867—but he wrote more of those letters during the passage home in the fall of 1867 (Powers 210, 222). He further revised them and expanded approximately 250 pages of letters into a 600-page book between January and June 17, 1868 (Powers 234–38). He invited Bret Harte and his friend Mary Fairbanks to help him revise the manuscript (Powers 239). The final manuscript went to Elisha Bliss, who helped him revise it still further, on July 30, 1868 (LeMaster and Wilson 400; Hill, *MT&EB* 1–4). His fiancée, Olivia, helped him read the proofs and make more changes in the spring of 1869, and the book was not published for a full two years after he had begun writing it. Most of Clemens's major novels were written in fits and starts such as this, with compulsive periods of writing interspersed with months or years of leaving the manuscript to lie fallow. Most of Alcott's novels for youth, on the other hand, were written in prolonged streaks that did not allow for significant revision.

Despite these differences in how they were composed, the 1869 books were both notably comic, *The Innocents Abroad* being much more so than *Little Women*, of course. But as Brodhead points out, *Little Women* is far more humorous than the domestic family stories that had preceded it, like Susan B. Warner's *The Wide, Wide World* (1850) or Catharine Maria Sedgwick's *Home* (1835) (92–103). For example, Amy, in *Little Women*, makes the same type of malapropisms that Twain's fellow passenger, the Oracle, commits. While Amy says "label" for "libel" (12), the Oracle elucidates upon the "Pillows of Herkewls" (1.105). Moreover, when Amy goes to Europe, her letters home evoke the same type of naïve and manic voyeurism that Twain depicts throughout *The Innocents Abroad*: on a train with her uncle and cousin, Amy writes, "we kept bouncing from one side to the other, trying to see everything while we were whisking along at the rate of sixty-miles an hour. . . . Amy flying up . . . Flo darting to my window, 'How sweet; we must go there some time, won't we pa?' Uncle calmly admiring his boots, —'No my dear, not unless you want beer; that's a brewery'" (247). Amy is energetic, and she is as innocent as any of the Innocents Abroad that Twain depicts.

The Innocents Abroad and *Little Women* were also both writers' first major successes—and both best sellers relied on their authors' reminiscences. Alcott had seen moderate success with *Hospital Sketches*, but her more fictional *Moods* was nowhere near as well-received. Clemens's first book, *The Celebrated Jumping Frog of Calaveras County and Other Sketches* (1867), contains some of the same type of Western humor that characterizes *The Innocents Abroad*, but it is neither an extended narrative nor narrated autobiographically. But Clemens and Alcott, however, must have understood by their phenomenal sales in 1869 that they had a selling formula if they wrote about their own lives in white-washed and sometimes comic ways. They mined their own experiences to generate salable fiction for the rest of their careers, even occasionally getting themselves in trouble in similar ways for reflecting real life a little too accurately. For instance, by 1875, Alcott was censored by a woman named Ariadne Blish for naming a minor character after her in *Eight Cousins*. She had been a passing friend in childhood, and Alcott remembered the name because of its uniqueness (Shealy, "Author-Publisher," Diss. 164–65). Alcott wrote to Blish, reassuring her that she would "rechristen" the character in all subsequent editions—and she does, indeed, appear in later editions as Annabel Bliss (*Selected Letters* 197).[30] In the same vein, Mark Twain describes in *Life on the Mississippi* how he and Charles Dudley Warner had to rename "Eschol Sellers" in *The Gilded Age* because of a real person by that name; "Eschol" became "Beriah Sellers" in all subsequent editions (*Life* 504). Both Alcott and Twain claimed innocence in the matter and rectified the situation as best they could. But both authors had employed what they considered to be comical names for comical characters: Sellers and Blish/Bliss are laughable characters.

Interestingly enough, given the extended comedy in *The Innocents Abroad* and the gentle comedy in *Little Women*, both books are at least partially influenced by John Bunyan's less-than-humorous religious allegory, *The Pilgrim's Progress* (1678–1684). Anne K. Phillips describes *Little Women* as an American retelling of the allegory, one that provides both children and adults with a paradigm for transcending "earthly frustrations and worldly concerns" by living as individuals whose spirituality puts them "in opposition to the larger society" because they are rejecting worldly temptations (214, 225). Thus, in Alcott's hands, *The Pilgrim's Progress* becomes a transcendental guide to the galaxy for reform-minded youth, which I discuss at greater length in a historical interlude on romantic evangelism in chapter 3. But in Twain's hands, *The Pilgrim's Progress* becomes a jest, a source for parody. In fact, the full title of the book is *The Innocents Abroad, or The New Pilgrim's Progress*. Twain's pilgrims are often thick-witted, materialistic, xenophobic, and comic. They have no pilgrimage other than the commodification of travel: they are gathering new experiences as if they were material objects so that they can return home to boast of their new possession, worldliness.

Portions of *Little Women* and *The Innocents Abroad* describe each author's experiences in Europe. Alcott had been to France in 1866; Clemens had been there in 1867. Predictably, those portions of *Little Women* based on Alcott's European experience tend to focus on people and domestic situations, while Twain describes more cultural differences than Alcott does. For instance, Alcott describes the Parisian cemetery Père la Chaise as "very curious,—for many of the tombs are like small rooms, and looking in, one sees a table, with images or pictures of the dead, and chairs for the mourners to sit in when they come to lament" (250). Twain, on the other hand, uses architectural metaphors rather than domestic metaphors to describe the graveyard: "It is a solemn city of wind-ing streets, and of miniature marble temples and mansions of the dead gleam-ing white from out a wilderness of foliage and fresh flowers" (188). Both of them describe Napoleon III, but Alcott contrasts him to his ill-clad wife, while Twain contrasts him (favorably) to the Sultan of Turkey. Alcott's character Amy writes home, "I've seen the imperial family several times,—the Emperor an ugly, hard-looking man, the Empress pale and pretty, but dressed in horrid taste, *I* thought" (250). Twain writes, "Napoleon, in military uniform—a long-bodied, short-legged man, fiercely mustached, old, wrinkled, with eyes half closed, and *such* a deep, crafty, scheming expression about them (1.172)"—while he claims the sultan looks like nothing more than a butcher (1.173). Alcott's pilgrim in Europe sees the beautiful, the sacred, and the gracious; Clemens's pilgrim sees beauty but also corruption.

When the two of them describe scenery or masses of people, however, they rely on rhetorical tropes, such as cataloguing, to such a similar effect that their efforts to appeal to the American public are apparent. Laid out side by side, the writers' styles bear a striking similarity.

Little Women

In Valrosa:

"It was a lovely drive, along winding roads rich in the picturesque scenes that delight beauty-loving eyes. Here an ancient monastery, whence the solemn chanting of the monks came down to them. . . . Valrosa well deserved its name, —for in that climate of perpetual summer roses blossomed everywhere. They overhung the archway, thrust themselves between the bars of the great gate with a sweet welcome to passers-by, and lined the avenue, winding through lemon-trees and feathery palms up to the villa on the hill. Every shadowy nook, where seats invited one to stop and rest, was a mass of bloom; every cool grotto had its marble nymph smiling from a veil of flowers; and every fountain reflected crimson, white, or pale pink roses, leaning down to smile at their own beauty. Roses covered the walls of the house, draped the cornices, climbed the pillars, and ran riot over the balustrade of the wide terrace, whence one looked down on the sunny Mediterranean and the white-walled city on its shore." (315)

Innocents Abroad

In Versailles:

"All about it rainbows of flowers, and colossal statues that were almost numberless, and yet seemed only scattered over the ample space; broad flights of stone steps leading down from the promenade to lower grounds of the park—stairways that whole regiments might stand to arms upon and have room to spare; vast fountains whose great bronze effigies discharged rivers of sparkling water into the air and mingled a hundred curving jets together in forms of matchless beauty; wide grass-carpeted avenues that branched hither and thither in every direction and wandered to seemingly interminable distances, walled all the way on either side with compact ranks of leafy trees whose branches met above and formed arches as faultless and as symmetrical as ever were carved in stone; and here and there were glimpses of sylvan lakes with miniature ships glassed in their surfaces. And everywhere—on the palace steps, and the great promenade, around the fountains, among the trees, and far under the arches of the endless avenues, hundreds and hundreds of people in gay costumes walked or ran or danced, and gave to the fairy picture the life and animation which was all of perfection it could have lacked." (1.204–05)

In Nice:

"Many nations are represented, many languages spoken, many costumes worn; and on a sunny day, the spectacle is as gay and brilliant as a carnival. Haughty English, lively French, sober Germans, handsome Spaniards, ugly Russians, meek Jews, free-and-easy Americans, —all drive, sit, or saunter here, chatting over the news, and criticising the latest celebrity who has arrived—Ristori or Dickens, Victor Emanuel or the Queen of the Sandwich Islands." (296)

In Gibraltar:

"There is an English garrison at Gibraltar of 6,000 or 7,000 men, . . . and one sees soft-eyed Spanish girls from San Roque, and veiled Moorish beauties (I suppose they are beauties) from Tarifa, and turbaned, sashed, and trowsered Moorish merchants from Fez, and long-robed, bare-legged, ragged Mohammedan vagabonds from Tetouan and Tangier, some brown, some yellow, and some as black as virgin ink—and Jews from all around, in gaberdine, skull-cap, and slippers, just as they are in pictures and theaters, and just as they were three thousand years ago, no doubt." (1.104)

Just as Alcott's pilgrim gushes about seeing such famous people as the "Queen of the Sandwich Islands," Twain rushes away from the International Exposition to see "the Empress of the French" (1.171). Both authors knew exactly what type of descriptions would appeal to their reading audience at home in the United States: elaborately florid and detailed landscapes of the scenery, name-dropping raves about celebrities, and adjective-heavy lists of foreign peoples described almost entirely in terms of otherness. Their knowledge of what would appeal to American audiences is not unrelated to their depiction of adolescence. Both value the potential that lies inherent in innocence, and their Americans in Europe are, indeed, the type of innocent and hopeful characters that bespeak the promise of change. Mark Twain in Europe is a youthful character, just as Amy is. For both characters, their innocence contrasts with the cynicism of European values, and Twain is particularly virulent in his social criticism of the Old World. But more important, Mark Twain's youthfulness and the youthfulness of the characters in *Little Women* imply not only the possibility of change but also the desirability of change. Thus, with both of these 1869 volumes, Twain and Alcott learned that writing hopefully about the potential for change would appeal to the American public.

Although they shared similar syntax, diction, content, and ideologies in 1869, no single point can demonstrate more clearly how very different Alcott's and Twain's goals were as writers than the different uses to which they put *The Pilgrim's Progress*. She used it allegorically; he used it comically. Alcott's writing is, in *Little Women*, as it often is in her writing for youth, frequently moralistic and earnest, even when she is being playful. On the other hand, Twain parodied moralistic behavior and was a skeptic—and nothing was too sacred to provide him with grounds for a joke. (His running riff on commercialism in the Holy Land includes the tour guide pointing out indentations in various walls that were allegedly made by the Savior's elbow.) No two books could have used *The Pilgrim's Progress* in more intertextually different ways.

But if Twain and Alcott had different goals in their writing, they still had similar values, including their faith in Americans' independence, their hope for reforming the country, and their conviction that the innocence of youth could be used to effect social change. They came from very different backgrounds and served on different sides of the Civil War, but they ended up experiencing similar pressures in their youths and in their adult lives. Their families frustrated their writing and supported it; both authors either experienced or were surrounded by ill health in ways that affected their productivity; and they both had antagonistic relationships with organized religion, which I will discuss at greater length in a later historical interlude. Both were continually beset by pressures to earn more money, which was a major factor in their decision to write juveniles. The pressure for Alcott was a result of her father's impecuniousness; the pressure for Clemens was a result of both his father's and his own bad business sense and his expectations about maintaining a certain standard of living. In fact, Ernest Hemingway once claimed that Twain and Henry James began writing "slop" so that they could earn the money necessary to maintain their households in the manner to which they were accustomed (23).[31] Clemens and Alcott wrote lovingly about youthful girls, and both also wrote about angst-ridden teenagers. Both learned in 1869 that Americans were willing to pay for narratives that contained within them social criticism based on youthfulness and hope. In part because of the frequency of their publishing, both became icons in their day, beloved authors whose popularity was sometimes a burden to them. And both of them felt ambivalence about writing for youth, even though they created two of the most important adolescent characters in the American canon, Huckleberry Finn and Jo March. Some of the stigma of writing for youth was alleviated by the communities in which they lived, but both of those communities were particularly influenced by Ralph Waldo Emerson. Like virtually every writer of the era, Clemens and Alcott were affected by burgeoning progressive ideals, but unlike most other writers, they used adolescents to define the reform potential in America. Their reliance on adolescence as a trope seems to have been motivated by intellectual values, psychological forces, and the economic practicality that juvenile publishing was lucrative. While many were writing successfully for youth in the nineteenth century, few did so for as wide an audience as Clemens and Alcott.

CHAPTER TWO

The Metaphor of the Adolescent Reformer
Adventures of Huckleberry Finn and *Little Women*

"I almost wish I hadn't any conscience."
—*Little Women*

"If I had a yaller dog that didn't know no more than a
person's conscience does, I would pison him."
—*Adventures of Huckleberry Finn*

The novels *Adventures of Huckleberry Finn* and *Little Women* were published seventeen years apart, which is almost a generation in terms of the readership of the juvenile market. But they are two of the most studied nineteenth-century American novels with adolescent protagonists. Neither book has ever been out of print, and both of them are the most canonical novel of their respective authors. The differences between the authors' personae and the novels' plot structures, however, create an ironic relationship of similarity between the two books, for despite one being characterized as a "girl book" of domestic fiction written by a literary bluestocking and the other being labeled a "boy book" written by a Western humorist who conjoins adventure with social critique, both novels rely on adolescent protagonists to advance the authors' reform ideologies. Moreover, the specifics of those ideologies emerge from the characters' moral development as they grow toward adulthood, so they share the same literary implication that youth is a time of greater potential for change than any other stage of life.

Jo and Huck experience moral conflicts in very similar terms. Jo says, "I almost wish I hadn't any conscience, it's so inconvenient. If I didn't care about doing right, and didn't feel uncomfortable when doing wrong, I should get on capitally" (281). Huck also laments his conscience, "If I had a yaller dog that didn't know no more than a person's conscience does, I would pison him. It takes up more room than all the rest of a person's insides, and yet ain't no good, nohow" (292). Both characters are being ironic—Jo more self-consciously than Huck—but both are performing a vital function in American literature. They are some of the earliest adolescent characters whose ironic moral crises serve as metaphors of the need for American social change.

The necessity of reform that those two novels establish emerges from two teenagers' moral development, so throughout this chapter I will focus on how both authors employed the concept of growth and moral development to imply the possibility of social change. An investigation of the qualities many writers shared when they wrote about social change in the nineteenth century precedes my analysis of the relationship between Clemens's and Alcott's lives and between their most famous novels.

Reform Writing and Adolescence

Scholars of nineteenth-century social change in American literature have identified several assumptions that help to define the type of reform literature that Clemens and Alcott wrote. First, nineteenth-century American authors of social reform fiction tended to base their motivation for writing in some permutation of Christianity that implied that "reform is simply the right thing to do" (Koistinen-Harris 3). In Clemens's and Alcott's cases, as with many reform writers, romantic evangelism influenced that ethos. Romantic evangelism is a broad term that describes many of the reform-oriented manifestations of Protestantism in nineteenth-century America, such as Methodism, Presbyterianism, Congregationalism, and Quakerism.[1] Much of the reform writing of the era emanated from the pen of authors who practiced some form of romantic evangelism. Their writing ranged from overtly didactic religious tracts to critically acclaimed novels and included a complex variety of narratives, genres, images, and style in many fictional assertions that certain behaviors or inequalities be eradicated from the culture (Reynolds 55).[2] Emphasizing as it does abolition, maternity, and the potential of youth to redeem their elders, *Uncle Tom's Cabin* is the most notable example of the antebellum reform novel.[3]

Furthermore, for many socially aware authors, reform had practical implications that were based on a desire to make the country's resources operate more efficiently and more fairly; in theory, the more people who had access to the country's abundance, the more productive the nation would be (Koistinen-Harris 3; Elbert, "Introduction" xviii). Thus, consumerism walked hand in hand with Christianity in providing a major impulse for reform (Shulman ix, 20). Another truism among critics of literary reform is recognizing the influence of the Civil War in inspiring reform movements. From abolitionism—which influenced the factionalism that led to the war—to the hygiene movements that occurred as a result of poor sanitary conditions for troops in the war, the Civil

War was the watershed from which many progressive movements of the Gilded Age emerged (Eiselein 3–5). Very significantly, within American literature, postbellum reform fiction also tends to revisit Civil War tensions in tracing conflict between the rights of the individual and the needs of society, especially focusing on the tension that exists when some people are more disempowered than others (Koistinen-Harris 3; Shulman 3–5). But most essential to these reform writers' functioning is their belief in social progress—their belief that humanity is capable of improvement, which principle is also related, in part, to nineteenth-century enactments of Christianity.

For my purposes, then, "reform" refers to any social movement that assumes that individuals in the society can be improved by a collective action that inspires greater social justice for some group of people. Greg Eiselein defines the goal of humanitarianism elegantly as "the reduction and elimination of suffering" (15).[4] Clemens and Alcott seem to have subscribed to this definition of humanitarian reform. Both of them, operating from memories of the Civil War and principles of romantic evangelism, democracy, and a belief that social groups can improve, wrote various reform novels for youth that relied on adolescent protagonists. In their novels, social reform becomes almost synonymous with a concept of social growth, i.e., a depiction of an improved or reformed society that could grow in the same basic sense that people grow, from dependency and solipsism into a greater awareness of community and altruism (Stephens 3).

Neither Clemens nor Alcott would have been familiar with the term "adolescence" when they were writing these novels, since it wasn't defined for the American public until G. Stanley Hall published a book on the subject entitled *Adolescence* in 1905. Nevertheless, both authors demonstrate repeatedly that they inherently understand the concept with characters like Jo March and Huck Finn, who are neither children nor adults. Like their Victorian peers, Clemens and Alcott would have been more comfortable with the term "youth" than such terms as "young adult" or "teenager."[5] (Interestingly enough, Olivia Clemens's well-known nickname for her husband was "Youth.") As writers, Clemens and Alcott knew that youth is a stage of life that is temporary; they knew that it involves more responsibility and therefore more social power than early childhood, but less than adulthood; and they knew that growth to adulthood is a normal goal for most youth. Most important, they knew that adult characters cannot be depicted growing in the same way that juvenile characters can.[6] While adolescents have the luxury of engaging in actions or introspections that allow for radical transformations of careers or relationships or morality or psychology, adulthood implies a permanence of commitments (to family, to home, to career, to conviction) that makes dramatic change less possible—and in a literary character, less believable. Ultimately, adolescence as a stage of life not only allows for the possibility of change, but it *assumes* the possibility of change—which is also a major element of reform writing. Adolescent characters are almost ideally suited to Clemens's and Alcott's reform agendas because their youthfulness implies the social possibility of hope, of change, and of growth.

Huck and Jo

Several basic similarities between Huck Finn and Jo March invite initial comparison between the two characters. Most notably, both are adolescents whose growth includes grappling with social issues in which many reformers shared an interest: for Huck, the dignity of the individual African American, and for Jo, the delimiting nature of femininity that led to the Suffrage movement. Both are also social misfits with ironic self-perceptions that help define their relationship with their culture. They live in cultures that condemn their behavior—Huck for his class-related delinquencies, Jo for her gender transgressions. For example, just as the Widow Douglas tries to cure Huck of swearing, Jo's sisters try to cure her of using slang. These critiques of their unconventional behaviors lead both adolescents to internalize self-perceptions that they are socially maladroit, which makes them vulnerable to the seductions of middle-class conventionality. Huck gets to liking the Widow Douglas's "ways" (22), and Jo acts like a stereotypical girl in love when she "[does] up her hair three times a day" for Professor Bhaer's benefit (363). But readers may also understand that Huck's and Jo's social discomfort is often a function of flaws in the culture itself rather than in the individual. Huck and Jo ironically think they are at fault for not comporting themselves appropriately, but the people they initially regard as their superiors are hardly models of an ethical citizenry. Miss Watson is mean-spirited; the Shepherdsons are vengeful; the Wilkses and the Phelpses are gullible to the point of stupidity. And the social arbiters of good society in *Little Women* are superficial snobs, as the March girls discover about virtually every middle- or upper-class family with whom they have contact, aside from their next-door neighbors.

Both Twain and Alcott base their social criticism in an adolescent's ironic self-perception that he or she is somehow inferior because of his or her nonconformity. As a result, the use of irony to depict adolescents as potential reformers is a unique point of comparison for the two. For example, Huck feels "bad and low, because I knowed very well I had done wrong," while readers understand that his not revealing that Jim is a runaway slave is, in fact, the right thing for him to do (133). Huck thinks he is wrong and his culture is right; Twain's intended reader knows the opposite to be true. While Huck's first-person misstatements about his own character create the irony that defines his character, the unnamed narrator of *Little Women* provides the ironic commentary about Jo's character: "Now, if she had been the heroine of a moral story-book, she ought at this period of her life to have become quite saintly, renounced the world, and gone about doing good in a mortified bonnet, with tracts in her pocket. But you see Jo wasn't a heroine; she was only a struggling human girl, like hundreds of others, and she just acted out her nature, being sad, cross, listless or energetic, as the mood suggested" (339). Jo yearns to do her duty and "secretly rebel[s]" against doing so (337)—though ultimately, she fulfills her duty by supporting her parents, emotionally and financially, *and* by becoming a romantic heroine who both publishes well and marries, despite thinking for most of her adolescence that neither success would ever be hers. She also becomes the reformer that she tells her sister she would like to be. When Amy claims, "I don't like reformers, and I hope you will never try to be one," Jo responds: "I do like them, and I shall be one if I can; for in spite of the laughing, the world would never get on without them" (235). Even though she considers herself socially awkward, she ultimately upholds the middle-class values of Protestant, reformist New England, proving that her individualism has a place within her society. Her ironic self-perception as an ugly duckling turns on the same irony as in Hans Christian Andersen's fairy tale: she proves to be a swan after all.

In the remainder of this chapter, I investigate how Twain's fictional commentaries on race and Alcott's fictional commentaries on gender are outgrowths of their biographies. Although some of the biographical material may be well trod, it does establish the connection between the two authors' reform impulses and their use of adolescent characters to serve as their mouthpieces. I trace the social tensions and moral issues that inform Clemens's and Alcott's lives in order to demonstrate how they employed adolescents as metaphors of the need for reform in *Adventures of Huckleberry Finn* and *Little Women*. With these novels, Twain and Alcott utilized adolescent growth meaningfully, implying parallels between the need for their characters to develop and the need for the character of their nation to develop.

Adventures of Huckleberry Finn

Twain employed Huckleberry Finn's immaturity as a platform from which to write about U.S. race relations. Huckleberry Finn's ambivalence about freeing

Jim mirrors Clemens's ambivalence about African Americans during his lifetime, which has been well-documented by most of his major biographers and
most thoroughly by Shelley Fisher Fishkin.[7] According to his own self-report,
the tales of three slaves in his childhood, one named Uncle Dan'l (Twain, *MT's
Autobiography* 112–13), one named Uncle Ned (Paine 15–16), and the other a
self-styled evangelist named Jerry (Twain, "Corn-pone" 583–84), provided his
indoctrination into the oral tradition. As a youth, he carried with him the virulent racism of most southerners at the time. When he first journeyed to New
York as a seventeen-year-old in 1853, Clemens wrote to his mother about the
street on which he lived: "Niggers, mulattoes, quadroons, Chinese, and some
the Lord no doubt originally intended to be white, but the dirt on whose faces
leaves one uncertain as to that fact, block up the little street; and to wade
through this mass of human vermin, would raise the ire of the most patient
person that ever lived" (*Selected Letters* 1.10).

As he matured, however, he began to develop some sensitivity to racial difference. For example, in San Francisco in the 1860s, he was appalled when white
policemen did nothing to stop bullies from attacking a Chinese man in front
of them (Fishkin, "MT and Race" 135–36), and the only tour guide he praised
on his first European tour was an African American who impressed him as
"the only [guide] we have had yet who knew anything" (*Innocents Abroad*
1.308).[8] Twain praises this guide's erudition and artistic values, then concludes:
"Negroes are deemed as good as white people, in Venice, and so this man feels
no desire to go back to his native land. His judgment is correct" (1.308). By
1867, when Twain wrote that passage, he perceived accurately the extent and
the effect of white racism on African Americans.

In 1874, Twain published in the *Atlantic Monthly* a poignant story spoken
in the voice of an ex-slave, called "A True Story." Mark Twain asks his family
servant, Aunt Rachel, how it is that she seems to have "never had any trouble"
(578). She responds with a chilling tale about being sold into permanent separation from her husband and seven children. She concludes, "Oh no, Misto
C——, *I* hain't had no trouble. An' no *joy*" (582).

Yet in 1876, Twain published *The Adventures of Tom Sawyer* with a stereotyped depiction of a Native American as the villain, who complains about being
"horsewhipped in front of the jail, like a nigger!" (208). In that novel,
Huckleberry Finn begs Tom Sawyer not to tell others that he thinks Uncle
Jake is "a mighty good nigger. . . . He likes me, becuz I don't ever act as if I
was above him. Sometimes I've set right down and eat with him" (200–01).
On the other hand, Clemens would be praised in his lifetime for being the

financial benefactor of the first black man who went to Yale Law School and for participating in a fund-raising event for Tuskegee Institute in 1906 (Fishkin, *Was* 90–91, 106).[9] Booker T. Washington expressed gratitude to Clemens for having called to the world's attention the racism at work in the Belgian Congo (Washington 349).

Nonetheless, Clemens thought nothing of employing the term "nigger," especially in his private writings, as Twain's posthumously published essay based on unpublished fragments of his *Autobiography* demonstrates. In an essay titled "The Minstrel Show," he writes: "Where now is Billy Rice? He was a joy to me, and so were the other stars of the nigger show. . . . [W]ith them departed to return no more forever, I suppose, the real nigger show—the genuine niggers show, the extravagant nigger show—the show which to me had no peer and whose peer has not yet arrived, in my experience" (111). Albert Bigelow Paine dates the essay as having been written November 30, 1906 (Twain, "Minstrel" 110). By that late date, Clemens had to have known the word "nigger" was inappropriate. In 1890, he wrote notes preparing for a speech introducing the journalist who found Dr. Livingstone, Henry Stanley, in which he used the word "black" to describe Africans: "—and delivered his humble black friends to the arms of their waiting wives and children" (*Notebooks* 3.589). In his published *Autobiography*, he wrote, "The black face is as welcome to me now as it was then" (101). When Clemens uses the word "black," he is being polite. When he uses the word "nigger," he intends either to be private or to startle the reader.

Because of Clemens's ambivalence about race, interpretations of the racial ideologies in *Adventures of Huckleberry Finn* have occupied literary critics for decades. Two of the most controversial arguments come from Leslie Fiedler, who argues ethnocentrically that Jim serves as the dark object of Huck's homo-erotic passion, and from Fishkin, who insightfully identifies the historical influences that led Twain to imbue Huckleberry Finn with the dialectical usages of a black character.[10] Ralph Ellison has also observed the intricacy of race as it recurs in *Huckleberry Finn*. Commenting on Twain's reliance on tropes of minstrelsy, Ellison believes that "it is from behind this stereotype mask that we see Jim's dignity and human capacity—and Twain's complexity—emerge" (50). Ellison, Fiedler, and Fishkin perceive how complicated race relations are in the United States, and so they read *Huckleberry Finn* as a complex novel.[11] Undoubtedly, racial prejudice is the most controversial topic surrounding the novel in our day. But when Twain was writing *Huckleberry Finn*, the religious skepticism of an America that was called to question faith by the Civil War and by Social Darwinism was also a tangible influence on his intellect.[12] Twain's inability to make a determinant reading of racial equality may well reflect his inability to make a determinant reading about his own religious faith.

Any one of a number of critics considers the burlesque ending of the novel to be motivated by racial ambivalence in America.[13] While I am no apologist for the ending of a novel that I sometimes wish Twain had ended the moment Huck decides to go to hell, those critics whose observations link race to the flawed ending of *Huckleberry Finn* have pertinence to an investigation of the relationship between religious intellectual thought in the United States and the development of the reform-minded adolescent novel. Without the moral imperative implied by the widespread romantic evangelism of his day, Twain might not have felt compelled to write a novel about an adolescent's growing awareness of the wrongs of slavery. Twain's struggle with black rights reflected the conflicted intellectual climate in which he operated and which could provide no easy justifications for how African Americans were treated during slavery or during Reconstruction. Twain's attempts at irony in the final section of *Huckleberry Finn* parallel his own inability to resolve the issues that the text attempts to resolve.[14]

Related to the issue of racism in the novel is the age-old question of whether Huckleberry Finn has grown (or grown up) at all. One key to the dilemma lies in Huck's growing ability to perceive Jim as a human being, despite the cultural conditioning that has taught the boy to consider African Americans to be chattel. The worst controversy about Huck's growth, of course, stems from Tom Sawyer's racist machinations to free a man who is already free, implicating Huck in a series of behaviors that makes him appear to forget that he has "humble[d]" himself to Jim (110), who has called him the "bes' fren' Jim's ever had" (131) only moments before Huck both protects his friend from being detected as a runaway and demonstrates their equality by splitting evenly with Jim the guilt-money he has extorted from two raftsmen, telling them there is smallpox aboard their craft (132–33). Huck's moral development progresses almost linearly in the novel, from his refusal to work actively to get into heaven in chapter 1 to his direct decision to go to hell for the sake of a friend in chapter 31.[15]

Huck's moral crises usually involve whether it is right for him to steal Jim out of slavery. He knows that "people would call me a low-down Ablitionist and despise me for keeping mum" (55) when he finds out that Jim is a runaway slave, but he cements their partnership when he finds out that slave-hunters are looking for Jim—not Huck—"Git up and hump yourself, Jim! . . . They're after us!" (81) But shortly before Jim calls Huck his best friend, Huck begins to worry about his life as slave-stealer: "I couldn't get that out of my conscience, no how nor no way. . . . it staid with me, and scorched me more and more" (129). His metaphor for a burning conscience that "scorches" him prefigures his later decision to go to hell, but after he fails at his effort to turn Jim in—because he discovers that he cannot betray someone who has just called him his best friend—Huck thinks: "A body that don't get *started* right when he's little, ain't got no show—when the pinch comes there ain't nothing to back him up and keep him to his work, and so he gets beat" (133). Twain casts Huck's ironically inaccurate moral self-perception in terms of his upbringing to indicate the boy's awareness of his own growth process. Huck then decides that his childhood has prepared him best to be hereafter expedient in matters of morals:

> Then I thought a minute, and says to myself, hold on;—s'pose you'd a done right and give Jim up; would you felt better than what you do now? No, says I, I'd feel bad—I'd feel just the same way I do now. Well, then, says I, what's the use you learning to do right, when it's troublesome to do right and ain't no trouble to do wrong, and the wages is just the same? I was stuck. I couldn't answer that. So I reckoned I wouldn't bother no more about it, but after this always do whichever come handiest at the time. (133)

But of course the "handiest" thing to do at the time when the duke and the king sell Jim back into slavery would be for Huck Finn to walk away. Instead, he thinks first that "it would be a thousand times better for Jim to be a slave at home where his family was, as long as he'd *got* to be a slave" (271), so he decides to write the letter revealing Jim's whereabouts to Miss Watson that he rips up after the moral epiphany in which he declares himself hell-bound.

In that chapter of his greatest moral crisis, Huck "couldn't seem to strike no places to harden me against" Jim and remembers the many kindnesses the man has showered on him (273).[16] It is those memories that lead Huck to conclude, "All right, then, I'll *go* to hell" (273). At the most basic level, growth in literature for youth amounts to the transition from self-absorption to concern for others (Stephens 3). Huck's willingness to go to hell for Jim demonstrates that Huck has turned from an orientation that is self-preoccupied to an orientation that is concerned with others. His growth, which comes in the form of moral development, has resulted entirely from having to confront racial injustice.

Three more things are salient about the concept of growth in *Huckleberry Finn*. First, Twain trains the reader to understand the irony of Huck's growth; second, Twain relies on the reader's understanding of romantic evangelism to stimulate the reader's awareness of that growth; and, ultimately, Twain implies that Huck's growth is as much about the nation's character as it is about Huck.

Twain carefully teaches the reader to interpret Huck's narration as ironic by raising "truth" as an issue in the first paragraph of the book and by detailing Huck's many lies.[17] Another notorious way that Twain provides that instruction is with comedy, as when Huck tells the reader that "Jim said bees wouldn't sting idiots; but I didn't believe that, because I had tried them lots of times myself, and they wouldn't sting me" (57). Even the youngest of readers can understand that such a statement depicts Huck as someone who is not meant to be believed literally at every moment. In a later and more important example of the reader being trained for ironic awareness, Huck thinks about his decision to go to hell: "It was awful thoughts, and awful words, but they was said. And I let them stay said; and never thought no more about reforming" (274). As a matter of fact, Huck very shortly thereafter thinks about reforming when he tries to reform Tom Sawyer out of the sin of "stealing" Jim in a passage that drips with irony: "That was the thing that was too many for me. Here was a boy that was respectable, and well brung up; and had a character to lose; and folks at home that had characters; and he was bright and not leather-headed; and knowing and not ignorant; and not mean, but kind; and yet here he was, without any more pride, or rightness, or feeling, than to stoop to this business, and make himself a shame, and his family a shame, before everybody" (295). Tom's actions in the following chapters are most assuredly more "mean" than "kind"; Tom displays himself as having precious little in the way of "rightness, or feeling." Twain the ironist expects the reader to understand, at the very least, that every moral perception Huckleberry Finn presents is skewed. Even in their first encounter with the book in high school, most students learn to regard Huckleberry Finn as better than the people around him, including Tom, even though Huck does not regard himself as superior to them. The irony of his inability to understand that he has morally transcended his culture is crucial to understanding the carnivalesque crisis of the book's final twelve chapters. Without Tom's moral certainty that his debasing actions of Jim are right and good—actions that we as readers recognize as flawed—we cannot appreciate the depths of Huck's good intentions. Huck genuinely means to save Jim; Tom does not because he knows that Jim is already free. Whether the irony succeeds in the final section depends entirely on how well the reader has been trained to perceive the irony surrounding Tom's inhumane treatment of Jim.

Second, the depiction of Huckleberry's growth is very consciously situated for a reader sympathetic to romantic evangelism—rather than for Huck himself—to discern. Many of the passages of moral crisis happen in direct address to the reader rather than in dialogue with another character, as when Huck tells the reader he won't "try" for heaven or when he claims he will "always do whichever come handiest" when he's making a moral decision (5, 133). Huck never has the type of awareness of his growth that Jo March has when she reassures her mother, "I'm not the scatter-brain I was; you may trust me" (340), or when she tells Laurie, "We never can be boy and girl again. . . . We are man and woman now, with sober work to do, for play-time is over, and we must give up frolicking" (346). Rather, Twain expects readers who share his values to do the necessary interpretive work about morality in dialogue with Huck, instead of having Huck perform in dialogue with another character. The expectations placed on the reader are demanding and ambiguous, so it is possible for some readers to conclude that Huck has not grown, and others to conclude that he has.[18]

Whether or not Huck has grown is almost immaterial to the most important point surrounding his growth: the reader is meant to understand that Huck *needs* to grow. Given that growth was a natural expectation of youth in the nineteenth century (as in our own), Twain's depicting a youth who *needed* to grow as a character in a novel marketed to an adult audience was most likely influenced by the Germanic tradition of the *bildungsroman* that also influenced Dickens and the Brontës to write about developing youth. But Clemens's religious background was also at work here. For example, Paul Carter demonstrates how Huck's decision to go to hell reflects Jonathan Edwards's concern with man's ability to make moral choices (61); Edwards was the progenitor of the branch of Presbyterianism to which Clemens's family subscribed. And Stone observes that Huck's morality develops because he is attuned to nature and the possibility of redemption to be found there in a very Emersonian fashion (140–44).[19] Thus, the former Presbyterian who has rejected the Calvinistic doctrine of predestination in favor of progressive beliefs about moral development depicts Huck choosing virtue because of the sentiments in the adolescent's heart that become available to him through his union with nature.[20] Twain requires any reader concerned about Huck's growth to connect the dots that his development hinges on an increased valuation of the individual and the redemptive power of nature.

But in most nineteenth-century *Bildungsromane*, the youth-who-needs-to-grow is on a path of maturation that involves his own evolution into the romantic notion of the self-aware and Other-oriented individual. Huck's moral crisis, on the other hand, is necessitated by a national crisis of morals, which brings

me to my third point about growth in *Huckleberry Finn*: the novel is as much
about the need for a nation to mature as it is about a boy's need to mature.
The national conflict about slavery and race relations—not the incipient conflict inherent to the *Sturm und Drang* of adolescent angst—creates the situation that forces Huck's need to develop. Huck's observations about his own
conscience, his underprivileged childhood, his need to grow, and his moral
decision-making all center around liberation, or as Huck might have it, stealing—either human beings or watermelons. (Huck's comic rationalizations
about stealing things like chickens or "a watermelon, or a mushmelon, or a
punkin" provide the reader with a running commentary that "stealing," that
is, liberating something, is sometimes justified [84–85, 305].) *Adventures of
Huckleberry Finn* implies that Jim deserves to be liberated and that the United
States has not made good on its promises of freedom and equality for all men.
Twain wants the readers who were his contemporaries to share his belief that
emancipation was a positive social good—and he wants his readers to perceive
the inhumanity inherent in racism. Twain confronts what he perceives as a
lack of moral development in his culture with an adolescent who is engaged
in the process of growth. He writes a novel about what it means for one man
to be liberated with the aid of a morally developing youth, implying that a
white teenager and his African American friend have more potential to understand racial equality than any white adult in the text.

While Jim expresses hope for the future in positive terms that allow for the
possibility that his own situation can improve, Huck acknowledges that human
nature is the root of the need for reform. The scene on the raft in which Huck
tries to trick Jim into believing that they have not really been separated during the fog demonstrates how their attitudes complement one another. While
Jim still believes that he is interpreting a dream, he thinks that the towheads
they have seen in the river represent the "troubles we was going to get into
with quarrelsome people and all kinds of mean folks, but if we minded our
business and didn't talk back and aggravate them, we would pull through and
get out of the fog and into the big clear river, which was the free States, and
wouldn't have no more trouble" (109). Jim believes that, if he keeps a low pro-
file in a world filled with bullies, he can still enter a "big clear" place that is
"free." His hope indicates how much he wants his present condition to change,
while it simultaneously humbles Huck, for the youth then realizes that he has
taken his joke too far and intruded on his friend's dream. Huck apologizes to
Jim—radical behavior for a southern boy, no matter how well-intentioned he
has been—and vows to "do him no more mean tricks" (110). Jim forgives him.

Huck's later comments about contemporary life validate both Jim's perception that society needs to change and the importance of forgiveness in enacting that change. For example, Huck doesn't want to describe all the details of the Shepherdsons laying in wait to kill Buck because "it would make me sick again if I was to do that. I wished I hadn't ever come ashore that night, to see such things. I ain't ever going to get shut of them—lots of times I dream about them" (160). Huck can't forgive the Shepherdsons, so their violence haunts him, just as the factions in the Civil War are haunted as long as they deny the possibility of forgiveness. Later in the narrative, however, Huck feels so much compassion for the king and the duke—even though they are the people in the story who have caused him and Jim the most trouble—that he can forgive them when they are tarred and feathered: "It made me sick to see it; and I was sorry for them poor pitiful rascals, it seemed like I couldn't ever feel any hardness against them any more in the world. It was a dreadful thing to see. Human beings *can* be awful cruel to one another" (292). This identification of human cruelty communicates how much people need to change, and Huck's and Jim's capacities for forgiveness communicate the possibility that people *can* change, given their willingness to do so.

Twain has combined remorse with racial politics about whether it is right to liberate (i.e., "steal") another human being because the author has an ideological intent, one that is articulated through the irony of Huck's moral growth. Twain chained the *bildungsroman* format to a reformer's wagon because his immersion in the culture of romantic evangelism made it impossible for him to write about moral growth without simultaneously recognizing his culture's need to develop what he regarded as more mature morals. If Huck needs to grow, so does anyone who shares his racial insensitivity. Huck's ignorance—and the far more malevolent ignorance of the southerners with whom he interacts—serves as a commentary on the ignorance of Americans in general (a topic that Twain had been exploring in his career as early as *The Innocents Abroad*). Twain implies that if Huck needs to grow, so does the nation that he represents. Perhaps the best proof of the parallel between Huck's and the nation's immaturity lies in Twain's inability to portray Huck as having achieved adulthood. Twain depicts Huck's need to grow, and he depicts the youth's moral growth, but Twain never depicts Huck as an adult. Twain's well-known cynicism about humanity was based on his perception that humanity needs to develop better morals but, en masse, is unlikely ever to do so. Huck—like the United States—needs to grow, but that need to grow will always-already be a social truth. Perhaps, then, Twain captured our cultural obsession with youth because he understood intuitively our need to believe that change is possible—and that change is a luxury that the fixity of adulthood does not always afford.

Little Women

Alcott, too, linked youth to social change. While she wrote far more about gender than she did about race in her novels for youth, because her suffragism emerged from her abolitionism, her commentary about race in *Little Women* helps to show that she shared Clemens's concerns about the fate of African Americans during Reconstruction. In *Little Women*, Alcott makes a limited number of references to race, all of which appear in the second book, "Good Wives." Amy agrees to work at a charity function because "it's for the Freedmen" (236). Symbolically, three paragraphs later, Jo makes the pronouncement that costs her a trip to Europe: "I don't like favors; they oppress and make me feel like a slave" (236). In a didactic and sexist passage that the narrator herself identifies as a soporific "homily," the narrator admonishes her male readers to "be courteous to the old maids, no matter how poor and plain and prim, for the only chivalry worth having is that which is the readiest to pay deference to the old, protect the feeble, and serve womankind, regardless of rank, age, or color" (343). Finally, Alcott embeds in the last chapter two references to a student at Plumfield who is a "little quadroon" (377, 379). The boy is at the school as a charity case, and his character serves as a tribute to her father's Temple School closing, in part, over the enrollment of Susan Robinson (Stern, *Louisa* 13). But the "merry little quadroon" who has "the sweetest voice of all" is notably absent from the book's sequels, *Little Men* and *Jo's Boys* (377, 379). Taken together, however, Amy's comment about working for the Freedmen at the charity ball, the narrator's sermon about "chivalry" being a matter of serving women "regardless of color" (343), and the unnamed African American child who serves as a signifier of Jo's charity (rather than serving as a fully developed character) all point toward Alcott's racial guilt and her method of dealing with it: by performing charitable actions.

Alcott had been raised in an abolitionist family that included her uncle, Samuel Joseph May. Her parents were friends with such abolitionists as William Lloyd Garrison, who delivered a eulogy at her mother's funeral (*Selected Letters* 226n1). After Harper's Ferry, in November 1859, Alcott wrote in her journal, "Glad I have lived to see the Antislavery movement and this last heroic act in it. Wish I could do my part" (95). Alcott's abolitionist principles seem at their most triumphant after Lincoln's assassination in 1865, when she wrote in her journal, "Saw the great procession, & though colored men were in it one was walking arm in arm with a white gentleman & I exulted thereat" (140). Alcott admired Lincoln, John Brown, Wendell Phillips, her uncle Samuel May, and Emerson because they upheld the ideals she held as central to her faith: people should live in the world reforming it as they go.

The grown-up Rose Campbell in *Rose in Bloom* epitomizes Alcott's sense of the ideal reformer: "Her heroes ceased to be the world's favorites; and became such as Garrison fighting for his chosen people; Howe restoring lost sense to the deaf, the dumb, and blind; Sumner unbribable, when other men were bought and sold: and many a large-hearted woman working as quietly as Abby Gibbons, who for thirty years has made Christmas merry for two hundred little paupers in a city almshouse, besides saving Magdalens and teaching convicts" (360).[21] Rose's goal is to be a philanthropist. Alcott employs the character's aspirations as a plot device that enables her to discuss educational reform (*Eight* 84–92, 179–90, 216–25), dress reform (*Eight* 204–15), suffrage (*Rose* 239), temperance (*Rose* 169–91, 259–61, 271–75, 276–90), and charity to the poor and orphaned (*Rose* 254–66).[22] Alcott's attitudes toward all these social reforms reside in a very white, middle-class, Protestant way of living. Her advocacy of self-sacrifice and charity never quite masks her staunch belief that people who feel as she does are superior to those who don't. She notes the debasing effects of poverty in *Little Women*, *Little Men*, and *Rose in Bloom* but cannot resist believing that some people deserve their poverty more than others. As Laurie tells Amy after they are married:

> "There's one sort of poverty that I particularly like to help. Out-and-out beggars get taken care of, but poor gentlefolks fare badly, because they won't ask, and people don't dare to offer charity; yet there are a thousand ways of helping them, if one only knows how to do it so delicately that it don't offend. I must say, I like to serve a decayed gentleman better than a blarneying beggar; I suppose it's wrong, but I do, though it is harder."
>
> "Because it takes a gentleman to do it," added the other member of the domestic admiration society. (357)

Alcott's Christianity compelled her to promote social justice as an act of charity. She did not appear to believe that social justice would ever be achieved, but she believed that Christians should work for racial and gender equality nonetheless.

One obvious social reform in the Alcott canon is her promotion of women's rights. The character Jo rebels against gender roles in scenes that involve her anger and her writing. Drawing on those combined motifs of anger and writing, Alcott depicts how the character's morality develops, despite Jo's relatively stable sense of self. For example, early in *Little Women*, Jo establishes her discontent with the confinement enforced on her by nineteenth-century mores surrounding femininity. Jo laments, "It's bad enough to be a girl, any way, when I like boy's games, and work, and manners. I can't get over my disappointment in not being a boy, and it's worse than ever now, for I'm dying to go and fight with papa, and I can only stay at home and knit like a poky old woman" (12–13). Her penultimate line of dialogue reflects that she still retains her self-identification with boys: "I have nothing to complain of, and never was so jolly in my life. Excuse the remark, but living among boys, I can't help using their expressions now and then" (380). The opening of *Little Men* describes her having such "peculiar tastes" as empathizing with boys: "She had a way of filling up a fellow's plate before he asked, of laughing at his jokes, gently tweaking him by the ear, or clapping him on the shoulder" (33). Jo is a character who is remarkably comfortable with masculinity for a nineteenth-century female.

Because of Jo's comfort with masculinity and discomfort with some aspects of femininity (but not others), many scholars have grappled with the question of whether or not *Little Women* is a feminist novel.[23] But even readers who are disappointed that Jo gives up her independence and saddles herself working for a house full of males cannot deny that Alcott's developing suffragist sentiments work their way into the novel. As with Huck Finn's, Jo's moral crises tend to correspond to the political convictions that the author is commenting on—in this case, gender. For example, Jo displays anger that is inappropriate for a woman, and she needs to find "some useful, happy work to do" within a sphere that is appropriate for a woman (337). Jo's moral crisis surrounding her temper is triggered by her sister Amy burning her book manuscript. While Jo is still angry at Amy, she thinks, "Let her take care of herself" (66). Jo's inability to be other-oriented at that moment results in Amy nearly drowning—and Jo subsequently developing a strong sense of remorseful compassion for the Other. Jo resolves the crisis with an evangelical moment of developmental conversion after her mother urges her to "learn to feel the strength and tenderness of your Heavenly Father as you do that of your earthly one" (70). Jo learns to think of God as "the Friend who welcomes every child with a love stronger than that of any father, tenderer than that of any mother" (70). Her definition of God is gendered as a strong father and a tender mother, but it nevertheless strives toward an androgynous balance of the genders.

Jo's writing also creates a crisis in *Little Women* when she mentally assumes the moral spectacles of the patriarchal Professor Bhaer and concludes that the sensation stories she has been publishing are "trash" (280). And this time, too, she ends up with a burnt manuscript, though she burns her papers herself and turns to writing more womanly—albeit financially unsuccessful—moral tales in the mode of "Mrs. Sherwood, Miss Edgeworth, and Hannah More" (281). The narrative persona addresses Jo directly with instruction about the importance of this act of moral development: "Pity from your heart those who have no such guardians [as your parents] to hedge them round with principles which may seem like prison walls to impatient youth, but which will prove sure foundations to build character upon in womanhood" (281). As it did with her fight with Amy, Jo's writing has been part of what has triggered the crisis. Nonetheless, her writing has been necessary to her family's well-being. She has needed to publish in order to help support them, and writing is one of the more lucrative ways that a woman of her station can earn money. The narrator even describes Jo's writing as a source of empowerment, after Jo begins receiving checks for her serial publications. She "began to feel herself a power in the house" because those checks can pay for the butcher bill and groceries and enable the family to buy new carpeting and clothing (215).

Jo values her independence, not just in terms of her artistic development, but also in terms of the financial security her career provides her: "Jo enjoyed a taste of this satisfaction, and ceased to envy richer girls, taking great comfort in the knowledge that she could supply her own wants, and need ask no one for a penny" (215). She cannot fight in the Civil War, and she cannot romp forever in masculine clothing as boys can, and she cannot avoid the social demands that she must observe the proprieties that cast her in the role of "Miss March." She cannot even avoid marriage and motherhood. But she does manage to find financial independence, first through writing, and second through the legacy of the strongest matriarch in the novel, Aunt March. Alcott communicates clearly to her readership that she values independent-minded women who are capable of self-support. Perhaps it is even the novel's ambivalence about gender that has made it so accessible to such a broad variety of readers over time.

Another reason that *Little Women* resonates with modern readers may be our perception that Jo—especially the vibrant Jo of the novel's first half—does not really need to change. Her aspirations, her goals, her interests, and her talent all seem admirable, as does her self-despised temper and inner strength. The reader is given to know that Jo's mannishness—which, crucially, she never completely outgrows—is a part of her character that is as important as her honesty. John Brooke, for example, praises young women in the United States to a visitor from England: "Young ladies in America love independence as much as their ancestors did, and are admired and respected for supporting themselves" (110). Readers, in turn, are meant to participate in the author's ideological valuation of female independence. But if the ideology were universally held, the statement would prove unnecessary. Alcott knows that not all members of the culture in which she lives value strength in young women. Jo learns to curb her temper, but she still feels anger in the final chapters of *Little Women*—and in *Little Men* and *Jo's Boys*. She returns to her self-identification as a storyteller throughout the trilogy whenever she needs either emotional solace or financial gain. She retains some measure of her androgyny, her independence, and her honesty in all three books. Although she learns to act in more socially acceptable ways and becomes more aware of the ethics involved in writing, her basic identity does not change all that much in *Little Women*.

In fact, throughout the novel, Jo is something of a transcendent character, a self-reliant nonconformist in the best Emersonian tradition. In that sense, Jo could be said to be more morally advanced than many of the representatives of society with whom she comes in contact: the Gardiners, the Moffats, the Vaughns, the Chesters, the Lambs—all upstanding families whose commitment to materialism and inability to articulate principles of social justice are notable. Jo is also often described in language that marks her as qualitatively different from those around her. For example, in the first chapter, Alcott describes all four sisters' eyes. Three of the sisters' she describes physically; but Jo's she describes in terms of vision. Meg's are "large," Beth is "bright-eyed," and Amy has "blue eyes," but Jo has "sharp gray eyes, which appeared to see everything" (13). Her eyes are not unlike the "transparent eyeball" in Emerson's essay "Nature" that sees "nothing" and "all," inspiring the individual to be spiritually transcendent (189). Jo's eyes are important for more than just their physical appearance: they are the symbols of her Emersonian capacity for transcendence because she sees with both the inner eye ("nothing") and with the outer eye ("everything"). Moreover, when Marmee first enters the novel, she expresses concern to each of her daughters: "Has any one called, Beth? How is your cold, Meg? Jo, you look tired to death. Come and kiss me, baby" (16). Only to Jo does Marmee express a metaphor that underscores the girl's ontological status as a living being: "you look tired to death." In the same chapter, Jo's father does something similar in eliciting with his letter home some sort of concern with the here-and-now from three of his daughters. Meg vows to be less vain and love work more; Amy vows to be less selfish; Beth simply wipes away the tears that she is then crying. But Jo's reaction reflects her awareness

of other planes of existence, other places she could be and longs to go: "I'll try
. . . [to] do my duty here instead of wanting to be somewhere else" (17). For
Jo, self-improvement is not only a matter of improving her moral character, it
is also a matter of choosing to be physically and emotionally present with those
whom she loves.

When the four sisters express their castles in the air, Jo's is, again, expressed
with a difference that implies her transcendence. Meg longs for a happy home;
Beth for safety in her family; Amy for artistic fame. Indeed, Amy, Laurie, and
Jo all long for artistic fame: Amy with painting, Laurie with music, and Jo
with writing. But only Jo introduces a fantastic element to her castle in the air:
she wants a "magic inkstand" (118). While everyone else in the group expects
to succeed by ordinary means, she expresses her own success as something that
would be magical. And when the castles in the air have begun to be built three
years later, Jo's is the only one "which was one day to place the name of March
upon the roll of fame" (191).

The novel concludes with the realization of Jo's potential for transcendence.
Jo is in "an unusually uplifted frame of mind" and describes her life as "quite
a little heaven on earth" (375). The school she and her husband have founded,
Plumfield, is a "boys' paradise"—even if all of the students "were not angels
by any means" (376). Jo is married to the sun and enacts Christ's injunction
to forgive "seventy times seven" (*KJV* Matthew 18:22): "No mortal boy could
hold out long with Father Bhaer shining on him as benevolently as the sun,
and Mother Bhaer forgiving him seventy times seven" (376). Jo and Bhaer
appear to have been apotheosized into god-like creatures. Jo tells her family,
"There's no need for me to say it, for every one can see that I'm far happier
than I deserve" (380)—but the statement seems ironic. She has worked hard
for what she has earned, and she has been rewarded for her faith in good works
the way any romantic evangelical might expect. There has been an earlier irony
in the novel surrounding Jo's spirituality when she tells Beth that she will get
to heaven easily: "I'm the one that will have to fight and work, and climb and
wait, and maybe never get in after all" (117). For the romantic evangelical, bat-
tling through life toward self-improvement was part of the religious process.
It is Jo's suffering that redeems her. From the beginning of the novel she has
been set apart—and sometimes above—those around her, but she earns her
salvation with her self-control and charity to others.

Jo's central problem, then, arises from living in a culture that cannot appreciate her as she is, which necessitates her development from rebelliousness to
adhering to appropriate gender mores. But because throughout the novel she

is a transcendent character who is at once self-reliant and redeemed by suffering, she is almost the ideal of Alcott's model adolescent. Jo is a character who serves as a metaphor for her culture's need to change. Alcott depicts negatively those characters who are haughty, dogmatic, lazy, or—worst of all—intolerant, while she values strength and courage and honesty and independence and the opportunity that the need for hard work provides the individual. When Jo and Laurie are in their early twenties, she tells him, "[We have] sober work to do," implying that the most significant difference between childhood and adulthood is concern for others (346).

Alcott provides Jo with an independent mind and a reformer's heart in the novel's opening chapters. Alcott also expects both genders to be respected for the functions that they performed in her culture, and she implies that greatness lies in engaging one's genius, regardless of gender. The narrator's didactic messages to the reader indicate how much Alcott thinks her audience needs moral instruction, but her depiction of Jo demonstrates that the protagonist has the innate qualities it takes to achieve the Emersonian ideal of the individual in "Self-Reliance" who has a "great soul. . . . To be great is to be misunderstood" (263–64). Jo does not need to grow and change in *Little Women* anywhere near as much as the country in which she lives does. She is, like the Emersonian ideal, simply misunderstood. She has within her all the qualities of greatness when the novel begins, and her putative growth is little more than her achieving her own potentiality and learning to live in such a way that she is less frequently ostracized by people who misunderstand her. But nothing in her interior life seems to have changed much by the end of the novel. She has grown more patient, but her personality remains otherwise stable.

Conclusion

If Jo March serves as Alcott's metaphor for the need for Americans to develop gender equality, Huckleberry Finn serves as Twain's metaphor for the need for Americans to outgrow their racism. Like Jo, Huck is a character that readers recognize almost immediately needs to grow far less than the racist culture in which he lives.[24] Like Jo, he grows more morally aware, but from the beginning to the end of the novel, Huck fights being civilized by running away from those who would require him to act with more propriety. At the end of the novel, as at the beginning, he still plays with Tom Sawyer; he still lies; he still steals; he still fails to recognize his moral superiority to those of a better class than he. The central irony of the book is Huck's inability to perceive that he does not have a problem; his culture does. Thus, like Alcott, Twain chose to write a social critique relying on a youth whose need to grow parallels the moral needs of the nation. And in both cases, the adolescent's growth is depicted with some irony.

Myra Jehlen describes *Huckleberry Finn* as an American classic because "almost uniquely it probes the lowest and most sensitive layer of the American mind, where individualism takes a first purchase on the world in some degree cognizant that the community will have to pay for it" (113).[25] Thanks to Jo March's obsessively reproving parents, she is all too aware that individualism comes at the cost of community, which may be why *Little Women* is also an American classic. Jehlen argues that Huckleberry Finn is performing for the reader the central conflict of the Civil War and Reconstruction: the will of the individual (slaveholder) opposing the will of the state (97). Saxton refers to the Civil War as one informed by an "adolescent morality" because, to people on both sides, good and evil were clearly demarcated (10). *Little Women*, she says, "outlines the adolescence of American morality" with its black-and-white, Dickensian ethos (9). But *Little Women* is influenced by the Civil War in the same way Jehlen describes it influencing *Huckleberry Finn*. The same could be said of Jo March as of Huck: she must learn to tame her individual passions for the collective good of the family order. Both characters thereby fit the standard definition of growth in youth literature: they move from some level of solipsism to an increased social awareness (Stephens 3). Indeed, in the chapter called "Experiments," Jo and her sisters learn that "the comfort of all depends on each doing her share faithfully"—or as Jo puts it, "Lounging and larking don't pay" (99). After a week of not having done any housework, a week that culminates in the pseudo-tragedy of Beth's parakeet dying, Marmee concludes: "Work . . . gives us a sense of power and independence better than money or fashion" (99). Having learned that lesson, Jo puts Beth ahead of her own ambitions when her sister is dying, and her sacrifice of selling her hair to pay for her mother's trip to nurse their injured father is one of the more critiqued passages of the novel.[26] The individual's responsibility to his or her culture was a central component of American romantic evangelism, and it is a narrative that both Jo and Huck fulfill while they are simultaneously critiquing American culture. It is impossible to imagine Clemens or Alcott writing in a different religious climate—but if they had, perhaps they could not have constructed such socially aware, reform-minded adolescent characters.

Samuel Clemens and Louisa May Alcott were the products of a reform culture that was based in the religious principles on which New England was founded. American horror at the excesses of the Civil War radically altered that culture, propelling the nation toward widespread social reform. Twain and Alcott's shared legacy was to create the two most enduring adolescent characters in American fiction: Huckleberry Finn and Jo March. Both of these characters are portrayed as youth who grow amidst—and despite—social turmoil. Their need for personal growth is metaphoric for both authors' beliefs that the society needed to reform, beliefs that were influenced by the authors' basic agreement with the value romantic evangelism placed on the individual and her or his responsibility to improve the world.

The similarities between *Little Women* and *Adventures of Huckleberry Finn* can thus be summarized as follows:

• Both novels demonstrate the American tension between individual and community;
• Both depict protagonists grappling with the romantic evangelical ideologies foregrounded by the Civil War;
• Both protagonists are adolescents;
• The adolescent protagonists are ethical characters whose moral development helps them transcend the corruption of the culture in which they live;
• Both have ironically negative self-images that the reader is meant to understand are inaccurate;
• Both novels imply that social change is not only possible but necessary;
• In both novels, the growth of the adolescent is a metaphor for the need for the nation's "social growth" (i.e., reform).

Jo thinks her worst flaw is her anger—but if everyone in her culture were as honest and androgynous and self-reliant as she, the culture would be transformed in Alcott's formulation. And if the southerners Huck encountered were as accepting and respectful of the individuality of African Americans as he, the Civil War would never have happened. The hypotheticals I am suggesting here are, of course, impossible: without the conflict between the individual and the culture, neither novel would exist. But the fact remains that Twain and Alcott both relied on adolescents when they wanted to write about the possibility of social reform because the temporary quality of adolescence as a stage of life implies the inevitable possibility of individual growth. Both of them wrote about adolescents in order to write about the inchoate nature of their own culture.

Multiple adolescent characters have followed in Jo's and Huck's footsteps, so the genre abounds with characters whose personal growth is a metaphor for the author's ideologies of social change. American adolescent literature is a reformist corpus because its earliest practitioners created prototypes that worked—prototypes that sold. American readers tend to believe that humans can learn to improve ourselves, an optimism that often results from religious training and the Judeo-Christian ideologies that inform our educations, even for those of us who are not religiously trained. American adolescents have been encouraged to think of adolescence as a movement toward the perfectibility of man since Alcott and Twain first defined the genre of adolescent literature for them. It seems likely that we will continue to value the ideology of reform in novels for youth in the United States. When we embrace such novels, we are paying tribute to the legacies initiated by Mark Twain and Louisa May Alcott.

CHAPTER THREE

Historical Interlude
Vita Religiosa and Romantic Evangelism

"Diligently train your ideals *upward* and *still upward.*"
— *What Is Man?*

"Keep innocency and take heed to the thing that is right,
for this will bring a man peace in the last."
— *Work*

H uck Finn and Jo March are the two most enduring adolescent figures in the canon of American literature. But how did it happen that authors such as Clemens and Alcott seized on the concept of adolescence as the nexus of moral choice and reform? Before moving on to analyses of the reformist adolescents that populate the rest of the Twain and Alcott canon, I would like to explore the history of ideas as a major factor in the evolution of both authors' reform-minded adolescent protagonists. *Adventures of Huckleberry Finn* and *Little Women* vary significantly in their use of generic conventions and in their settings, plot, and structure. But both novels are informed by the intellectual climate—specifically the nineteenth-century American obsession with religion—in which the two authors were writing.

What initially led both post–Civil War writers to use youthful characters as a symbol for the possibility of social hope was undoubtedly a result of the Romantic belief in the purity of youth. Little Eva's inspirational piety in *Uncle Tom's Cabin* is perhaps the most famous example of the Romantic child inspiring social change in nineteenth-century American literature. Although Eva is not an adolescent like Huck and Jo, but a child character who is "between five and six years of age" (161), Alcott's construction of Jo as being at fifteen "as innocent and frank as any child" fits squarely into the same tradition of the innocent child functioning as a symbol of moral purity (46).[1] Far more interesting to me than the effect of the inspirational child, however, is the relationship between moral growth, spirituality, and reform that occurs in *Little Women* and *Adventures of Huckleberry Finn*. Ultimately, Alcott and Clemens's greatest legacy to American literature may be their use of the adolescent as a metaphor for social growth, which I discussed in the previous chapter. But that metaphor grew out of the Protestant theology that most affected Clemens's and Alcott's attitudes toward religion.

Romantic Evangelism

If people can be said to share a similar theological ancestry, Alcott and Clemens shared one that led them to have comparable views about reform, charity, and the individual's responsibility to improve the world. The influence of various theologians on both of them has historically been well-documented, but origins of influence for the theologians that most affected the authors can be traced back to the same religious figure: Jonathan Edwards. Something of a family tree of religious leaders demonstrates this phenomenon (see Fig. 1). The men who influenced Clemens's and Alcott's spirituality each had an important mentor who was, in turn, someone who embraced some aspect of Edwards's theology but who also broke away from some of Edwards's beliefs to create a schism in Congregationalism.

Samuel Clemens attended Joseph Twichell's Asylum Hill Congregational Church in Hartford. While Clemens never formally joined the church, he did rent a pew for his family and regularly went to church there. More important, he had an intimate friendship with Twichell that influenced Clemens's spirituality throughout his adult life (LeMaster and Wilson 757). Twichell himself had studied under Horace Bushnell, one of the most influential theologians of nineteenth-century American Protestantism, and Bushnell had studied under Nathaniel William Taylor, a follower of Jonathan Edwards's grandson, Timothy Dwight, who had served as a president of Yale from 1785 to 1817. Louisa May Alcott, on the other hand, widely acknowledged the spiritual influences of Ralph Waldo Emerson and Theodore Parker, whose transcendentalism was directly affected by William Ellery Channing, who in turn had been influenced by—and rejected many of the tenets of—one of Jonathan Edwards's most ardent disciples, Samuel Hopkins. The part of Hopkins's Congregationalism that influenced Channing the most was his abolitionism. The part Channing rejected was the Calvinism that the Unitarians rejected but the Congregationalists continued to embrace. What follows, then, is an account of the historical relationships among these religious leaders and a subsequent analysis of Clemens's and Alcott's religious lives in ways that help explain their motivation to create youthful reformers.

The theologians who most influenced Alcott and Clemens were immersed in the dominant religious milieu of their day, romantic evangelism. If evangelism

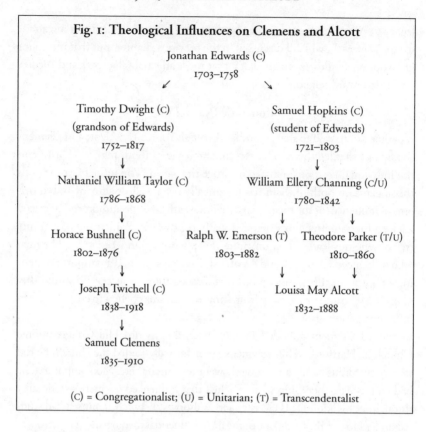

Fig. 1: Theological Influences on Clemens and Alcott

Jonathan Edwards (C)
1703–1758

Timothy Dwight (C)
(grandson of Edwards)
1752–1817

Samuel Hopkins (C)
(student of Edwards)
1721–1803

Nathaniel William Taylor (C)
1786–1868

William Ellery Channing (C/U)
1780–1842

Horace Bushnell (C)
1802–1876

Ralph W. Emerson (T)
1803–1882

Theodore Parker (T/U)
1810–1860

Joseph Twichell (C)
1838–1918

Louisa May Alcott
1832–1888

Samuel Clemens
1835–1910

(C) = Congregationalist; (U) = Unitarian; (T) = Transcendentalist

describes the religious practice of creating converts by preaching the New Testament as it was written by the evangelists who wrote the four gospels, romantic evangelism is the specifically Protestant manifestation of conversion-based religions that developed in the aftermath of the eighteenth-century Great Awakening and that grew even more fervent during the nineteenth-century Second Great Awakening. Let me hasten to add that neither Clemens nor Alcott could ever be described as being religious zealots interested in the conversion of sinners. Rather, both were affected by the philosophers and clerics such as Emerson and Bushnell who were active in influencing the intellectual history of romantic evangelism.

Inspired in America largely by Jonathan Edwards and his followers, romantic evangelists emphasized the primacy of the individual and his or her relationship with God as a fundamental factor in conversion. Those touched by God's light through their gospel-based conversion would be expected to live better lives, to become people who were themselves evangelicals, reaching out to others and reforming them, either through quiet example, like the Quakers, or with public exhortations, like some Methodists. Many of the major abolitionists—the Beechers, the Grimké sisters, Frederick Douglass, William Lloyd Garrison, Sojourner Truth—practiced some sort of religious faith that could be identified as functioning within the tenets of romantic evangelism: they were Congregationalists, or Unitarians, or Baptists, or Presbyterians, or Methodists, or Quakers, or Campbellites, or any one of a number of sects that linked abolitionism to Protestantism. Much (but not all) of the history of nineteenth-century reform movements that started with abolitionism and eventually evolved into suffragism, the temperance movement, and health reform parallels the history of an American people obsessed with the individual's obligation to improve the world because of his or her knowledge of the Christian gospel.[2]

Clemens was raised in a branch of Presbyterianism that had joined with the Congregationalists in 1801 only to split again in 1837 over schisms about original sin, slavery, and the role of the presbytery (see Ahlstrom 466–68). As an adult, Clemens was to ally himself more closely with the Congregationalist faction that held that "sin is in the sinning,"[3] not inborn in the sinner. The notion that sin is an action rather than an inborn condition emerged from the work of Congregationalist theologian Nathaniel William Taylor. The split he created in Congregationalism was very similar to the split William Ellery Channing created in Congregationalism with his Unitarian repudiation of the Trinity. It is not incidental that Taylor was a professor at Yale Divinity School—the New England bastion of Congregationalism in Connecticut, where Clemens lived—while Channing was from Harvard, the Unitarian university in Massachusetts, where Alcott lived and where Ralph Waldo Emerson nurtured transcendentalism and its rejection of Unitarianism.

Unitarianism had grown out of Puritan Congregationalism following the Great Awakening, which was inspired in large part by Jonathan Edwards's insistence on original sin, from which humanity is saved only by dint of God's grace: "That state of man's nature, that disposition of the mind, is to be looked upon as evil and pernicious, which, as it is in itself, tends to extremely pernicious consequences, and would certainly end therein, were it not that the free mercy and kindness of God interposes to prevent that issue" (227). Unitarians such as Channing (and later Emerson) split from Edwards's theology, believing in the perfectibility of man, while Congregationalists such as Nathaniel William Taylor split from Edwards over the issue of sin as a choice—but Edwards had nonetheless left both the Unitarian and the Congregational heirs of Puritanism with a legacy of believing emotion to be essential to conversion and believing humanity to be tied to the natural world.[4] As Edwards put it, "Virtue primarily consists, not in love to any particular beings, because of their virtue or beauty, nor in gratitude, because they love us; but in a propensity and union of heart to being simply considered; exciting *absolute* benevolence . . . to being in general" (246). That is, the greatest virtue lies in feeling benevolence for all creation. It followed logically that loving the beauty in creation—especially in nature—was a component of spirituality. Thus, from Jonathan Edwards, the romantic evangelicals learned to regard nature and its beauty as a spiritual force that inspired virtue in people.

Three generations younger than Jonathan Edwards, Nathaniel William Taylor determined that rejecting virtue was a choice the sinner made rather than one to which the sinner was predestined. Taylor was the mentor of Horace Bushnell, the nineteenth-century Congregationalist who was one of the greatest religious thinkers of his day (Wells 232–33; Ahlstrom 610–13) and who has been called the "Emerson of Hartford" (Andrews 29). In Bushnell's view, the Trinity was three manifestations through which God reaches out to humanity, and conversion was almost a developmental process achieved through education, rather than a dramatic conversion that occurred only once in a Christian's life (Ahlstrom 610–11; Phipps 122). Conversion was an affective matter, an emotional one: "The heart was the organ of his religion" (Clebsch 116). Moreover, Bushnell found in Christ's crucifixion an example of the redemptive power of God's love rather than an example of God's retribution exacted for Adam's sins (Phipps 122–23). Influenced by Coleridge's *Aids to Reflection*, Bushnell was also a romantic in his belief that spirituality and language are inseparable (Ahlstrom 611; Clebsch 116). Charles N. Feidelson notes that for Bushnell, language is "social and symbolic," while for Emerson it is "metaphysical" (151–52; qtd. in Ahlstrom 611), but for both of these influential religious thinkers, language is a primary condition of one's relationship to God. Emerson writes in "Nature": "Words are finite organs of the infinite mind. . . . Words and actions are not the attributes of brute nature. They introduce us to the human form" (207). In other words, language is the catalyst between the divinity in nature and the divinity in people. Linking Emerson to Bushnell, Sydney Ahlstrom writes: "Through [Bushnell] the romantic movement made its entrance into theological seminaries and pulpits just as, in a more indirect though perhaps more pervasive way, Emerson brought it into the nation's schoolrooms and parlors" (Ahlstrom 613).

Emerson's thinking about childhood was also a crucial component of the romantic evangelism that influenced Bushnell, and in turn, Twichell and

Clemens (Stone 11–12)—and Alcott. In "The Over-Soul" Emerson wrote, "To the well-born child, all the virtues are natural, and not painfully acquired. . . . If I renounce my will, and act for the soul, setting that up as umpire between us two, out of [my child's] young eyes looks the same soul; he reveres and loves with me" (284, 286). Emerson's understanding of the divinity present in all people stemmed from his belief in the divinity of all children. Emerson's attention to youth inspired Bushnell to investigate the importance of childhood in religious conversion, and it was because of Emerson's and Bushnell's imprimatur on childhood as a topic that authors like Stowe and Hawthorne could write about childhood with dignity (Stone 11–14). It follows that Samuel Clemens could then write about childhood with impunity (Stone 14)—and so could Alcott.

Of the transcendentalists, certainly Emerson had the broadest impact on American thinking in the nineteenth century. Like Emerson's, Bushnell's writings were also widely read and affected the religious lives of many Americans in the nineteenth century. It was through the direct influence of Emerson and Bushnell that Clemens and Alcott became products of American romantic evangelism: believers in redemption through social action, believers in the importance of youth being able to develop an independent relationship with God, and believers in the redemptive power of understanding how humanity is tied to nature. Although Clemens was more sporadic than Alcott in his religious convictions, both of their reform impulses sprang from a common wellspring of Puritanism and were largely centered around issues of social justice: for Clemens, racial justice, and for Alcott, racial and gender justice. Both believed that individuals had a moral imperative to improve the world—and that youth growing toward adulthood were capable of perceiving that concept. They were inspired by the religious views of the communities in which they lived, and both communities were influenced by a similar theological impetus. Emerson and Parker would not have influenced Alcott without Jonathan Edwards's influence; Bushnell and Twichell would not have inspired Clemens without it.

Alcott and Clemens: *Vita Religiosa*

Louisa May Alcott and Mark Twain were criticized by their contemporaries for failing to adhere to the religious orthodoxies of the day. The *Ladies Repository* wrote in 1868 that no Sunday school library should contain *Little Women* because it presented "religion without spirituality, and salvation without Christ" ("From" 549), just as the Concord Public Library banned *Adventures of Huckleberry Finn* because Huck makes the un-Christian decision to go to hell. And both authors professed themselves to be skeptical of organized religion. Both, however, commented on their own faith more than once.

Louisa May Alcott

When Alcott was twelve years old, she experienced what she reported was a conversion experience:

> I had an early run in the woods before the dew was off the grass. The moss was like velvet, and as I ran under the arches of yellow and red leaves I sang for joy, my heart was so bright and the world so beautiful. I stopped at the end of the walk and saw the sunshine out over the wide "Virginia meadows."
>
> It seemed like going through a dark life or grave into heaven beyond. A very strange and solemn feeling came over me as I stood there, with no sound but the rustle of the pines, no one near me, and the sun so glorious, as for me alone. It seemed as if I *felt* God as I never did before, and I prayed in my heart that I might keep that happy sense of nearness in my life. (*Journals* 57)

Forty years later, Alcott added an emendation to this entry in her journal: "I have, for I most sincerely think that the little girl 'got religion' that day in the wood when dear mother Nature led her to God.—L.M.A., 1885."

In 1856, after the distressing year in which her sisters Lizzie and May suffered from scarlet fever, Alcott found her spirits raised by listening to Theodore Parker's sermons and joining him after church at his home with people such as Harriet Beecher Stowe and U.S. senator Charles Sumner—the man who had been caned on the floor of the Senate by Preston Brooks of South Carolina for taking a strong anti-slavery position.[5] After one of these events, when a friend said Parker was not a Christian, Alcott responded, "He is my *sort*; for though he may lack reverence for other people's God, he works bravely for his own, and turns his back on no one who needs help, as some of the pious do" (*Journals* 81). Two years later, after her sister died, Alcott reported herself again buoyed up both by Parker's sermons—this time one called "Laborious Young Women"—and by his good works in helping Alcott secure a position as a tutor. In a journal entry in which she describes having heard Parker and others lecture, Alcott writes, "The past year has brought us the first death and betrothal, —two events that change my life. I can see that these experiences have taken a deep hold, and changed or developed me. Lizzie helps me spiritually, and a little success makes me more self-reliant" (*Journals* 91). This passage links Parker with Alcott's sense of being spiritually uplifted and more financially independent—and demonstrates her usage of the familiar language of transcendentalism, "self-reliant," to describe her own success.

As Estes and Lant observe, Alcott's relationship with her father ensured that she grew up steeped in the tenets of transcendentalism (98–101).[6] Alcott's faith was based on twin concepts: Emerson's theistic concept that self-reliance can only come to those who understand the each-and-all in nature and in Theodore Parker's twist on transcendentalism that involvement in social activism was a necessary component of spirituality.[7] The split in Unitarianism that William Ellery Channing initiated in 1815 by claiming that "the Unitarian believes that there is but one person possessing supreme Divinity, even the Father"—by which he meant *only* the Father—reached fruition in Parker's assertion that Christ was a historical figure, not a divine manifestation of God, so Christians did not need to believe in Christ in order to be saved (Channing qtd. in Ahlstrom 395).[8] According to Parker, if Christ were divine, it would be impossible to imitate him and so his sacrifices and pain would become meaningless (126). Parker believed that Jesus of Nazareth defined Christianity as "a simple thing, very simple. It is absolute, pure morality; absolute, pure religion—the love of man; the love of God acting without let or hindrance. The only creed it lays down is the great truth which springs up spontaneous in the holy heart—there is a God" (128). Parker was the most socially active of the major transcendentalists, and Alcott acknowledged his influence over her in such a way that she evolved from the Romanticism of the individual that Emerson heralded to the social awareness of the national reform movement that Parker represented (Elbert, *Hunger* xvii, 113). Alcott's shift of allegiance from Emerson to Parker eventually influenced the social progressivism in her novels for youth. For example, Demi's description of Christ to Nat, a new student in the school Jo and Professor Bhaer run in *Little Men*, puts Parker's theology of "pure morality" in the mouth of a nine-year-old:

"That is Christ, the Good Man, and He is blessing the children. Don't you know about Him?" said Demi, wondering. . . .

"What makes Him bless the children?" asked Nat. . . .

"Because He loved them."

"Were they poor children?" asked Nat, wistfully.

"Yes, I think so; you see some haven't got hardly any clothes on, and the mothers don't look like rich ladies. He liked poor people, and was very good to them. He made them well, and helped them, and told rich people they must not be cross to them, and they loved Him dearly, dearly," cried Demi with enthusiasm. . . .

"He was born in a barn, and was so poor He hadn't any house to live in when He grew up, and nothing to eat sometimes, but what people gave Him, and He went round preaching to everybody, and trying to make them good, till the bad men killed Him." (48–50)[9]

Demi's depiction of Christ emphasizes his humanity, almost completely ignoring the possibility that he was divine.

Demi's aunt, Jo March, and Jo's husband, Professor Bhaer, believe in God, if not necessarily in the Trinity. In *Little Women*, when confronted with metaphysical agnostics, Professor Bhaer rejects their logic: "Somehow, as he talked, the world got right again to Jo; the old beliefs that had lasted so long, seemed better than the new. God was not a blind force, and immortality was not a pretty fable, but a blessed fact" (278). Faith is important to Jo, which becomes even more evident when Beth dies and Jo's belief in God and heaven sustain her through her grief. But Alcott's depiction of Christianity as being not a matter of belief in Christ's redemption of humanity but as a matter of belief in God motivating us to live charitably in the world would have scandalized those evangelical readers who recognized that she was depicting Christ as a man, rather than as a divine savior. And she was certainly no Trinitarian: she praised one of Moncure Conway's sermons in 1876 for "showing how false" much of the New Testament is and excoriating the exclusionary practices of theologians who ignore "the most learned scholars & thinkers because they will tell the honest truth & upset the old theories of the Trinity, Incarnation &c which have no foundation in fact as some of them were ideas & beliefs that didn't exist till after Christ's time & are not spoken of at all in the letters of Paul which are ackno[w]ledged to be the truest accounts" (*Selected Letters* 215–16).[10]

Alcott's representation of her religious beliefs demonstrates how the many religious controversies of the mid-nineteenth century in America operated in her own life. By 1852, Unitarianism had split into two factions: the Christian and the theistic Unitarians (Ahlstrom 606–07). Alcott, following Emerson and Parker, would have allied herself with the theistic Unitarians, who believed God exists in all living things and who disavowed Christ's divinity. She called Parker "my beloved minister and friend" and wrote, "To him and R.W.E. I owe much of my education. May I be a worthy pupil of such men" (*Journals* 95). Her transcendental take on Unitarianism appears when Jo talks about spirituality with one of the boys at her school, telling him, "Nature is your God now; she has done much for you; let her do more, and lead you to know and love a wiser and more tender teacher, friend, and comforter than she can ever be";

after listening to her, Dan can't speak but she sees in him "a glimpse of the divine spark which smoulders or burns clearly in every human soul" (*Jo's* 129). Alcott even bases Mr. Power, the minister in one of her novels written for an adult audience, *Work*, on Theodore Parker.

> Laying his hands together, with a peculiarly soft and reverent gesture, [he] lifted up his face and prayed. Christie had never heard a prayer like that before; so devout, so comprehensive, and so brief. A quiet talk with God, asking nothing but more love and duty toward Him and our fellow-men; thanking Him for many mercies, and confiding all things trustfully to the "dear father and mother of souls." (207)

Power's androgynous god is both "father and mother," like Jo's god in *Little Women*, and his theology focuses more on virtuous actions than on doctrinal belief. For example, one of his sermons is about the pitfall of commercial success in transforming promising youth into hypocrites and money changers; he speaks "with the indescribable effect of inward force and true inspiration" (207). At another point, he preaches that people should "keep innocency and take heed to the thing that is right, for this will bring a man peace in the last" (213). Like Parker, Power posits humanity's ability to do good within each individual's conscience.

Alcott developed as a writer influenced by most of the major transcendentalists, including her father. In fact, Louisa attended Thoreau's school when she was a child (Stern, *Louisa* 20–21), and she seems to have shared the opinion of the father of her friend Anna Ricketson, who referred to Thoreau as "an angel or an evangelist (he is probably both)" (Ricketson 194). But if Alcott respected Thoreau's spirituality, she respected and adored Emerson. She regarded his poetry as some of "the best . . . we have" and referred to his writings as "my minister & friend" after his death (*Selected Letters* 231, 302).[11] She characterized Emerson's transcendentalism this way:

> He is called a Pantheist or believer in Nature instead of God. He was truly *Christian* & saw God *in* Nature, finding strength & comfort in the sane, sweet influences of the great Mother as well as the Father of all. I too believe this, & when tired, sad, or tempted find my best comfort in the woods, the sky, the healing solitude that lets my poor weary soul find the rest, the fresh hope, or the patience which only God can give us. (*Selected Letters* 277)

Whether Alcott's interpretation of Emerson's theology is accurate matters less than the testimony of her own faith that is embedded in this description of

Emerson. She considered herself a Christian, but one who found God's presence in nature more easily than in people or in churches.[12] She did feel connected with one church, however, the 28th Congregational Society of Boston, where Parker preached. Parker—like Emerson and Bronson Alcott—shared some beliefs common to transcendentalism, especially in his faith in the power of nature to affect religious conversion, his belief in the need for the individual's self-reliance to lead him to God, and his understanding that Christ was human rather than divine.

In the sense that Alcott managed to write any number of stories about spirituality without ever once mentioning Christ as anything more than "the best life ever lived" (*Little Women* 19) or "the Good Man" (*Little Men* 43), she was an apt pupil of the transcendentalists' theism. In *Under the Lilacs* Celia tells Ben that "being kind and cheerful, doing one's duty, helping others, and loving God, is the best way to show that we are pious in the true sense of the word" (102), and Jack and Jill are told that Jesus is "the children's saint to pray to, love, and imitate, for he never forgot them but blessed and healed and taught them all his life" (*Jack* 56). The *Ladies Repository*'s remark about the first book of *Little Women* could apply to the whole Alcott canon: she consistently presents salvation without Christ. But she also always does so in a context that insists that youth have faith in God and work to improve the conditions of humanity.

Samuel Clemens

Clemens's religious skepticism has been far more widely analyzed than Alcott's.[13] *What Is Man?*, "To the Person Sitting in Darkness" (1901), "Reflections on Religion" (1906), and *Christian Science* (1907) are among the works written later in his life in which he denounces either religion or "The Mysterious Stranger" for having created man as he is: sinful and flawed and therefore necessarily corrupt. These works contain notorious expressions of anger at organized religion. Clemens asserted that organized religion is a failure because people can only be motivated to act ethically if they see charitable behavior as a matter of self-interest rather than as a matter of behaving as part of a social group. For example, in *What Is Man?*, one character claims that self-interest is the only motivating force in the world, but he articulates one principle (based on his belief in self-interest) that he claims most religions in the world share in common: "Diligently train your ideals *upward* and *still upward* toward a summit where you will find your chiefest pleasure in conduct which, while contenting you, will be sure to confer benefits upon your neighbor and the community" (54–55). Even at his most skeptical, Clemens with that statement postulates a morality not unlike Alcott's: good works make the world a better place, regardless of whether religious faith motivates us or not. Phipps refers to this manifestation of Clemens's morality as emanating from his "ethical monotheism" (374); Clemens's belief in one god was linked to his value system. Ultimately, Clemens seems convinced that God existed in some form and that man's most important work is to live ethically.

Clemens was raised Presbyterian by a mother reputed to have attended church more for the sociability than the spirituality (Sanborn 8, 39). If Alcott's youthful conversion story is the narrative of an Emersonian maiden who found God in nature, Clemens's story about his childhood conversion is marked by its comic depiction of an angry and vengeful Presbyterian God. He claims in *Life on the Mississippi* to have repented of his own sins during a "ferocious thunder-storm" that followed the drowning of Lem Hackett, who fell from a boat on the Mississippi: "Being loaded with sin, he went to the bottom like an anvil" (543). Clemens's childhood religion was the religion of damnation and repentance, of sinfulness and renunciation.

Already quite skeptical by the time he boarded the *Quaker City* to tour the Mediterranean and the Holy Land in 1867, Clemens found much in the trip to affirm his cynicism. Despite his disgust with his fellow passengers' hypocrisy on the cruise, Clemens found himself attracted to the purity he perceived in Olivia Langdon's picture that her brother, Charles, carried on the cruise. In courting her, Clemens developed an acute and perhaps expedient case of Christianity. He told his fiancée on November 28, 1868, "I believe in you, even as I believe in the Savior in whose hands our destinies are," equating his love for her with his newfound love for God (*Selected Letters* 2.289). Exactly three months later, he told her, "You are very, very useful to me. . . . Necessary to my dreams when they are pure and beautiful; necessary to my moments of doubting the promises of God, as showing a hope & a blessing realized" (*Selected Letters* 3.127). In these letters, Clemens cultivates Livy's dependence on him by maintaining that his religious faith is dependent on her.

That he equated Christianity with a change in his social status is clear in a letter he wrote to Mary Fairbanks, a friend he made aboard the *Quaker City*:

I shall seek the society of the good—I shall be a *Christian*. I shall climb—climb—climb—toward this bright sun that is shining in the heaven of my happiness until all that is gross & unworthy is hidden in the mists & the darkness of that lower earth whence *you* first lifted my aspiring feet. . . . I believe in *myself*. I believe in God—& through the breaking clouds I see the star of Hope rising in the placid blue beyond. (*Selected Letters* 2.284)

The upward-climbing Christian anticipates the philosopher training his ideals "upwards and still upwards" in *What Is Man?* (54). Clemens wrote to his future mother-in-law in February 1869, "But now I never swear; I never taste wine or spirits upon any occasion whatsoever; I am orderly, & my conduct is above reproach in a worldly sense; & finally, I now claim that I am a Christian" (*Selected Letters* 3.90). Note that Clemens defines his Christianity not just as a matter of faith but also as a matter of action, as a matter of behavior, even as a matter of climbing—and possibly even social climbing, at that. His actions, following his conversion, have become more refined, he implies. That sentiment—of Christianity as a matter of action rather than faith—manifests itself in Clemens's writing as late as 1889, when the Connecticut Yankee says, "And as for me, all that I think about in this plodding sad pilgrimage, this pathetic drift between the eternities, is to look out and humbly live a pure and high and blameless life, and save that one microscopic atom in me that is truly *me*: the rest may land in Sheol and welcome, for all I care" (208). Living a "pure and high and blameless" life matters far more than faith does.

After Clemens and Olivia married, he wrote to his sister in 1874 that he considered himself an "entire & absolute unbeliever" (qtd. in Webster 131), and he wrote the following conflicted passage to his brother Orion in 1878: "Neither Howells nor I believe in hell or the divinity of the Saviour, but no matter, the Saviour is none the less a sacred Personage, and a man should have no desire or disposition to refer to him lightly, profanely, or otherwise than with the profoundest reverence" (qtd. in Phipps 278). Like Alcott, he doubted the divinity of Christ, although he considered him sacred. And like Alcott, he still believed in heaven, even if he did not believe that one earned a berth there with faith in Christ's divinity. Clemens's biographer Albert Bigelow Paine reports that Clemens told him in 1907:

> "As to a hereafter, we have not the slightest evidence that there is any—*no* evidence that appeals to logic and reason. I have never seen what to me seemed an atom of proof that there is a future life."
>
> Then, after a long pause, he added:
>
> "And yet—I am strongly inclined to expect one." (Paine 1431)

Clemens's inner debate about whether man was "an automated or an autonomous being," predestined either by a Calvinistic God or a moral free agent in a universe devoid of divinity, informed much of the intellectual inquiry in his life (Tuckey 533). The conclusions he sometimes came to were skeptical because he was so often disappointed in his expectations of other people. Moncure Conway once described Clemens as having composed "a sentiment which he claims to be 'quite Emersonian.' It is this:—'The ease with which I perceive other peoples [*sic*] religion to be folly, makes me suspect that my religion may be folly also'" (Twain, *Selected Letters* 6.601). Clemens had even less faith in religion than he did in God.[14]

Clemens's religious life was dominated in his adulthood by his friendship with the Reverend Joseph Twichell. Clemens, in fact, chose to move to the Nook Farm community in Hartford in part because of his friendship with Twichell (*Selected Letters* 3.102–03). Harold K. Bush Jr. describes Clemens's minister as "orthodox and evangelical in his faith," but also "funny, rigorous, and muscular" (71). Clemens wrote to Twichell that they "share[d] a companionship which to me stands first after Livy's" (qtd. in Paine 632). Twichell's importance in Clemens's religious life cannot be underestimated, for it was largely through their ongoing theological debate (which the humorist often staged to twit Twichell) that Clemens's childhood Presbyterianism evolved into an adult spirituality that insisted on the importance of moral choice.

James L. Johnson also observes how powerful Emerson's influence was on Clemens: "Twain and Emerson were much preoccupied, in the course of their respective careers, with the same problem: that of realizing in practical terms the capabilities they believed man harbored within him" (5). Johnson offers as examples the characters Hank Morgan and Tom Sawyer, who appear to embody the ideal of the hero that Emerson articulates in his essay about Napoleon: in two different books, Tom Sawyer proves the "malevolent possibilities for a protagonist who could treat the globe as his toy," but he does so only at the expense of his own character, a phenomenon that is even more clear with Hank Morgan (121).[15] With Hank Morgan, the Emersonian empowered self—the man who is solely self-reliant and impervious to social pressure—becomes a narcissistic terror capable of enough callousness to ultimately cause other people's destruction, which limitation of power, Johnson argues, Clemens understood (185–92). Harris also describes Clemens's image of childhood in terms that are couched in the romanticism of the transcendental movement that glorifies individuality: "Twain celebrates the child who refuses to compromise his integrity, creating a mythic otherworld as a substitute for the community for the child who reflects the author's own alienation from conventional ideas. . . . Only in flight from other people and their values can the solitary child discover his unity with the organic universe" (*MT's Escape* 98). Harris refers to Clemens as neither an anti-materialist, like Thoreau, nor a philosopher like Emerson, but she nonetheless demonstrates his responsiveness to the ideals of transcendentalism, especially in the creation of his child characters (97). Furthermore, Phipps shows how Clemens relies on transcendentalism to depict youth when he compares Huck to Thoreau for being willing to be "out of step with most of the church people around him" (177). Johnson, Harris, and Phipps demonstrate that Huck Finn, in marching to the beat of his own drum, is a transcendental nonconformist influenced by Emerson—just like Jo March.

Other critics have documented how Clemens responded to transcendentalism, both by creating idealized child characters and in being willing to write for children. But what these analysts of the relationship between Clemens and transcendentalism have missed is how Clemens's depiction of the Over-soul at work in an adolescent also has the net effect of creating a socially responsive and socially responsible character. As with Alcott, transcendentalism made it possible for the author to create a youthful protagonist whose soul, as Emerson would have it, "is the perceiver and revealer of truth"—particularly of the author's perception of social truth (286). The romantic strain of transcendentalism brought childhood, and especially the purity of the child, to prominence as a social construct, but Clemens and Alcott developed that romantic child into an adolescent figure whose awareness of the relationship between self and society, i.e., whose awareness of the Over-soul, made it possible for a youth to function actively as a reformer.

Some romantic evangelicals' commentary on sin provides one additional piece of contextual data that is pertinent to understanding Clemens's and Alcott's religious lives. Bushnell believed that Christ's suffering was—as Theodore Parker also postulated—a matter of example for others to live by, rather than a source of redemption for the sins of all believers. David F. Wells interprets this theological position as a "theodicy for the Civil War: America was atoning for its national sins" (233).[16] In other words, the horror of the Civil War required spiritual justification, and those who believed that Christ lived to set an example could find a better explanation in why a brutal war would devastate a sinful nation than those who believed that faith in Christ ultimately redeems people's sinfulness. Perhaps the greatest of these sins was the American legacy of racial strife. For white authors such as Alcott and Clemens, racial guilt was never to subside throughout their lives. Certainly, nothing in the orthodoxies of the organized religions surrounding them provided either author with an adequate explanation for why one people should maintain dominance over another. Moreover, Alcott understood the logic that if whites should not disfranchise blacks, males should not disfranchise females, either.

The religious contexts that influenced Clemens and Alcott to write about social reform shared several elements. Although both authors were skeptical of organized religion, both were influenced literarily and philosophically by some of the major tenets of transcendentalism: respect for the role of the individual's consciousness in his or her relationship with the divine, respect for nature, and respect for the child's ability to have an independent relationship with God. Moreover, both adhered to some basic reform principles that were two of the major factors of the Civil War: a growing social belief in equality before the law and a belief in the individual's obligation to improve social conditions for other people. Ultimately, both Clemens and Alcott subscribed to some subset of romantic evangelism that led them to create moral youths as protagonists who were reformers. Huck Finn and Jo March are the two most enduring of the many youthful protagonists who advance reform ideologies in Twain's and Alcott's novels. Other examples include Tom Sawyer, Polly Milton, the prince and the pauper, Rose Campbell, and Joan of Arc.

CHAPTER FOUR

Education and Reform
Victorian Progressivism in Youth Literature

"A full belly is little worth where the mind is starved."
—*The Prince and the Pauper*

"The least of us have some influence in this big world."
—*An Old-Fashioned Girl*

M ark Twain and Louisa May Alcott demonstrate repeatedly their shared belief that education is the most powerful tool for reform available to the American public. Their belief was such a widely held ideology that it was seldom questioned in the nineteenth century—or since. Henry J. Perkinson identifies Americans' faith in education as having its roots in both Puritanism and the rationalist thinking that influenced the Revolution and the Constitution. He refers to Americans' ideological faith in education as an "imperfect panacea" because U.S. citizens so often—and so wrongly—turn to education as the best possible cure for all social ills (xi, 6–10). Perkinson notes that Jacksonian democrats promoted public schools as something that could make America more democratic in the 1820s, and Anne Scott MacLeod demonstrates how the common school system established by the Jacksonians created a literate nation (MacLeod 188–90). When de Tocqueville toured America in 1831, he wrote, "The first duty imposed on those who now direct society is to educate democracy" (12). From 1870, which marked the beginning of the decade in which Twain began publishing for youth audiences, to 1915, five years after his death, the number of children enrolled in schools jumped from seven million to twenty million (Mintz 174). Americans increased their financial commitment to education during the same years by raising their school expenditures from $63 million to $605 million (Mintz 174).

Twain's and Alcott's faith in education was as common as faith in American democracy and probably more common than faith in God during the Gilded Age. While it is no great intellectual feat to observe either author (or any of their contemporaries who wrote juveniles) in the act of writing about education ideologically, it is certain that Twain and Alcott were more widely read both during their lifetimes and afterwards than perhaps any other juvenile author of their age. As a result, the ways that Twain and Alcott employ children or childlike characters to help proliferate the ideology of the imperfect panacea seem to have been particularly influential on the development of the adolescent novel in the United States. For Alcott, liberal education almost invariably leads to improved morality, while for Twain, education is a double-edged sword that can bestow great wisdom and/or create great corruption. But for both, the purpose of education is to allow the individual to reach his or her greatest potential. And even though these two authors write in different genres, they imbue the protagonists of their novels for youth with a heavy responsibility to use their education to reform other people and, in the process, improve the world. Their ideological observations about education take two forms: in some novels, their adolescent characters are reformers whose actions or observations convey ideology overtly, while in other novels, the need for educational reform is only implied. But either way, Twain and Alcott rely on novels for youth to provide them with platforms from which to advocate reform. When they employ adolescent characters as reformers, they do so because of the adolescent's potential for growth and the hope that youth represents.

In this chapter, then, I investigate the educational ideologies at work in Twain's and Alcott's novels that specifically employ adolescence to convey the ideology of education as a panacea: *An Old-Fashioned Girl, The Prince and the Pauper, A Connecticut Yankee in King Arthur's Court, Little Men,* and, briefly, *Tom Sawyer Abroad* and *Tom Sawyer, Detective.* Throughout these novels run several shared themes. First, as I have noted, liberal education is a panacea for most social ills. Second, these novels present the Emersonian concept that the educated individual is an empowered individual. Third, youth who are "improving souls" can educate those around them in moral improvement. Fourth, children learn more from inductive teaching methods than they do from rote memorization. Fifth, education effects social mobility. Sixth, misapplied education is a dangerous thing. Finally, virtually every one of these novels also touches on some other aspect of Victorian progressivism: hygiene, dress reform, penal reform, Magdalene reform. Informing all the novels under discussion in this chapter is an insistence that educated youth are capable of themselves being reformers. The patterns Twain and Alcott established with Huck and Jo serving as youthful metaphors for the need for cultural reform appears quite noticeably in other novels they have written for youth.

Improving Souls

The "improving child" was a staple of Victorian literature. The little Evas whose death brought others closer to salvation and the What-Katy-Dids whose illnesses taught forbearance were familiar characters to any reader of Anglo-American fiction during the Gilded Age.[1] The child whose purity improved the lives of others around him or her made perfect sense to readers in a culture steeped in late romanticism and evangelical piety. Twain's *The Prince and the Pauper* was a standard manifestation of the improving child, but Alcott's Polly Milton beat Twain's prince and pauper into print by thirteen years.[2] *An Old-Fashioned Girl* was serialized in *Merry's Magazine* in 1869; Roberts Brothers released it as a novel in 1870. The novel was a well-received third book by the author of *Little Women* and *Good Wives*, as the second volume of *Little Women* was titled when it was released in 1869. *An Old-Fashioned Girl* describes how Polly Milton, something of a country mouse, improves the lives of her city-mouse friends, the Shaws. Polly begins the novel with a level of maturity that obviates her need to grow. She is the ideal adolescent: even from the beginning of the novel she is a wise, generous, hardworking, stoic, and devout little woman. Most important, she educates others by example, which provides Alcott an opportunity to provide a pedagogical alternative to the direct instruction that occurs in a classroom. In privileging the power of indirect instruction and in exemplifying the importance of one-on-one instruction, Alcott transforms into fiction some of the pedagogical theories on which her father's Temple School was founded.

For example, the three Shaw children, Fanny, Tom, and Maud, are rich and relatively spoiled Bostonians who try to make a pet out of Polly. She, however, teaches them to value "health, intelligence, and modesty" (128) and to recognize how much more important "talent, energy, and character" are than "money, fashion, and position" (228). By the time Mr. Shaw loses the family fortune and must work to repay his creditors, Fanny, Tom, and Maud are young adults who learn from Polly how to help their parents uncomplainingly. Polly is ever conscious of her role as an improving soul whose responsibility it is to teach others by example. Her mother tells her, "The least of us have some influence in this big world; and perhaps my little girl can do some good by showing others that a contented heart and a happy face are better ornaments than any Paris can give her" (49–50). Polly makes "sunshine" for the others (55, 71) and teaches them how to self-entertain, how to sew, how to study, how to forgive, and how to avoid jealousy. She even "unconsciously" teaches Mr. Shaw how to show love to his children (57). Mr. Shaw asks Polly to "set this silly child of mine a good example" when Fanny acts inappropriately (76). Later he tells her, "I can't tell you how, exactly; but you brought something into my house that makes it warmer and pleasanter" (142). His words leave her feeling "proud and happy at this proof of the truth of her mother's words, when she said that 'even a little girl could exert an influence, and do some good in this big, busy world'" (142–43). Polly also prefigures Pollyanna by proclaiming, "I just try to look on the bright side of things; that helps one amazingly. Why, you've no idea how much goodness and sunshine you can get out of the most unpromising things, if you make the best of them" (258). Polly has learned all these skills from her mother, who "only explains things to us, and helps us be good, and never scolds" (122). Absent from any appearance in the plot, Polly's mother is a Marmee-figure who sends letters from a town suspiciously Concord-like and whose ideologies are most certainly influenced by the theistic strain of Unitarianism. Polly teaches others simplicity and goodness and charity because her mother values those things so highly, conveying implicitly a message about the power mothers have to indoctrinate their children ideologically.

Polly's ability to improve the world is expressed as clearly as are her maternally influenced views on charity. She helps save a young woman who has attempted suicide rather than turn to prostitution, and Polly takes as her role model a charitable spinster named Miss Mills: "In the likeness of this plain old maid she saw the lovely charity that blesses and saves the world" (181). Miss Mills demonstrates that she practices practical (and theistic) Christianity when she tells Polly, "This love and thought and care for those weaker, poorer or worse than ourselves, which we call Christian charity, is a very old fashion, my dear. It began eighteen hundred years ago, and only those who honestly follow the beautiful example set us then learn how to get genuine happiness out of life" (212). Polly, in turn, convinces Fanny's frivolous friends to help support the young woman. Her action on Jane's behalf becomes the first of many charitable acts in her life, and the text didactically extols the virtues of charity. When Fanny asks Polly how she endures working among the impoverished, Polly answers, "But it isn't all dreadful. There are good and lovely things among them, if one only has eyes to see them. It makes me grateful and contented, shows me how rich I am, and keeps me ready to do all I can for these poor souls" (261). Polly vows to show Fanny "the sunny side of poverty and work" (271). Alcott implies that the old-fashioned girl's most important virtue is her ability to conduct charity in the style of Theodore Parker.

The twins-born-of-separate-mothers in *The Prince and the Pauper* have the same ability to influence those around them to act more charitably. But unlike

An Old-Fashioned Girl, The Prince and the Pauper directly extols the virtues of formal instruction. *The Prince and the Pauper* also differs from *An Old-Fashioned Girl* in that the prince and the pauper fit the traditional model in children's literature: unlike Polly, they are protagonists who themselves need to grow.

Tom Canty, the pauper, has delusions of grandeur. He is identified early in the text in language very much like the description of Alcott's old-fashioned girl. Especially noteworthy is his apparently innate ability to influence other people for the better:

> By and by Tom's reading and dreaming about princely life wrought such a strong effect upon him that he began to *act* the prince, unconsciously. . . . Tom's influence among these young people began to grow, now, day by day; and in time he came to be looked up to, by them, with a sort of wondering awe, as a superior being. . . . Withal, he was so deep and wise! Tom's remarks, and Tom's performances, were reported by the boys to their elders, and these also presently began to discuss Tom Canty, and to regard him as a most gifted and extraordinary creature. Full grown people brought their perplexities to Tom for solution, and were often astonished at the wit and wisdom of his decisions. (6–7)

Prince Edward also influences his elders for the better. His first charitable action is to defend Tom from the guards who have hurt him before the boys change clothes and create their own misidentification. As Tom becomes prince and then king of England against his will, he grows to understand how heavy adult responsibility is; Edward finds Tom's parents, and although he cannot convince them that he is the true prince, in his wanderings before he is restored to the throne, he grapples with a variety of social ills, as does the usurper who is serving as king. Through the boys' eyes, the text comments on poverty, child abuse, crime and punishment, religious persecution, and sanitation. Both boys value education, charity, and merciful justice, and their youth is one factor that makes it possible for them to perceive the need for change and to have enough hope to act on those changes.

Tom's first action when Henry VIII dies is to enact gentler justice. "Then shall the king's law be law of mercy, from this day, and never more be law of blood," the pauper tells the court (83). When he tries prisoners, he introduces rules of evidence into a legal system that has heretofore relied heavily on hearsay. One peasant describes Tom in his role as king as "a dear and gracious little urchin . . . and whether he be mad or no—and they say he mendeth daily— his praises are on all men's lips; and all bless him, likewise, and offer prayers that he may be spared to reign long in England; for he began humanely, with saving the old Duke of Norfolk's life, and now is he bent on destroying the cruelest of the laws that harry and oppress the people" (232–33). A chronicler at his coronation writes, "Wonderfully transported were the people with the loving answers and gestures of their king" (255). Tom Canty, the pauper, improves the entire nation with his charitable sense of justice.

Twain credits King Edward's generosity as having its roots in his experiences as a pauper: only from having lived the abjection of poverty and abuse is a king able to be compassionate. What Twain's history of King Edward VI lacks in accuracy, it makes up for with its reflection of nineteenth-century American ideologies of democracy and social progressivism. Prince Edward has the reformer's heart of any nineteenth-century Progressive. Early in his travails he mutters to himself, "When I am king, [children] shall not have bread and shelter only, but also teachings out of books; for a full belly is little worth where the mind is starved, and the heart . . . for learning softeneth the heart and breedeth gentleness and charity" (24). While he is still a victim of mistaken identity, he says, "When I am come to mine own again, I will always honor little children, remembering how that these trusted me and believed in me in my time of trouble; whilst they that were older, and thought themselves wiser, mocked at me and held me for a liar" (171). True to his word, when he is king he founds Christ's Hospital "for the *education* and maintenance of orphans and children of indigent persons" (294) so that they "shall have their minds and hearts fed, as well as their baser parts" (286).

Edward rails against the lack of hygiene, the miscarriage of justice, the brutality of the penal code, and the ignorance of his people. His zeal for sanitation, penal reform, and public education make him sound like a youthful John Howard, Sylvester Graham, and Horace Mann, all rolled into one.[3] When Edward finally assumes the throne, he effects justice for religious dissenters, potential victims of capital punishment, and falsely dispossessed nobility who have crossed his path. He advocates for those who suffer and are oppressed: "Yes, King Edward VI lived only a few years, poor boy, but he lived them worthily. . . . The reign of Edward VI was a singularly merciful one for those harsh times" (289). Edward is an improving soul, a literary character whose growing social consciousness makes it possible for him to reform the legal system of an entire nation. But he is a youth who never grows into adulthood, and it is this youthfulness that allows him to be the character whose voice implies how the nineteenth-century United States needs to reform itself. Because he is a youth, he never needs to contend with the corruption adulthood conveys in the Twain canon. In reviewing *The Prince and the Pauper*, Howells actually recommends the book as a children's textbook for social justice in a democracy: "This is the sort of manual of republicanism which might fitly be introduced in the schools" (Budd, *MTCR* 200). As an arbiter of Victorian progressive values in America, Howells could not have predicted more accurately the prescriptive ideological role that Twain's novels would eventually have in influencing the shape of adolescent literature.

Like *The Prince and the Pauper*, *A Connecticut Yankee in King Arthur's Court* is also a textbook for republican idealism set in a historically inaccurate England. J. D. Stahl speculates that Twain relied on British settings when he wanted to write directly about social class because the author perceived England as more socially stratified than the U.S. (85).[4] That is, just as writing about youth freed Twain to write about optimism and hope, writing about Europe liberated him as a social critic to condemn European social problems that American adults were replicating, especially in failing to live up to the ideals of the democracy as it was founded.

In *Connecticut Yankee*, the narrator, Hank Morgan, is a character who selfconsciously desires to be an improving soul: he wants to improve all of England out of its ignorance, provincialism, and hierarchical social class system. Although the novel has often been appropriated by youth, it does not necessarily fit the conventions of adolescent literature because the narrator is an adult whose growth is minimal: he ends the novel as convinced of his culture's superiority to medieval England's as he is when he first arrives in Camelot. His unreliability as a narrator and his grandiosity, however, make him seem at times quite adolescent. Although he thinks of himself as a reformer, the text ironically demonstrates how lethal some of the inventions he introduces to the British, like electrification and explosives, are to them. And, consistently, Hank justifies his own adolescent behavior by infantilizing the people of England: "Plainly, too, they were a childlike and innocent lot" (66). Later, he says, "Look at the opportunities here for a man of knowledge, brains, pluck and enterprise to sail in and *grow up with the country*. The grandest field that ever was; and all my own; not a competitor . . . not a man who wasn't a baby to me in acquirements and capacities," while in the nineteenth century he could "catch a hundred better men" than himself anytime (109, emphasis added). Although Hank claims to be a man, he recognizes his own need to "grow up with the country." He considers himself "a man among children, a master intelligence among moles" and chafes at the thought of a "sheep-witted earl" having more social power than he in the sixth century, but his self-assertions of his maturity make him seem, at times, like a man protesting too much (113). Although much of the text critiques social stratification and ignorance, the Yankee technology that Hank introduces proves to be the most destructive force in the novel. Twain's ambivalence about the role of technology and education in educating the masses emerges in the cataclysm of the novel's ending.

In the final chapter that Hank narrates, he has at his side fifty-two loyal soldiers who share his reform ideologies and his hopeful faith in Yankee ingenuity. He calls all the rest of England "human muck" (473), but the fifty-two soldiers are "fresh, bright, well-educated, clean-minded young British boys" (472); they are "a darling fifty-two! As pretty as girls, too" (476). When he writes to King Arthur's forces, who are marching against them, he refers to himself, his adolescent assistant Clarence, and these boys this way: "We number 54. Fifty-four what? Men? No, *minds*—the capablest in the world; a force against which mere animal might may no more hope to prevail than may the idle waves of the sea hope to prevail against the granite barriers of England" (480). Hank feels his superiority is mandated in this age simply because he knows more than anyone else in the sixth century. The destruction Hank wreaks upon Camelot with his *übermensch* mentality may well be Twain's critique of the unbridled industrialization of the Gilded Age destroying the agrarian values on which the nation was founded. Nonetheless, the medieval setting provides Twain with ample fodder to suggest social reform, especially in the form of education. And Hank expects youth—fifty-three adolescent boys, including Clarence—and himself, an overgrown adolescent, to do the work of reforming the culture. That his expectations fail may well be a function of the fact that he is not an adolescent but an adult, and therefore, by Twain's definition, corrupt.

Initially, Hank has the same reformer's agenda as Prince Edward and Tom Canty. His first accomplishment is to establish a patent office. As he explains it, "The first thing you want in a new country, is a patent office; then work up your school system; and after that, out with your [news]paper" (120). Later, Hank introduces the telephone and telegraph, and he argues in favor of penal reform. But education of youth, through public schools and reformed religion, is his favorite topic:

> In various quiet nooks and corners I had the beginnings of all sorts of industries under way—nuclei of future vast factories, the iron and steel missionaries of my future civilization. In these were gathered together the brightest young minds I could find. . . . I was training a crowd of ignorant folks into experts—experts in every sort of handiwork and scientific calling. . . . I had started a teacher factory

and a lot of Sunday schools the first thing; as a result, I now had an admirable system for graded schools in full blast in those places, and also a complete variety of Protestant congregations all in a prosperous and growing condition. Everybody could be any kind of a Christian he wanted to. (127)

At the heart of Hank's reform movement is education. Educated people need patent offices for the mighty inventions their unleashed imaginations will produce; educated people value newspapers to help protect them from the tyranny of government manipulation; educated people (in Twain's economy) think for themselves and are therefore necessarily Protestant. Hank Morgan despises Merlin, whom he considers a pawn of the Catholic Church. The Church is Hank Morgan's greatest enemy because, in his estimation, it mitigates against education: "It means death to human liberty, and paralysis to human thought" (127). Whether Twain intends to be ironic in promulgating the notion that all Protestant sects foster intellectual freedom is never resolved in the text. But Twain is unwavering in his ideological valuation of education—and the first person Hank educates is an adolescent boy named Clarence. Hank communicates many of his goals and values in conversations with Clarence, leaving readers to understand that youth is a time of pliability, a stage of life in which education can effect change. While the text is often cynical about the so-called advances that follow from gunpowder and advanced machines of war, never once is education portrayed in anything but a positive light.

The racist commentary in the text, for example, invariably justifies racism in terms of the moral superiority that comes from an Anglo education. When he is in prison, Hank notices that the prisoners do not complain because they expect this form of justice from having treated other people with the same barbarity they are experiencing in prison: "Their philosophical bearing is not an outcome of mental training, intellectual fortitude, reasoning; it is mere animal training; they are white Indians" (66). Similarly, he describes the woman he eventually marries as uncivilized, and adds, "Measured by modern standards, they were merely modified savages, those people. This noble lady showed no impatience to get to breakfast—and that smacks of the savage, too. . . . Those Britons were used to long fasts, and knew how to bear them; and also how to freight up against probable fasts before starting, after the style of the Indian and the anaconda" (154–55). Yet despite his own racism, Hank critiques the Church for treating people like slaves (110, 185–86), and he rails against the way British citizens are so used to being treated like slaves that they do nothing to protest their plight (111). He discourses on the depersonalizing nature of slavery and criticizes the Britons for being inured to the horrors enacted on those who really are slaves: "This was what slavery could do, in the way of ossifying what one may call the superior lobe of human feeling" (246). Presumably, his horror is related to the fact that these slaves and near-slaves are Anglos. One might cynically observe that, were they Native Americans, Hank might have had no objection to their enslavement.

Hank proclaims that loyalty should be "to one's country, not to its institutions or its officeholders. The country is the real thing, the substantial thing, the eternal thing; it is the thing to watch over, and care for, and be loyal to; institutions are extraneous" (159). How he believes a country is anything but an institution is unclear. But he reminds the reader that he is from Connecticut, whose constitution guarantees citizens the right to change forms of government, if they deem it necessary. He rejects any idea of immediate revolution because he knows that "the Jack Cade or the Wat Tyler who tries such a thing without first educating his materials up to revolution grade is almost absolutely certain to get left" (160).[5] Instead, he focuses his revolutionary ideals on the education of the masses. And because he is unable to educate the nobility, he is defeated. He annihilates 25,000 of them, winning the battle but losing the war, because their stinking, rotting, corrupt bodies will suffocate him, Clarence, and the "darling" fifty-two soldiers who are with him in the bunker from whence they have staged their siege. The tool of the Church, Merlin, infiltrates their hiding place and places a spell on Hank, leaving him to sleep for centuries.

Hank Morgan fails because he is crushed by the corruption of the nobility and the Church. His failure to reform the culture has ironic implications about the imperfectibility of mankind. But he is unique within the Twain canon for being a self-conscious reformer who ultimately reforms nothing. If, as Stone argues, the primary purpose of children in the Twain canon is to provide "moral commentary on adult society" (270), perhaps Hank's failure as a reformer is a function of his being an adult. He does not have the idealism of youth that would allow him to be a successful metaphor for reform, nor does he have the youthful voice with which Twain's most successful ironic commentaries on American culture are annunciated. Perhaps Twain is implying that the stirrings of social awareness that Prince Edward and Tom Canty and Huckleberry Finn experience emerge from their being adolescent and that a burgeoning awareness is necessary to successfully enacting change. If a growing awareness is necessary to Twain's conception of the literary reform character, then adolescence becomes the ideal staging ground for reform. Adolescents perceive social problems and still have enough faith to believe that their actions can make a difference. Hank Morgan, on the other hand, is an adult who ultimately knows better.

Children's Literature and Education

Embedded in *The Adventures of Tom Sawyer* is an ideology of education very similar to those found in *The Prince and the Pauper* and *A Connecticut Yankee in King Arthur's Court*: educated people are more deserving than uneducated people. Although Tom himself is never the actively engaged social reformer that the prince and the pauper are, his situation allows Twain to develop a variety of commentaries on the relationship between education and social mobility. For example, the villain in *Tom Sawyer* is a Native American and uneducated. Huck calls him a "murderin' half-breed" even before Joe kills Doc Robinson, on whom Joe has vowed revenge for accusing him of ill intentions when he had only been begging (74). Injun Joe is uneducated but crafty enough to finger Muff Potter—a drunk and also uneducated—as Doc Robinson's murderer. Muff is eventually saved by Tom Sawyer's testimonial, and Injun Joe receives divine retribution when he is sealed in McDougal's Cave and starves to death. But the lawyers and the judge involved in the case earn the boys' respect. Their education gives them social status—as it has the murdered Doc Robinson. Part of the outrage the townspeople feel when Robinson is murdered is a function of class. Injun Joe and Muff Potter are lower class because they are uneducated—or are uneducated because they are lower class.[6]

But while the text links education and class in tying social position to the amount of schooling a citizen has had, Twain has little praise for the forms of education that Tom Sawyer must endure. Tom Sawyer's educational experiences become the occasion for Twain to advocate for educational reform—even though Tom himself is no reformer. For example, Twain parodies the Sunday School Movement when he portrays Tom's Sunday school as having a system of tickets that are meant to reward students for memorizing verses of the Bible. In Tom's hands, the system becomes a capitalistic system to be manipulated by commerce rather than knowledge. When his sister bribes him with a Barlow knife if he memorizes his verses, he obliges, "and under the double pressure of curiosity and prospective gain, he did it with such spirit that he accomplished a shining success" (27). Tom is certainly bright enough to memorize the Bible. (He appears to have the entire corpus of Sir Walter Scott's novels memorized.) But the relatively valueless exercise of rote memorization provides Twain with comic material that has a social edge to it: children motivated to learn for profit rather than pleasure are likely to end up as embarrassed as Tom is when he tells the Sunday school superintendent that David and Goliath are the first two of Jesus's disciples (36).

Twain also has something to say about the hypocrisy of the Sunday school teachers who are motivated to behave more kindly when they are visited by Judge Thatcher: "The young lady teachers 'showed off'—bending sweetly over pupils that were lately being boxed, lifting pretty warning fingers at bad little boys and patting good ones lovingly. The young gentleman teachers 'showed off' with small scoldings and other little displays of authority and fine attention to discipline" (33). The satire on superficial teachers is comic, but it nevertheless communicates an ideology about how teachers should act. These teachers undoubtedly have something to do with Tom's lack of motivation.

Additionally, Tom's hypocrisy in mistaking education for a salable commodity is underscored by Judge Thatcher's observation that:

> knowledge is worth more than anything there is in the world; it's what makes great men and good men; you'll be a great man and a good man yourself, some day, Thomas, and then you'll look back and say, It's all owing to the precious Sunday-school privileges of my boyhood—it's all owing to my dear teachers that taught me to learn—it's all owing to the good Superintendent, who encouraged me, and watched over me, and gave me a beautiful Bible—a splendid elegant Bible, to keep and have it all for my own, always—it's all owing to right bringing up! . . . And you wouldn't take any money for those two thousand verses then—no indeed you wouldn't. (36)

The comedy resides in the reader's knowledge that Tom *has* no knowledge of these verses and that, if he did, he very likely *would* sell the knowledge of those two thousand verses for money, if he could. But the comedy only works for a reader who believes the judge's faith in education is well-founded; a reader who places little value on formal education could not enjoy the passage's irony.

Twain also critiques the provincial pedagogies of the one-room schoolhouse when he demonstrates Tom's "slow suffering in school" (44). When Tom arrives at school, his teacher is "throned on high in his great splint-bottom arm-chair" and is "dozing, lulled by the drowsy hum of study" (52). After Tom is sent to sit with the girls as punishment for being late, "the accustomed school murmur rose upon the dull air once more" (54). Later in the same morning, "the drowsing murmur of the five and twenty studying scholars soothed the soul like the spell that is in the murmur of bees" (57). The only punctuation of the soporific monotony are the times when Tom is punished, usually corporally.

As vacation draws nearer, Mr. Dobbins, the schoolmaster, "always severe, grew severer and more exacting than ever. . . . Only the biggest boys, and young ladies of eighteen and twenty escaped lashing. Mr. Dobbins's lashings were very vigorous ones, too; for although he carried, under his wig, a perfectly bald and shiny head, he had only reached middle age and there was no sign of feebleness in his muscle" (153). Mr. Dobbins is portrayed as a frustrated medical student and a sadist who takes "vindictive pleasure in punishing the least shortcomings," so the children live in terror of him (153).

Examination Evening reveals the superficiality of the children's education, which Twain's description enunciates when he describes the students' writing: "A prevalent feature in these compositions was a nursed and petted melancholy; another was a wasteful and opulent gush of 'fine language'; another was a tendency to lug in by the ears particularly prized words and phrases until they were worn entirely out; and a peculiarity that conspicuously marked and marred them was the inveterate and intolerable sermon that wagged its crippled tail at the end of each and every one of them" (156). Twain's critique of the clichés and conformity that proliferate in public school is consistent with his valuation of the individual and the potential of the individual's mind. He rails particularly hard against the evangelical tendency toward didacticism in student writing:

> No matter what the subject might be, a brainracking effort was made to squirm it into some aspect or other that the moral and religious mind could contemplate with edification. The glaring insincerity of these sermons was not sufficient to compass banishment of the fashion from the schools, and it is not sufficient today; it never will be sufficient while the world stands, perhaps. There is no school in all our land where the young ladies do not feel obliged to close their compositions with a sermon. (156)[7]

School structures Tom Sawyer's life—and the story of his adventures. Twain uses that opportunity to communicate his beliefs about education and to offer social commentary about how school needs to be reformed. Tom is not a self-conscious reformer in the way that Tom Canty and Polly Milton are, but his youthfulness provides Twain with an opportunity to write about the need for school reform, nonetheless. Tom Sawyer bears witness to the panacea that education improves everyone.

The great exception to Twain's ideology of education improving the masses seems to be Huckleberry Finn, who is "idle, and lawless, and vulgar and bad" (47). He "did not have to go to school or to church, or call any being master or obey anybody" (48), and yet he and Tom are rewarded with Injun Joe's treasure. Huck gets his reward because he has the good sense to think about reforming his evil ways. After hearing Injun Joe threaten to mutilate the Widow Douglas, Huck tells the Welchman, "You see, I'm a kind of a hard lot,—least everybody says so, and I don't see nothing agin it—and sometimes I can't sleep much, on accounts of thinking about it and sort of trying to strike out a new way of doing" (213). This passage is the key to Huck's success. Huck is not educated, and he is common, but he aspires to a better way of life, to a "new way." He admires Tom Sawyer's fluency with language: he is "filled with admiration of Tom's facility in writing, and the sublimity of his language" (80). Huck's admiration of Tom's education and his desire to "try a new way" of improving his social position is enough to earn that status for him. Because he regrets that he is poor and uneducated, he is allowed to participate in the Horatio Alger ideology of social mobility coming to those who try.

Huck tells Tom that he is not going to live with the Widow Douglas, who "kept him clean and neat, combed and brushed, and they bedded him nightly in unsympathetic sheets that had not one little spot or stain which he could press to his heart and know for a friend," because he is not consciously interested in social mobility (255). Huck can only endure the "miseries" of using utensils and not cussing for three weeks because, as he tells Tom, "I ain't everybody, and I can't *stand* it. It's awful to be tied up so. . . . Being rich ain't what it's cracked up to be. It's just worry and worry, and sweat and sweat, and a-wishing you was dead all the time" (257–58). Huck's youthful innocence makes possible his ironic social critique of the pretensions of the middle class. But Tom's American values trump Huck's initial rejection of social mobility. Tom tells Huck that he cannot join their band of robbers if he "ain't respectable" (258). Huck succumbs to peer pressure and—at least as this novel ends—agrees to move up the ladder of putative social success that includes manners, good clothes, and education.

While *Adventures of Huckleberry Finn* depicts Huck rejecting social mobility by "light[ing] out for the Territory" so as to avoid being "sivilize[d]" by Aunt Sally, the other two sequels to *Tom Sawyer* that Twain completed demonstrate Huck as having hopped back on the bandwagon of respectability in St. Petersburg (363). Highly derivative of Jules Verne's *Five Weeks in a Balloon* (1887), *Tom Sawyer Abroad* depicts what happens when Tom, Huck, and Jim venture to the Holy Land in a balloon—although the story occasionally evokes *Huckleberry Finn*, especially in the scene in which Tom yells about Egyptians who are shooting at Jim, "Huck, they're after Jim!" (97). The story is so episodic that it is virtually devoid of plot, and a recurring riff of humor involves Jim and Huck arguing with Tom's logic. One of the boys usually starts with the sort of invalid premise that characterizes Jim and Huck's argument on the raft in *Huckleberry Finn* about whether or not all men should speak English.[8] The rest of the arguments in *Tom Sawyer Abroad* are delivered and concluded with Jim and/or Huck employing perfectly valid logic and Tom bullying his friends with appeals to his own higher wisdom. In every case, the joke depends on the reader having enough erudition to analyze the faulty logic. The reader's education is again being assumed—and valued.

For example, Tom tells Huck and Jim that they are going on a crusade to "recover the Holy Land from the paynim" (9). Huck cannot understand how it's right to take land from someone who already owns it, and Tom responds with derision, "Oh, shucks! you don't know enough to come in when it rains, Huck Finn. . . . They own the land, just the mere hand [*sic*], and that's all they *do* own; but it was our folks, our Jews and Christians, that made it holy, and so they haven't any business to be there defiling it. It's a shame, and we ought not to stand it a minute. We ought to march against them and take it away from them" (10).

Jim does not understand how it can be "religious" to steal someone's land, but Tom dismisses him: "It's enough to make a body sick, such mullet-headed ignorance" (10). Huck says, "We knowed well enough that he was right and we was wrong, and all we was after was to get at the *how* of it, and that was all; and the only reason he couldn't explain it so we could understand it was because we was ignorant—yes, and pretty dull, too, I ain't denying that; but, land! that ain't no crime, I should think" (12). The once-illiterate Huck eventually reads *The Talisman*, the Walter Scott novel on which Tom Sawyer has based his colonialist notions, and concludes that "most of the folks that shook farming to go crusading had a mighty rocky time of it" (12). Huck's pragmatism trumps Tom's romanticism—but at the end of the day, Huck is still smart enough to read Scott's novel. Throughout their adventures in the balloon and the Holy Land, Tom's education, derived from the books he loves, competes with Jim's and Huck's pragmatism. While Tom wins most of the arguments, common sense prevails because the reader understands that Jim and Huck are right, despite being less bookish. In fact, the matter of common sense trumping formal education is a motif in *The Adventures of Tom Sawyer*, *Adventures of Huckleberry Finn*, *The Prince and the Pauper*, and *Connecticut Yankee*, too. In all of these novels, Twain implies that any education divorced from pragmatism can lead the individual to be at best insensitive and at worst destructive.

First published in *Harper's New Monthly Magazine*, *Tom Sawyer, Detective* was written for a more adult audience than *Tom Sawyer Abroad*, which was published in *St. Nicholas* magazine for children. The whole plot of *Tom Sawyer, Detective* turns on Tom's abilities of logical deduction. Huck plays Watson to Tom's Sherlock Holmes when Uncle Silas is accused of murdering a local man. Tom Sawyer has spring fever because "his aunt Polly wouldn't let him quit school and go traipsing off somers wasting time" (116). Tom and Huck eventually drive her to enough distraction that she ships them back down to Uncle Silas's farm, where they uncover a mystery. As Huck explains it, Tom was always attracted to a good mystery: "If you'd lay out a mystery and a pie before me and him, you wouldn't have to say take your choice; it was a thing that would regulate itself. Because in my nature I have always run to pie, whilst in his nature he has always run to mystery" (122). When Tom eventually reveals that the murder involved an identical twin relying on his brother's identity to keep his own hidden, the judge calls Tom a "very remarkable boy" (186). Tom insists that he was "just noticing the evidence and piecing this and that together, your honor; just an ordinary little bit of detective work; anybody could 'a' done it" (186). Three times, however, Tom refers to the prosecuting attorney at the trial as the "lawyer for the prostitution" (171, 174, 175), so the novel contains humor that precludes its adherence to nineteenth-century conventions for juvenile literature. But the elitism of the intellectual is even more pronounced in this book than in Twain's *Tom Sawyer* novels marketed to youth: only those capable of logical deduction can understand the truth behind something like a murder.

Twain's novels for youth valorize logic and critique rote memorization as a method of instruction largely because no one has ever learned logic from rote memorization. Twain's novels link social progress and social class to education: the more education a citizen or citizenry has in a Twain novel, the more likely it is to be civilized. At odds with Twain's promotion of education are his two most Romantic characters, Huck and Jim, who seem to be highly evolved moral characters largely because they have not been educated out of their common sense and into the ways of logic and corruption that Tom Sawyer and Hank Morgan represent. But what all of these characters have in common with Twain's misplaced faith in education as a panacea is the potential of their individual minds. Influenced by Emerson to revere the empowered self, Twain believed that education is essential for most people to reach their full potential.[9]

Educating Little Men

In at least three ways, Alcott's *Little Men* is an antecedent to Twain's *Tom Sawyer* books: Tommy Bangs anticipates Tom Sawyer, Dan Kean prefigures Huckleberry Finn, and both books comment on pedagogical reform using a similarly overeducated character as a trope. Tommy Bangs is the most mis-chievous character at Jo March's school for boys, Plumfield. Tommy is a jun-ior Tom Sawyer whose smoking almost sets the house on fire and who passes snuff around in church to make the other boys sneeze. Tommy gets in trou-ble with the African American servant, Asia, for "luxuriously skimming a pan of cream with half a stolen pie" and then tying her up to the clothesline as a joke in a scene as insensitive as Tom Sawyer's treatment of Jim at Phelps Landing (26). Tommy Bangs drops hot pennies down the dress of another ser-vant; he chops the end of one of his own fingers off and puts white pebbles in the sugar bowl. Like Tom Sawyer, he is obsessed with teeth pulling and pre-maturely tries to pull another boy's tooth out. He feeds the chickens rum-soaked bread and gets them drunk. He is "as full of mischief as a monkey, yet so good-hearted that one could not help forgiving his tricks" (26). The great-est reason he is so forgivable, however, is his keen intelligence: "If he did not know his lessons, he always had some droll excuse to offer, and as he was usu-ally clever at his books, and as bright as a button in composing answers when he did not know them, he got on pretty well at school. But out of school, — Ye gods and little fishes! how Tommy did carouse!" (27). Tommy Bangs shares Tom Sawyer's energy level, his sense of humor, his intelligence, his entrepre-neurial spirit, and his annoying overconfidence.

Another character in *Little Men,* the ragged orphan Dan Kean, prefigures Huckleberry Finn. Dan is a social outcast who has trouble conforming to the rules of Plumfield; he does not want to give up cussing or smoking, and he defies authority on more than one occasion. While Linda Black considers Mark Twain's rebel less socially inhibited than Alcott's (16), Dan spends much more time in trouble with authority than Huck because Huck runs away from rather than confronting it as Dan does. To be sure, Dan does run away for a time—and learns to love nature during his time of escape from Plumfield. However, when Dan regrets that he has not "had folks to tell him things" (173), he sounds for all the world like Huck Finn lamenting that "a body that don't get *started* right when he's little, ain't got no show" (133).

In *Jo's Boys*, Dan becomes a conscious advocate for the racially dispossessed. He serves as an agent to Native Americans in the Dakotas: he "lived, bravely and usefully, among his chosen people till he was shot defending them" (365). Just as Fishkin traces Huck's language to a minority racial identity, Dan's affin-ity for the Native Americans is well-established by a textual positioning of him as biologically linked to them: "Mrs. Jo often thought that Dan had Indian blood in him, not only because of his love of a wild, wandering life, but his appearance; for as he grew up, this became more striking. At twenty-five he was very tall, with sinewy limbs, a keen, dark face, and the alert look of one whose senses were all alive" (*Jo's* 66). Alluding to his dark skin, the narrator refers to him as "Othello" (*Jo's* 99), and he has the stoicism of a stereotyped Native American. He takes pride in "hiding [his inner self] as an Indian does in concealing pain or fear" (*Jo's* 130), and when he was in jail, "he faced the terrible strait he was in with the dumb despair of an Indian at the stake" (*Jo's* 210).[10] The stereotyped images of Native Americans are as obvious as those of the racially stereotyped slaves in *Huckleberry Finn*, but both adolescents—Huck and Dan—are engaged in seeking justice for their friends among a racial minority.[11] Dan's vengeful spirit is finally transformed into a forbearing kindness by two things: his prison term and the love of an improving soul, Amy and Laurie's daughter Bess. The family considers it inappropriate for their precious "pearl of great price" to be married to an ex-convict of such low social station, so she is whisked off to Europe while Dan completes his quest to serve the Native Americans as an agent (355). At his death, he carries in his pocket a lock of Bess's sanctifying hair. Like Huck, Dan is a rebel in the cause of racial justice—but he dies for the cause, rather than running away from it.

Little Men also shares *Tom Sawyer*'s critique of education, though *Little Men* is far less comic in its critique than *Tom Sawyer*. The two books share virtually the same image of a child victimized by extreme educational methods. One boy in Tom Sawyer's Sunday school suffers brain damage as a result of too much study: "a boy of German parentage . . . once recited three thousand verses without stopping; but the strain upon his mental faculties was too great, and he was little better than an idiot from that day forth" (32). At Plumfield, thirteen-year-old Billy Ward is

> like a child of six. He had been an unusually intelligent boy, and his father had hurried him on too fast, giving him all sorts of hard lessons, keeping him at his books six hours a day, and expecting him to absorb knowledge as a Strasburg goose does the food crammed down its throat. He thought he was doing his duty, but he nearly killed the boy, for a fever gave the poor child a sad holiday, and when he recovered, the overtasked brain gave out, and Billy's mind was like a slate over which a sponge has passed, leaving it blank. (25)

Granted, Twain tells the story of the biblically overdosed "idiot" for comic effect, while Alcott melodramatically describes Billy for the sake of pathos, but both descriptions advance the authors' ideologies about education. Both authors are criticizing parents who push their children too hard; both are criticizing the emptiness of rote memorization. Although their delivery differs dramatically, their message is identical.

Alcott absorbed most of her theories about education from her father. Influenced by the Zurich-born educational philosopher Johann Pestalozzi, Bronson Alcott advocated gentler forms of education in which children were motivated to learn by their own interests.[12] Pestalozzi advocated a concept he called *Anschauung*, a principle by which children learn from direct observation of concrete phenomena. His followers (Maria Montessori, among them) described the pedagogy as moving from "the concrete to the abstract." Alcott, following Pestalozzi, believed that educators must love the children they teach and must respect their innate uniqueness in order to teach them what they are ready to learn at a given time.[13] Pestalozzi was unusual in his day for rejecting corporal punishment, and Bronson Alcott's disciplinary tactic of having students ferrule the teacher instead of the teacher ferruling the child appears in *Little Men* as a means of teaching one boy to stop lying. The girl who loves to run away is tied to the bedpost by a tether in the same way Alcott herself was tied as a child (Saxton 100).

The concept of *Anschauung* pervades *Little Men*. Wild Dan is tamed in two ways: by himself taming a wild colt in a chapter that is directly allegorical and by studying nature closely. He has been influenced by a Thoreau-like naturalist, and Jo and Professor Bhaer provide him with materials to further his biological endeavors because they believe, as Professor Bhaer tells his nephew Demi that "we live in a beautiful and wonderful world, Demi, and the more you know about it the wiser and better you will be" (303). But the text makes clear that Dan cannot understand the natural world fully until he has learned "patience and a love of nature," two things that he has gained during his education at Plumfield (303). Demi is the star pupil of *Anschauung*: his grandfather has "cultivated the little mind with the tender wisdom of a modern Pythagoras, —not tasking it with long, hard lessons, parrot-learned, but helping it to unfold as naturally and beautifully as sun and dew help roses bloom" (20). When another of Bhaer's nephews falls in love with the sea, Bhaer centers his education—mathematics, astronomy, navigation, and geography— around the boy's interest in becoming a sailor. A budding musician is supplied with a fiddle, and entrepreneurial aspirants are trained in the importance to their profession of both mathematics and honor.

Alcott's descriptions of Plumfield identify it as a haven of *Anschauung* with a strong component of Emerson's transcendental emphasis on self-reliance thrown in:

Boys at other schools probably learned more from books, but less of that better wisdom which makes good men. Latin, Greek, and mathematics were all very well, but in Professor Bhaer's opinion, self-knowledge, self-help, and self-control were more important, and he tried to teach them carefully. People shook their heads sometimes at his ideas, even while they owned that the boys improved wonderfully in manners and morals. But then, as Mrs. Jo said to Nat, it was an "odd school." (28)

The children are gently led to believe one of the basic tenets of romantic evangelism, that doing good for others improves one's own soul. Jo's goal is for her boys to "be good, and to love to be good" (31). She believes that "though we may begin by being good for the sake of the reward, if it is rightly used, we shall soon learn to love goodness for itself" (169). The purpose of morality, then, is to improve the self and in doing so, to improve the world.

Transcendental values also permeate the book in the recurring imagery of the children as gardens. For example, Jo pats the cheek of one boy whose health is improving and tells him that "this is the crop I like best" (54). Later, the narrator generalizes, "when kind hands gently began to cultivate [the garden], all sorts of green shoots sprung up, promising to blossom beautifully in the warmth of love and care, the best climate for young hearts and souls all the world over" (125). Each child plants his own garden, and one of the culminating chapters is entitled "Crops," which describes the fruits of the boys' labors, but "Father and Mother Bhaer's crop was of a different sort, and not so easily described; but they were satisfied with it, . . . and by and by had a harvest that made them very happy" (316). Jo speaks her transcendental values in the book's final page in language evocative of Emerson's description of what it takes for a man to be a hero: "Honesty, courage, industry, faith in God, their fellow-creatures, and themselves; that is all I try for" (*Little Men* 375). That is all, indeed.

The pedagogy at Plumfield also relies on the children teaching one another. For example, Jo reassures Dan that he is a good friend to Demi because Demi "will help *you*, because he is so innocent and wise in his small way, and has what I am trying to give you, dear—good principles. It is never too early to try and plant them in a child and never too late to cultivate them in the most neglected person. . . . Demi will unconsciously strengthen your moral sense, you will strengthen his common sense" (272). As Jo puts it, "Half the science of teaching is knowing how much children do for one another, and when to mix them" (115). Daisy teaches the boys to appreciate domesticity; Nan teaches them justice; and Bess teaches them aesthetics. In reciprocity, "Nat does much for Daisy with his music; Dan can manage Nan better than any of us; and Demi teaches [Bess] so easily and well that Fritz calls them Roger Ascham and Lady Jane Grey" (374).[14] Pestalozzi's pedagogy decenters the authority of the teacher in the classroom and elevates the potential of each child to make a unique contribution to society.

From that decentering of authority emerged Bronson Alcott's and other followers of Pestalozzi's advocacy for coeducation. Jo tells her husband, Fritz Bhaer, "You know we believe in bringing up little men and women together, and it is high time we acted up to our belief. . . . [The boys] must learn gentle ways, and improve their manners, and having girls about will do it better than any thing else" (113). Alcott is not as fully committed to the ideals of coeducation in 1871 when *Little Men* is published as she will be when *Jo's Boys* appears in 1886. In 1871, she still values domestic skills so much that the girls in Jo's school "shall learn all I can teach them about it, even if they give up the Latin, algebra, and half-a-dozen ologies it is considered necessary for girls to muddle their poor brains over now-a-days" (226).[15] For similar reasons, the school's benefactor, Laurie, has been skeptical of coeducation succeeding at Plumfield, but he later admits that Jo's instincts on the matter have been right. She tells him, "One of my favorite fancies is to look at my family as a small world, to watch the progress of my little men, and, lately, to see how well the influence of my little women works upon them. . . . Dear me! if men and women would only trust, understand, and help one another as my children do, what a capital place the world would be" (373–74).

Jo's words reveal the ideological intent Alcott has had in describing Plumfield. She is not simply depicting a pastoral school that reflects her father's transcendental pedagogical values; she is consciously taking a political stance about the importance of gender equality. Thus, Alcott's insistence on the relationship between education and suffrage brings me to my next chapter, which is a discussion of gender in some of Alcott's and Twain's more notoriously conflicted novels. Alcott's views on education—and Twain's as well—were influenced by the sense of social justice that motivated them both. Though Twain complicates the negative possibilities of education creating an over-empowered and corrupt citizenry, ultimately both Twain and Alcott display more faith in the educated American individual than in any other type of person.

The types of narrative structures on which Twain and Alcott rely to make their ideological points are distinct from one another. Twain writes historical novels and adventures; Alcott writes domestic dramas and school stories. Twain's tone is often comic; Alcott's rarely is. Twain is satiric; Alcott is not. Twain's texts have come to be thought of as "boys' books" because the characters in them are so action-oriented; Alcott's are considered "girls' books" because the plots are more focused on how characters grow and what they feel than on what they do.[16] But despite these differences in their books' style and structure, both authors communicate a significant number of related values about education, including their shared belief that education can improve humanity and their disrespect for corporal punishment, rote learning, and reason misused in the name of logic. Both authors rely on the trope of the "improving child" in similar ways, and they create parallel characters, including Polly Milton and Tom Canty; Tommy Bangs and Tom Sawyer; and Dan Kean and Huckleberry Finn. Significantly, they depict youth as a time of hope and a time during which people's ability to learn makes it possible for them to become reformers. Because reform depends on a belief in the possibility of social change, Twain and Alcott employ the educable and hopeful nature of youth to write novels at once about the importance of education and about reforms that would make education even more effective as a platform for further social change.

CHAPTER FIVE

Gender and Reform
New Women and True Womanhood

"We don't need girls to teach us anything."
—*Jo's Boys*

"There have been other young generals, but they were not girls."
—JOAN OF ARC

Alcott's efforts to reconcile coeducation, careers, and choices about marriage in her novels *Little Men* and *Jo's Boys* reflect one of the central debates of postbellum America about the role of what would eventually be called the "New Woman."[1] The debate would also engage Twain, especially later in his career. Emerging as a result of the suffrage movement, the New Woman was the antithesis of the woman immersed in the Cult of True Womanhood—that early nineteenth-century embodiment of romanticism that conflated domesticity and piety.[2] The True Woman was pure, pious, and homebound; she wanted nothing more than to serve those she loved. The New Woman was strong, politically convicted, and independent of thought. Her critics charged her with wanting to destroy that sacred bastion of American values, the family, which is why Alcott is so careful to have her incipient New Women articulate their respect for family and the sanctity of marriage.[3] For instance, in the same year that *Jo's Boys* appeared, Alcott wrote to a young friend describing how her neighbor Sarah Ripley "used to rock her baby's cradle, shell peas, or sew, & fit a class of young men for college at the same time. One can discuss Greek poetry & chop meat as I saw her doing once with Mr Emerson & Margaret Fuller & the one task ennobled the other because it was duty" (*Selected Letters* 297). Alcott's novels *Jo's Boys*, *Eight Cousins*, and *Rose in Bloom* demonstrate the tensions at work between the New Woman and the Cult of True Womanhood; Mark Twain's *Personal Recollections of Joan of Arc* is his most extended investigation of the topic. Twain's Joan and Alcott's characters Josie, Nan, and Rose are all adolescent girls; they are all reformers; and they all call to the reader's attention the gender imbalances that disempower women by denying them political parity. Alcott's and Twain's explorations of gender are, therefore, another example of their reliance on youth as symbols for potential social reform.

Truly just, and free, and great

In 1883, Twain praised coeducation in *Life on the Mississippi*, describing a Minneapolis university that educates four hundred students, "and, better still, its good efforts are not confined to enlightening the one sex" (582). Three years after *Life on the Mississippi* appeared in book form, Alcott published *Jo's Boys*, an entire novel on the subject that is even more direct about coeducation than *Little Men* is. With *Jo's Boys*, Alcott concludes the March family trilogy. More important, however, she participates in the dialogues about education for women that recurred throughout the nineteenth century in the United States. For example, Doyle observes that Alcott's arguments about coeducation were responses both to Catharine Beecher's assertion that women should be educated in order to better carry out their domestic functions and Edward Clarke's *Sex in Education; or, a Fair Chance for the Girls* (1873), which argued that educating women caused them to become physically more weak ("Transatlantic" 273–74). Alcott articulates directly the pedagogical philosophy of the coeducational school her novel describes: the founders of Plumfield "believed so heartily in the right of all sexes, colors, creeds, and ranks to education, that there was room for every one who knocked" (*Jo's* 281–82). Jo says bluntly, "It is all nonsense about girls not being able to study as well as boys" (288). As in *Little Men*, Alcott takes as her primary justification for coeducation the moral stance that studying together gives both genders a chance to improve the other: females soften males; males strengthen women. Given that the most common objections to coeducation involved defilement of feminine purity, Alcott's rationale is an ingenious one in the way that it completely sidesteps the basic premise on which most opponents of coeducation relied—the idea that women would be corrupted by too much knowledge. How could innocent lasses be made less innocent by purifying the lads who needed their refining touch? And wouldn't innocent lasses who are made stronger be better able to protect their purity? Alcott understood that men would not be willing to grant women suffrage until they deemed the majority of women in America well enough educated to handle the responsibilities of the ballot box. But although suffrage is discernibly her goal in the 1880s—as is evidenced by her journals, her letters, and the increasing volume of suffrage ideology in her fiction—in *Jo's Boys*, she bases her argument more on improving both genders than on preparing women for the vote.

Nan, formerly a tomboy but studying to be a doctor in *Jo's Boys*, is Alcott's most feminist character. Nan says, "If we girls have any influence we should use it for the good of these boys, and not pamper them up, making slaves of ourselves and tyrants of them" (108). She is annoyed by Tommy Bangs's professions of love for her, and she disrespects those who flirt, which Jo reinforces when she says that "the girls who love to study wish to be treated like reasonable beings, not dolls to flirt with" (273). Daisy's love interest, Nat, is a male who also demonstrates how women are moral souls who improve men. He says, "I should be the most ungrateful fellow alive if I did not love, honor, and serve women with all my heart and might, for to them I owe everything I am or ever shall be" (111–12). Jo assesses gender in terms of economics: "It takes three or four women to get each man into, through, and out of the world. You are costly creatures, boys" (22)—and she ensures that they know that it is women who have improved them, at a cost. Jo's nephew Emil also concurs with this rhetoric of females being superior to males: "I'll ship a crew of girls any time you say so. Are n't they worse than a press-gang to carry a fellow to his moorings? Don't we all need one as pilot to steer us safe to port? and why shouldn't they share our mess afloat and ashore since we are sure to be wrecked without 'em" (111). His commentary extends Alcott's logic of the improving soul to the debate about suffrage: since the genders improve each other, shouldn't they have equal rights?

Nan's friend Alice is direct about equal rights: "Let us have equal opportunities, and in a few generations we will see what the judgment is. I like justice, and we get very little of it" (108). The girls at Plumfield admire the many post-Civil War spinsters who have "proved that woman is n't a half but a whole human being, and can stand alone" (285). More than one male character also helps communicate ideologies about gender equality. For instance, Tommy Bangs is a convert to his female friends' political beliefs: "I believe in suffrage of *all* kinds. I adore *all* women, and will die for them at any moment if it will help the cause" (112). Nan quenches his ardor—again reminding the reader that suffrage is a matter of daily life, which includes education—when she responds to Tommy: "Living and working for it is harder, and therefore more honorable. Men are always ready to die for us, but not to make our lives worth having" (112). Nan calls his statement "cheap sentiment and bad logic" (112). Additionally, Jo's father describes sexism as an "old-fashioned belief" and comments that change will be slow in coming (39). Without acknowledging that she ultimately loses the race, he compares the women students at Plumfield to Atalanta, saying, "I think the woman's hour has struck; and it looks to me as if the boys must do their best, for the girls are abreast now, and may reach the goal first" (39). Josie, Meg's youngest daughter, echoes his sentiments: "I'll never own that *my* brain is n't as good as [Ted's], though it may be smaller" (40).[4] Josie later implies that the students at Harvard aren't as good as the students at Plumfield because the male students don't have the benefit of coeducation, which she believes "keep[s] you lazy things up to the mark" (270). Suffrage and coeducation are inseparable rights in Alcott's mind, and she is as direct about that fact in *Jo's Boys* as she is anywhere in her oeuvre.

Alcott was proud of being the first woman in Concord to register to vote at a meeting in 1879, and she expressed annoyance that other women, including Ralph Waldo Emerson's daughter Ellen, refused to register (*Journals* 216, *Selected Letters* 236). In 1880, however, Alcott wrote with joy in *Women's Journal*, a periodical edited by suffragette Lucy Stone and her husband Henry Blackwell, that twenty-eight women had intentions of voting—very significantly—on the membership of the town's school committee. Most of the voting women came to the town meeting "with husbands, fathers or brothers as they should; all in good spirits and not in the least daunted by the awful deed about to be done" (245). The women were accorded the "respect" of being able to drop their ballots in the ballot box first: "No bolt fell on our audacious heads, no earthquake shook the town, but a pleasing surprise created a general outbreak of laughter and applause, for scarcely were we seated when Judge Hoar rose and proposed that the polls be closed" (246). The women had been allowed to vote only on the membership of the school committee and not on any other civic matter. The judge's action presumably implies that women were expected to have an interest in the education of children, if nothing else.[5] But his grand gesture was undercut by the superintendent of schools being informed that it did not matter whether or not the men voted because "it made no difference as the women had all voted as the men would" (246). Nonetheless, Alcott predicted that this day would pave the way for greater suffrage. To her dismay, it did not do so immediately. By 1881, she disparaged her hometown for taking "no active part in any of the great reforms of the day" (*Selected Letters* 256), and by 1883, she reported that only seven women had registered to vote in Concord, "a poor show for a town that prides itself on its culture & independence" (*Journals* 239).[6]

Alcott's work on behalf of suffrage extended far beyond the city limits of Concord, however. She attended the Women's Congress in Syracuse in October 1875, along with Susan B. Anthony, Elizabeth Cady Stanton, and Julia Ward Howe, and she later encouraged her publisher, Thomas Niles of Roberts

Brothers, to publish a book on the history of the suffrage movement (Stern, *Feminist* xix–xxi). He agreed to do so, writing to Alcott, "I am a suffragist to the extent of allowing the ladies, dear creatures, to do just what they have a mind to do, but I believe the bayonet and the ballot go together & I should hate to see you shouldering a musket" (Roberts Brothers, February 14, 1881). She responded:

> I think we shall be glad by and by of every little help we may have been able to give to this reform in its hard times, for those who take the tug now will deserve the praise when the work is done.
>
> I can remember when Anti slavery was in just the same state that Suffrage is now, and take more pride in the very small help we Alcotts could give than in all the books I ever wrote or ever shall write.
>
> "Earth's fanatics often make heaven's saints," you know, and it is as well to try for that sort of promotion in time. . . .
>
> I, for one, don't want to be ranked among idiots, felons, and minors any longer, for I am none of the three. (*Selected Letters* 253)

Alcott wrote to Lucy Stone, "I earnestly desire to go forward on . . . [women's Suffrage] as far & as fast as the prejudices, selfishness & blindness of the world will let us" (*Selected Letters* 291). Alcott was enraged by assertions that suffragists were anti-family: "The assertion that suffragists do not care for children and prefer notoriety to the joys of maternity is so fully contradicted by the lives of the women who are trying to make the world a safer and a better place for both sons and daughters, that no defense is needed. Having spent my own life from fifteen to fifty, loving and laboring for children, as teacher, nurse, storyteller and guardian, I know whereof I speak" (*Selected Letters* 269). One can only imagine how Alcott would react if she knew that feminists in the twenty-first century are still fighting that same straw man of an argument.

In *Jo's Boys*, written in the year following Alcott's most active work for suffrage, Nan is Alcott's consistent mouthpiece. Nan insists on talking about women's rights, saying, "The women of England can vote, and we can't. I'm ashamed of America that she is n't ahead in *all* good things," even though placid Daisy pleads with her not to talk about suffrage, since "people always quarrel over that question, and call names, and never agree" (82). Nan tells a group of male students who are jestingly begging her to be nicer to them, "We'll be kind to you if you will be just to us. I don't say generous, only just. I went to a suffrage debate in the legislature last winter; and of all the feeble, vulgar twaddle I ever heard, that was the worst; and those men were *our* representatives. I blushed for them, and their wives and mothers. I want an intelligent man to represent *me*, if I can't do it myself, not a fool" (109). In the students' tableau, she is depicted as Minerva, holding signs that read "Women's Rights" and "Vote early and often" (250). The narrative voice proclaims that "even in glorious America there is still plenty to be done before she is what she should be,—truly just, and free, and great" (293).

But the novel also contains a cautionary tale about the problems that beset women who seek equal rights. Alcott describes how women involved in the movement are often discouraged by others: "No one objects to plenty of domestic work or fashionable pleasure, I find; but the minute we begin to study, people tell us we can't bear it, and warn us to be very careful" (288). Alice laments that women have not been fully educated to assume the responsibilities of citizenship and yet are expected to be the intellectual equals of males. She understands that women have not had the same advantages as men and she doesn't like having to plead on behalf of her gender: "Only give us a chance, and have patience till we can do our best" (108). Josie dislikes being teased by her cousin that women should "always obey men and say that they are the wisest, just because they are the strongest" (39), and she has to endure two of the least accomplished boys she has grown up with telling her that "we don't need girls to teach us anything" (270). Later, one of these boys warns another, "Better not try to fence with these superior girls" (319). The narrator describes the "prejudice, ridicule, neglect in high places, and prophecies of failure" that the women of Plumfield face, but the faculty persist in their beliefs because they have "seen greater reforms spring from smaller roots" (282). *Jo's Boys* is as politically direct a novel as any written in the nineteenth century. The adolescent reformers in the text are numerous, so the message to youthful readers directly addresses the possibility—and responsibility—of youth to change a nation's prejudices.

To alleviate the fears of those who might resist the role of reformer, however, Alcott advocates one traditional response to gender. In *Little Men* and in *Jo's Boys*, both, she emphasizes that women must be trained in domestic arts as well as academic arts. In *Little Men*, Jo introduces Daisy and Nan to the "splendid new play" of cooking (72). In *Jo's Boys*, Mrs. Meg institutes a sewing circle in which the women mix conversation of "cooks and chemistry, table linen and theology, prosaic duties and good poetry" (283). Meg invites a broad circle of female students to the sewing circle so "the usual sneer at learned women" will not be applied to the graduates of Plumfield, even if they do wear "blue stockings" (283). Naturally, the female students take well to the domestic lessons, so "the hands that dropped the thimbles for pens, lexicons, and celestial globes, were better fitted for life's work, whether to rock cradles, tend the sick, or help on the great work of the world" (284). The novel also accords equal respect to marrying or remaining single, openly acknowledging both options as necessary because of the gender imbalance in the U.S. created by the Civil War.[7] The girls at Plumfield may not have used the kindest adjective when they discuss the number of "superfluous women" in New England, but their comment bears a certain degree of accuracy (285). As a response to this idea of unmarried women being "superfluous," the text praises many unmarried women with careers, including Frances Power Cobbe, Florence Nightingale, Elizabeth Stuart Phelps, Harriet Martineau, and the actress Charlotte Cushman (thinly disguised as the actress Miss Cameron in the novel).[8] Jo also praises social work as an occupation for women; it was, after all, Alcott's mother's profession (286). Just as Alcott wrote to some of her admirers, "I . . . believe in [w]omens' [sic] right to any branch of labor for which they prove thier [sic] fitness" (*Selected Letters* 168), Jo says the goal for the girls at Plumfield should be to "become noble, useful, and independent women, and earn for themselves some sweet title from the grateful lips of the poor, better than any a queen could bestow" (294). They should not worry about "their sphere, but make it wherever duty calls them" (294). In other words, even women who remain single have much to contribute to society.

But Alcott is equally willing to praise married women with careers, including the writers Charlotte Brontë, George Eliot, and Elizabeth Barrett Browning. Jo Bhaer has learned how to balance a family with two careers: running a school and writing. The plot itself extols the virtues of marriage, since all but two of the major characters end up married. Nan has a successful career as a doctor and is a "busy, cheerful, independent spinster," and Dan lives "bravely and usefully" among the Native Americans he has chosen to serve (365). The narrator lets her "gentle readers" know that "many weddings, few deaths" are included to please them (365). At the most basic level, one of the goals of coeducation has been to provide well-educated wives for the boys in the Bhaers' school. Jo hopes that "some of the new ideas of education will produce a few hearty, happy, capable, and intelligent girls for my lads" (182). But Alcott is extraordinarily careful to ensure that the balance between ennobled tasks and duty is always maintained by her female characters, even though none of her male characters show even remote interest in domestic duties in *Jo's Boys*. Moreover, although Jo speculates that if all women writers had husbands as supportive as hers "they would live longer and write more," she concludes that "perhaps that wouldn't be a blessing to the world though, as most of us write too much now" (54).

The legacy of the Cult of True Womanhood shines in through the text's inability to avoid gender stereotypes. Jo describes herself as "always ready to talk, should n't be a woman if I were not" (124), and she warns the boys against decadent women who "will unfit you for [the society] of good ones, and lead you into trouble and sin and shame" (277). Motherhood is also confused with perfection in all three books in the March trilogy. For example, after Marmee refers to God as the "best lover," Jo gently disagrees with her, calling mothers "the *best* lovers" (*Little Women* 341). Teddy is completely confident that his mother will find and rescue him when he is lost in *Little Men*, and the text assures readers that "mothers can forgive and forget every thing as they fold [their sons] in their fostering arms" (209–10). Alcott repeats that sentiment in *Jo's Boys* when Jo tells Dan that "mothers can forgive *anything*" because of "the blessedness of mother love—that divine gift which comforts, purifies, and strengthens all who seek it" (*Jo's* 336). Although motherhood has improved her character, Jo still struggles with her sharp tongue and her temper. She is rewarded finally with the ability to make "Professor Bhaer's busy life quite a bed of roses" when she finally resolves "never to be impatient or fretful" with her "beloved husband" again (254). In a comic scene, Laurie teases her for her "domestic infelicity, her meddlesome disposition, sharp tongue, bad temper, and jealousy," linking poor housekeeping with an unwomanly personality (251). Throughout *Little Women*, Jo's temper is the sin that has kept her from achieving the femininity and domestic happiness her sisters have. In the sequel written eighteen years later, Alcott is unable to abandon the notion that expressing personal anger is unfeminine. Daisy and Bess are upheld in the text as ideals of femininity: Daisy is "as sweet and domestic as ever," while Bess is "graceful . . . and dainty" (11). They embody the ideals of the True Woman, and sharp-tongued Nan and hoyden Josie serve as their New Woman foils.

Although the narrator of *Jo's Boys* insists that women can have both a career and domestic happiness, Alcott only describes this as a reality for two of these four girls—and she gives the topic only one sentence: "Bess and Josie won honors in their artistic careers, and in the course of time found worthy mates" (365). Throughout the novel, girls are depicted either as sweet, loving, and obedient to their parents, or outspoken, independent, and uninterested in family life. While either domestic women or independent women are preferable to immoral women in Alcott's view, the tension between the True Woman and the emerging concept of the New Woman permeates the text of *Jo's Boys* and is never completely resolved. Nonetheless, readers of both genders can observe adolescent reformers at work who strive to make the world less sexist. Like the characters in most of Alcott's other novels for youth, these adolescent characters serve as reformers who are willing to model progressive behavior for the reading audience.

Yours for reforms of all kinds

Perhaps the most reform-minded of all Alcott's improving souls is the one who most clearly straddles the fence between the Cult of True Womanhood and the New Woman: Rose Campbell.[9] Rose is the protagonist of two novels, *Eight Cousins* and *Rose in Bloom*. She is a girl who has seven male cousins; together, the eight of them comprise the children of the Campbell clan. Rose's parents are dead, so she is raised by her guardian, Uncle Alec. Her six aunts also have considerable say on Rose's upbringing. For example, Aunt Clara—mother of the intemperate Charlie—is a fashion plate of a woman who wants nothing more than for Rose to assume the position in society that she can claim as an heiress. Aunt Myra is dyspeptic and cranky; Aunt Jane is stern and difficult. Great-aunts Peace and Plenty share the domestic duties of their home. As the only representatives of an older generation, they are the novels' most unadulterated examples of the Cult of True Womanhood: Peace is a model of virtuous suffering and Plenty cares more about domestic economy than almost anything. Aunt Jessie, however, joins Uncle Alec in training Rose to be a New Woman. They want her to be well-enough educated to spend her money wisely, they encourage her to dress sensibly and to eat and exercise healthily, and they train her in the joys of charity: "'They who give to the poor lend to the Lord,' and practical Christianity is the kind He loves the best" (*Rose* 14).[10] It is through the charity based in romantic evangelism that she becomes a reforming New Woman: "She certainly did not look unpleasantly strong-minded, for she *was* beautiful in spite of her modest denials. Beautiful with the truest sort of beauty; for nobility of character lent its subtle charm to the bloom of youth, the freshness of health, the innocence of a nature whose sweet maidenliness Mac felt but could not describe" (*Rose* 28). The danger of being a strong-minded New Woman never overtakes Rose because of her beauty, both external and internal.

The training of the New Woman is also at odds with the traditional marriage plot that informs the narrative, especially of *Rose in Bloom*. One of the major tensions in the novel involves which of the cousins she will marry. Rose expresses anger at the cousin who assumes the right to marry her will be his and who treats her like chattel. She tells Charlie she will never have a husband "if I must give up the liberty of doing what I know is right" (*Rose* 94). Later, she says, "I don't choose to be taken possession of in that lordly way" (103), and adds, "My heart is my own, to dispose of as I please" (188). Nonetheless, her aunts and uncles spend a considerable amount of time plotting about which marriage would be best for her emotionally and for the family financially. Rose talks the talk of being tough-minded and independent, but she ultimately marries exactly as her uncle has hoped she would. When she finally agrees to marry her cousin Mac, the young man concludes, "I'll be proud to own that my best inspiration comes from the beneficent life of a sweet and noble woman" (374). He is a medical student and a poet inspired by her philanthropy because she is still thoroughly feminine, "sweet and noble"—more True Woman than New Woman.

In fact, Mac has been able to write poetry of a Thoreauvian stature only because he has been inspired to do so by Rose's improving him. For her sake, he learns to become more socially polished and less brusque; he even deigns to learn dancing from his brother so he may successfully dance with Rose. And, while Rose is improving Mac, he improves her. They read Emerson's essays together (304, 309) because he has "done more to set young men and women thinking, than any man in this century" (305), and Mac reads Thoreau to Rose, calling him "sane, simple, and sagacious" (301). Moreover, Thoreau is Mac's model as a poet: "Having proved that he *could* write poetry, he might drop it for some new world to conquer, quoting his favorite Thoreau, who, having made a perfect pencil, gave up the business, and took to writing books with the sort of indelible ink which grows clearer with time" (346). Rose believes that "every woman has her own little circle and in it can use her influence for good, if she will" (228); furthermore, Rose "felt her power, and wanted to use it wisely" (109). Rose is an improving soul—like Polly in *An Old-Fashioned Girl*—whose ability to improve men derives more from her adherence to traditional femininity than to her stance on equal rights.

But *Rose in Bloom* is as ideologically direct about gender equality in marriage as *Jo's Boys* is about suffrage. Rose is "not quite like other girls, and rather startled them now and then by some independent little speech or act, which made them look at one another with a sly smile" (8). Her uncle says, "To me there is something almost pathetic in the sight of a young girl standing on the threshold of the world, so innocent and hopeful, so ignorant of all that lies before her, and usually so ill prepared to meet the ups and downs of life. We do our duty better by the boys; but the poor little women are seldom provided with any armor worth having" (10). Rose concurs in a speech that shows her balancing traditional notions of femininity with developing concepts of New Womanhood: "Phebe and I believe that it is as much a right and a duty for women to do something with their lives as for men; . . . for we've got minds and souls as well as hearts; ambition and talents, as well as beauty and accomplishments; and we want to live and learn as well as love and be loved" (12). Mac also provides a social critique of contemporary practices regarding marriage: "It is very unreasonable in us to ask women to be saints, and then expect them to feel honored when we offer them our damaged hearts, or, at best, one not half as good as theirs"—for which Mac's brother accuses him of "preaching 'Women's Rights'" (238–39).

Rose endures many travails tied to traditional femininity. Charlie patronizes her career goals, and she is hurt by young men who have been taught to believe that "girls with beauty or money are brought to market to sell or buy as the case may be" (*Rose* 75). But she is also temporarily tempted to be a social gadfly because "the spirit of Eve is strong in all her daughters" (*Rose* 55). Not only is Rose weak before temptation, but she also enjoys self-abnegation: "The spirit of self-sacrifice . . . makes women love to give more than they receive" (*Rose* 258).[11] She also has a strong mothering instinct; she adopts an orphan and raises her because she cannot ignore the essentialism of her maternal feelings. After Charlie's death, Rose experiences a moment that crystallizes the textual tension between the True Woman and the New Woman: "The time had not yet come when the knowledge that a man's heart was in her keeping would make the pride and joy of her life; and while she waited for that moment she enjoyed the liberty she seemed to have recovered" (277). The love of a man is meant to be the pinnacle of her life's achievement—even though she can't help enjoying her independence while she still has it. In the novel's climactic chapter, she finally feels like a woman: "Was not life very rich that day, when uncle, friend, and lover were coming back to her together? Could she ask anything more, except the power to be to all of them the creature they believed her, and to return the love they gave her with one as faithful, pure, and deep?" (364). Rose's whole life has been spent in training for marriage, which makes her something of a failure as a New Woman, but at least she has moments of awareness that enable readers to consider issues of gender equality.

Rose's training—i.e., her education—is tied to her gender. As in *Jo's Boys*, Alcott articulates an educational reform agenda that is more pronounced for girls' than for boys' education. Rose first arrives at her aunts' house "miserable" because the more lessons she completes, the more her teacher at school gives her (*Eight* 6). She misses her father because "he taught me so pleasantly I loved to study" (6). The school she has been attending rushes her through "French and German, history and arithmetic, grammar and music," but Rose's uncle would rather have her study fewer subjects and learn them more thoroughly (86). He criticizes her former teacher for "cram[ming] her pupils like Thanksgiving turkeys" (87). Rose teases him, "You shall teach me, and when I am a woman we will set up a school where nothing but the three Rs shall be taught, and all the children live on oatmeal, and the girls have waists a yard around" (89). In Alec's mind, education reform is linked to dress reform and health reform; he does not believe that Rose can learn effectively if caffeine makes her jittery and her corset stifles her breathing. Alec tells one of Rose's aunts, "I mean to teach her how to manage her nerves so that they won't be a curse to her, as many a woman's become through ignorance or want of thought. . . . Rose shall understand and respect her body so well that she won't dare to trifle with it as most women" (217).

Not only does Alcott use education to link health and dress reform to gender, but she also ties education to social class and morality. For example, Rose teaches her maid Phebe, to which Aunt Plenty responds, "My blessed mother used to sit at work with her maids about her, teaching them many a useful thing in the good old fashion that's gone by now" (*Eight* 258). Furthermore, Uncle Alec communicates Bronson Alcott's pedagogical idealism, making clear that an education that builds moral character is far more important than any other aspect of learning: "Less Greek and Latin and more knowledge of the laws of health for *my* boys, if I had them. Mathematics are all very well, but morals are better" (221). Alcott equates the American ideology of education as a form of social mobility with the *Anschauung* at work in *Eight Cousins* and *Rose in Bloom*. Every individual's best and most moral potential is achieved through an education tailored to that person's need. Ultimately, education serves as the platform for Alcott's feminism. And although Madeleine Stern considers Alcott's thrillers to articulate her feminism "far more boldly than in the succession of domestic novels she produced" (*Feminist* xxi), *Eight Cousins*, *Jo's Boys*, and *Rose in Bloom* left a far more widely read feminist legacy, especially among impressionable youth, than Alcott's early serials could ever hope to have accomplished.

If Alcott is ultimately unable to abandon the Cult of True Womanhood for all of her New Woman characters but Nan, that inability reflects the tensions in Alcott's life that required her to be both the strong-minded financial supporter of her family and, simultaneously, Duty's Faithful Child, as her father once referred to her in a sonnet. Alice's comment in *Jo's Boys*, perhaps better than any other, typifies Alcott's perception of the underlying problem for women seeking equality in the late nineteenth-century United States: "Now we are expected to be as wise as men who have had generations of all the help there is, and we scarcely anything" (108). Women have not had the help—and especially not the education—that men have had. Alcott acknowledges the impossibility of progress without education by employing a hopeful adolescent to reform other adolescents. Like Alcott's other reform characters, the adolescent is self-aware, honest, motivated by a sense of justice, and politically aware. The implications about Alcott's construction of adolescence are noteworthy, for she implies that youth have the awareness and the power to change a culture. The construction is at once optimistic and idealized.

Joan of Arc: The Creating Mouth

Twain's most openly reform-minded adolescent characters share the same traits. Tom Canty, Prince Edward, Huckleberry Finn, and Joan of Arc are all, to some degree, self-aware of the political implications of their anger at injustice. If Tom Canty and Prince Edward dwell on injustice created by social class and Huckleberry Finn has a growing moral discomfort about racial inequality, Joan of Arc rebels against her societally proscribed gender role. Granted, Clemens sympathized more with the Cult of True Womanhood than with the New Woman.[12] Indeed, he referred to his wife as "my 'Angel in the House,'" referencing Coventry Patmore's poem of that name, which was the defining poem of the Cult of True Womanhood (Gribben, *MT's Library* 2.536).[13] But Harris traces how Clemens evolved from a man who would satirize women for wanting suffrage in 1867 to a man who would write in his notebooks in 1895, "No civilization can be perfect until exact equality between man and woman is included" (qtd. in "MT and Gender" 183).[14] In 1909, he articulated an odd sort of feminist logic in complaining that adultery laws are calculated to rob women of their sexual freedom:

> [Man] observes certain facts. For instance, that in all his life he never sees the day that he can satisfy *one* woman; also, that no woman ever sees the day that she can't overwork, and defeat, and put out of commission any *ten* masculine plants that can be put to bed with her. He . . . draws this astonishing conclusion:
>
> *The Creator intended the woman to be restricted to one man.*
>
> So he concretes that singular conclusion into a *law*. . . . And he does it without consulting the woman, although she has a thousand times more at stake in the matter than he has. . . . You have heretofore found out, by my teachings, that man is a fool; you are now aware that woman is a *damned* fool. ("Letters from the Earth" 915–16)

While Twain is being astonishingly insensitive to his own implications about rape, he still believes himself to be protecting the rights of women.

Twain was the husband of an emotionally strong and intelligent woman and the father of three ambitious daughters. It is nonetheless an understatement to say that he had a conflicted relationship with femininity. His daughters were smart and articulate; Susy and Clara were particularly so. Clemens paid tribute to Susy in writing *Joan of Arc*: the character Joan is modeled on Susy, who died of meningitis when she was twenty-four. In truth, *Joan of Arc* demonstrates some of the same gender tensions that are present in suffragette Alcott's work. Just like Rose Campbell, Joan has the independence, intelligence, and strength of a New Woman but the kind-hearted moral values of a True Woman.[15] Both of them are women who are surrounded by men—and it is in the context of the masculinity around them that their femininity emerges. Rose grows up with seven male cousins as peers; Joan's peers are also all male, especially when she moves from her hometown to lead an army. Whenever the males in their lives become too omnipresent, both characters resort to feminine behavior to assert themselves. And neither Joan nor Rose is allowed to enter adulthood as a New Woman: Rose marries, fulfilling at least some aspect of True Womanhood, while Joan dies and remains "pure." Nonetheless, both are characters who demonstrate the benefits of enacting gender equality. Rose is a stronger, healthier, and more balanced girl than the rest of the girls in her social set, and Joan's androgyny allows her to save a nation from oppression and colonization.[16] Most important, both characters serve as role models for youthful readers—especially adolescent girls—so Twain and Alcott again rely on adolescents as metaphors for social change.

Perhaps it is significant that Mark Twain called this conflicted novel about the need for social change his favorite: "I liked *Joan of Arc* best of all my books; and it is the best; I know it perfectly well" (qtd. in Cooley xxiv).[17] He seems to have adored Joan in a very personal way and depicts her as the most virtuous person who has ever lived.[18] She was "the greatest soul in the universe" (*Personal* 102); she "was built on a grander plan than the mass of mankind, and moved on a loftier plane" (119). She is also the smartest military strategist of all time. But she is allowed to be articulate and intelligent and courageous in battle only because of her virtue. Hers is the type of virtue so profound that it improves the people around her, so she is another of Twain's "improving souls." She has a "spotless and beautiful character" (116) that even inspires her troops to quit swearing and philandering. The narrator tells a friend, "When a person in Joan of Arc's position tells a man he is brave, he *believes* it; and *believing* it is enough; in fact to believe yourself brave is to *be* brave; it is the one only essential thing," to which his friend replies, "Now you've hit it! . . . She's got the creating mouth as well as the seeing eye! . . . Joan of Arc has spoken, and France is marching, with her head up" (151). With her perceptive eye and her vocal proclamations, Joan—like Prince Edward in *The Prince and the Pauper*— has improved an entire nation. Even as a young child, she has an improving soul. When the local priest exorcises a ring of fairies from a magic tree in her village, Joan points out the error of his logic: God must have created the fairies or they would not have been allowed to live for five hundred years. The priest excoriates himself and begs God's forgiveness; he will now be an improved priest because of Joan.

Joan's piety is the key to her virtue. Never once does she waver in her faith in God—or in the King of France as God's designee. Her devotion makes it possible for her to improve others: "In her eye was stored all charity and compassion . . . when her glance fell upon you it seemed to bring benediction and the peace of God" (157). Twain is intrigued by the eye that perceives and the mouth that bespeaks a truer perception than the object of the gaze has ever had of himself: "Joan's eyes were deep and rich and wonderful beyond anything merely earthly. They spoke all the languages—they had no need of words. They produced all effects—and just by a glance, just a single glance: a glance that could convict a liar of his lie and make him confess it; that could bring down a proud man's pride and make him humble; that could put courage into a coward and strike dead the courage of the bravest. . . . Ah, there it is—*persuasion!* that is the word" (169). Joan is so omnipotent that she transcends the need for language. This faculty makes her almost godlike—and it also makes the book almost irresistibly ripe for a Lacanian reading.

According to Lacan, we all experience "Lack" because we are separated from our Imaginary belief as infants that we are one with our mothers (203–15). This separation occurs as a result of our entry into the Symbolic Order (reductively described as "language"). Joan appears to have no Lack (also reductively described as "castration anxiety"). She accomplishes everything she says that she will; she is all-knowing in strategy and all-powerful in battle. She makes no bones about the fact that it is voices from God that give her power: angels and saints speak to her and from them she learns the knowledge that is power. Joan is, as it were, unified with the "Name-of-the-Father," which is, in Twain's paradigm, God. Unlike the rest of us who must suffer imperfection because we live outside of God's grace, Joan resides completely in unity with it and is "the most noble life that was ever born into this world save only One" (28).

Joan is as perfect as Christ. She is like God in that she is above language and so can create—"producing all effects"—with her "creating mouth."

Twain had great familiarity with the King James Version of the Bible. He would have understood the syllogism that opens the gospel of John: "In the beginning was the Word, and the Word was with God, and the Word was God. . . . All things were made by him; and without him was not anything made that was made" (*KJV* John 1:1, 3). The major premise of the syllogism is "the Word and God are the same." The minor premise is "God made all things." The conclusion is "therefore, the Word made all things." Nothing is made without language, which is a conclusion compatible with Lacan's premises. In endowing Joan with the power to create something out of nothing with a wordless language that transcends ordinary speech, Twain is depicting Joan as divinity. Indeed, the Ignatius Press edition of *Joan of Arc* has a slightly grumpy footnote when Twain's narrator refers to Joan as second only to Christ in nobility: "Mark Twain seems to have overlooked Our Lady in making this statement; he was not a Catholic" (28n1). Joan is blessed in being one with The (Name-of-the-) Father. She feels "divine . . . joy" (270) and is like the lilies of the field: "To know Joan of Arc was to know one who was wholly noble, pure, truthful, brave, compassionate, generous, pious, unselfish, modest, blameless as the very flowers in the fields—a nature fine and beautiful, a character supremely great" (377). On her way to the stake, the masses adore her as a martyr and a saint.

And yet, despite having achieved all this perfection, Joan still has two unmet desires that motivate her. She does not want to die by fire, and she wants to be reunited with her mother. When she is on trial, and when she is in prison and guarded only by male guards, she wants to see her mother. Her desire, in Lacanian terms, is the simple desire to return to Imaginary oneness with our mothers that we all experience, as Lacan would have it. And it is through this desire that a rupture enters Twain's character. She cannot be both perfectly united with God-the-Name-of-the-Father who is the Symbolic Order and still desire reunion with the maternal body. Her desire is an impossibility. But Twain uses this impossibility, this rupture, to dichotomize the True Woman and the New Woman. As New Woman, Joan is powerful and omnipotent and holy and perfect; she is one with the Word, a creating mouth who wholly partakes of the Symbolic Order. As True Woman, however, she is a perfectly normal child who wants to be comforted by her mother, and she impossibly desires Imaginary reunion with the maternal body.

Joan's fear of dying by fire is imagery that further reinforces this rupture between the New Woman and the True Woman. Joan does not fear death; she fears fire. She fears burning, feeling hot and inflamed. She does not fear the fire at the stake as the flames of hell because her voices have guaranteed that she is going straight to heaven. Rather, she fears the fire as the flames of passion. And it makes sense for Mark Twain's angelic and virginal warrior-hero to fear passion as any True Woman should. While Twain finds it perfectly appropriate for her to ride valiantly in battle, he cannot have her enduring a death that might "defile" her body, which Joan asserts is virginal (427).[19] Twain writes that when Joan heard her death sentence, "she sprang wildly to her feet, and wound her hands in her hair, and began to writhe and sob, oh, so piteously, and mourn and grieve and lament. . . . 'Oh, cruel, cruel, to treat me so! And must my body, that has never been defiled, be consumed to-day and turned to ashes?'" (427). A group of men is watching the adolescent girl writhing and pulling her hair, agonizing over her own defilement. Bells have been "throbbing" in the distance (427), and the bishop who has sentenced her is "not shamed, not touched" (428). The scene is sexualized, with almost sadistic undertones that imply the pleasure at least the bishop gains from watching the objectification of this female body. Moreover, the way that Joan uses the word "defiled" equates the fire with male corruption of the female body. In historic terms, Joan's fear of burning would be legitimately based in believing that without a body to rise again at the time of the Second Coming, she would never enter heaven. But Twain never explains that theological horror. Indeed, he has Joan claim what was a very Protestant belief in the nineteenth century, that she will "be in Paradise" that very night" (428).[20] Twain describes Joan's panic as a matter of the fire consuming her when she has never been defiled. Her desire for purity is the plea of a True Woman—and a virginal one, at that.

Twain's descriptions of how virtuous and gentle Joan is border on the tedious. As Henry James would have it, Twain relies too heavily on exposition to reveal Joan's character. The adjective to non-adjective ratio in this book probably reaches a higher number than in any other of his novels, as if when Twain writes about a female character, he must rely more on modification than when he writes about males. She is a "gentle little creature" (57), "modest, gentle, shrinking" (114); she "always protected her modesty from hurt" (79); her "hero-heart was a young girl's heart too, with the pity and the tenderness that are natural to it" (190); she has a "loving and merciful nature" (232). Additionally, Twain writes, "what a dainty little figure she was, and how gentle and innocent, how winning and beautiful in the fresh bloom of her seventeen years" (323); that she is "full of a human girl's sensitivenesses and tendernesses and delicacies" (356); "what a gentle and innocent little thing she looked" (346);

that she is an "innocent creature" (367). Even on the way to the stake, "she looked girlishly fair and sweet and saintly in her long white robe" (430). She has a "blameless mind" (433)—and like any maidenly girl, she blushes profusely (214). Twain's female warrior, his military strategist, claims, "I was not ever fond of wounds and suffering, nor fitted by my nature to inflict them; and quarrellings did always distress me, and noise and tumult were against my liking, my disposition being toward peace and quietness, and love for all things that have life" (277).

Moreover, Joan is as beautiful—and as slender—as the most feminine of True Women. The narrator claims that she is "shapely and graceful, and of a beauty so extraordinary that I might allow myself any extravagance of language in describing it and yet have no fear of going beyond the truth" (62). Later, when the narrator sees Joan wearing a beautiful dress, he writes, "She was a poem, she was a dream, she was a spirit when she was clothed in that" (121). The narrator praises her "beauty and extreme youth" (154) and writes, "she so youthful . . . hers so fair and pink, so fresh and smooth; she was so gracious" (157). She is a "dainty little figure" with a "lovely face" (164); her face is "smooth and pure and girlish, beautiful beyond belief" (326); she is "so little and slender" (284). Lest we forget her size, Twain repeats that she is a "slender girl" (300) and refers to her "delicate little self" (346) and her "slender body" (433). She goes to the stake "with the grace of her comely youth still unmarred" (433); she was a "lithe young slender figure" (452). Twain, in a 1904 appendix to his story, assures the reader how wrong are the depictions of Joan as a "strapping middle-aged fishwoman, with costume to match, and in her face the spirituality of a ham" (452). He bases his conviction in what seems to him an undeniable fact: "The supremely great souls are never lodged in gross bodies" (452). It seems fair to conclude that Mark Twain held a deep-seated prejudice against the overweight. His ideal True Woman must be delicate to be feminine.

Twain also reinforces Joan's femininity by having her act girlishly after any major scene in which she has acted particularly martial. For example, after the king proclaims her general in chief, the narrator compares her to a "small gray kitten" who has grown into a cat (143). After Joan lifts the Siege of Orléans, the narrator finds her crying among the corpses of the soldiers who have died. She is thinking about "the mothers of those dead friends and enemies" (190). After the Battle of Patay, she eases a British soldier to his death with "womanly tears running down her face all the time" (250). Through the narrator, Twain articulates a belief that Hamlin Hill describes throughout *Mark Twain: God's Fool* as being one that Clemens personally held: that women are emotionally stronger than men. The narrator says, "Men can have eyes and yet not see. All their lives those men had seen their own womenfolks hitched up with a cow and dragging the plough in the fields while the men did the driving. They had also seen other evidences that women have far more endurance and patience and fortitude than men—but what good had their seeing these things been to them? None. It had taught them nothing. They were still surprised to see a girl of seventeen bear the fatigues of war better than trained veterans of the army" (*Personal* 102).

The narrator describes Joan as "great in courage, fortitude, endurance, patience, conviction, fidelity to all duties—in all things, indeed, that make a good and trusty soldier and perfect him for his post" (118), but in the following paragraph praises her "sweetness and simplicity and unconscious eloquence" (119). Twain's vision of Joan as Word-of-God with an "unconscious eloquence" is gendered by her feminized "sweetness and simplicity."

Added to the New Woman/True Woman split that leads Twain to depict Joan as both one with the Name-of-the-Father but desiring reunion with the maternal body is Clemens's ongoing inner debate about "nature vs. nurture"— which was exacerbated by the tenets of Social Darwinism. *Pudd'nhead Wilson* is Twain's most extended—and confused—exploration of this topic: is Tom Driscoll bad because of his drop of Negro blood or because he was raised in a corrupt white culture?[21] In that novel, race calls Social Darwinism into question; in *Joan of Arc*, femininity does. Joan is clearly born feminine and acquires her masculinized knowledge and strength from God's nurturance. The narrator effuses about "the enchantments which were hers by nature, of youth, sincerity, a voice soft and musical, and an eloquence whose source was the heart, not the head" (137). The narrator also gives her myth of origin a slightly transcendental twist in that Joan is a child of nature (as in Mother Nature): she has been "born child of the sun, natural comrade of the birds and of all happy free creatures" (323). In his appendix, Twain elaborates Joan's myth of origin: "She is the Wonder of the Ages. And when we consider her origin, her early circumstances, her sex, and that she did all the things upon which her renown rests while she was still a young girl, we recognize that while our race continues she will be also the *Riddle* of the Ages" (448). Twain observes that when we evaluate the talent of "a Napoleon or a Shakespeare or a Raphael or a Wagner or an Edison or other extraordinary person," we know that "talent will not explain the whole result": "It is the atmosphere in which the talent was cradled that explains; it is the training which it received while it grew, the nurture it got from reading, study, example, the encouragement it gathered from self-recognition and recognition from the outside at each stage of its development" (448). Twain says that he can believe that Joan was born with "the orator's gift of eloquence, the advocate's gift of presenting a case in clear and compact form, the judge's gift of sorting and weighing evidence, and finally, something recognizable as more than a mere trace of the statesman's gift of understanding a political situation and how to make profitable use of such opportunities as it offers" (449). In other words, he can understand how she would be born with the talents of his most autobiographical character, Tom Sawyer. But what confounds him is how she was able to access these talents as "immediately usable and effective" without "teaching, study, practice—years of practice" (449). Joan of Arc appears to be a character who—like Huck—develops her Emersonian empowered self without the benefits of education. Thus, in Twain's amazement that she could be so evolved without formal education, he claims to be siding with nurture, but he clearly believes in nature as well. He believes women are born kinder and gentler and stronger than men, which is why it is so odd that Joan should become a military leader: "There have been other young generals, but they were not girls" (450). Although Twain concludes that "she is easily and by far the most extraordinary person the human race has ever produced," the implications throughout the novel are that God has produced Joan (452). She was endowed with her talents by nature (God) and nurtured by God. Perhaps the ultimate tension that tortures this novel is the agnostic Clemens's inability to admit the conclusion that he has been driving at for over four hundred pages: to believe in Joan's perfection, the reader must believe that God created her.

Joan of Arc's story is the one historical narrative that could allow Twain to explore female gender roles so thoroughly. As a woman, she is the epitome of Twain's "improving souls": "Whatever thing men call great, look for it in Joan of Arc, and there you will find it" (242). Twain can conceive of transcendent individuals—even adolescents—who are capable of changing entire cultures, but he expects education to be a key component of that transcendence. He cannot write about gender without relying on stereotypes, and Joan of Arc is the only completely intelligent female he describes in his novels for youth.[22] Ultimately, he believes the ideologies that a work ethic and education create social mobility, as does Alcott.[23] For Alcott, education is the most important means of achieving gender equality. But her depiction of the improving soul is more limited than Twain's: none of her characters improve a nation; they only help others outgrow character flaws. On the other hand, Twain thinks God must be involved to create such a paradoxical combination of the New

Woman and the True Woman as Joan of Arc, but Alcott asserts the combination of New Woman and True Woman as a matter of course that is not paradoxical at all, but a simple matter of females not having had equal opportunity with males.

Conclusion

Both Twain and Alcott create reform-oriented adolescent characters when they write for youth, but the scope of the narratives they write nevertheless defines the differences between action novels and domestic novels. Over time, both authors have been identified with the gendered patterns of boys' stories being about adventure and girls' stories being about family (Townsend 67; Hunt 52–57; Mott 102–03, 155–58). Both of them participated in the codification of gender in the nineteenth century, even at the moments when they were most vocal about protesting gender inequities. Indeed, perhaps the directness of many of their ideological statements—about gender, about education, about religion, about social class—explains why many of the novels they wrote for youth are not as critically acclaimed as *Adventures of Huckleberry Finn* and *Little Women*. At times, it seems that Alcott and Twain both strained too hard to identify youth as the hope of America and the metaphor for how society might improve itself. Alcott claimed, for example, that the moral of one of her most didactic novels, *Jack and Jill*, is "the influence for good or ill that even young people can exert over one another" (*Selected Letters* 239). The explanation is an unnecessary one, since her intention is applied so heavy-handedly in that novel. Phillips further identifies Alcott's impulse in *Jack and Jill* as transforming children into missionaries to convert children to "conventional, middle-class values" (226). That transformation seems to recur throughout much of the Alcott and Twain canons. Tom Sawyer sets out to turn Huck Finn into a literate participant in middle-class culture; Prince Edward provides the same opportunity for Tom Canty. Rose helps Phebe elevate her social class; Jo March does the same for Nat and Dan. Regardless of whether their novels have male or female protagonists, Twain's and Alcott's fiction for youth extols the virtues of upward mobility, which can best be gained through the panacea of education. And the adolescent reformers in these novels teach those around them—and presumptively, also the reader—that social change is possible for those who are educated and aware and who believe in the possibility of change.

The ambivalence Twain and Alcott felt about reform and its possibilities also reflects their own ambivalence about writing for youth, which I will explore in the next chapter. But regardless of their ambivalence, both authors left a reform legacy in American literature so commonly understood that it goes largely unremarked, which I will explore in the final chapter. The adolescent character who is a reformer is such a common trope in American literature that we don't even notice its existence; we just take the phenomenon for granted. But Twain and Alcott were instrumental in defining adolescent literature in the United States as something that assumes youth are interested in and capable of enacting social change. *An Old-Fashioned Girl*, the *Tom Sawyer* novels, the sequels to *Little Women*, *The Prince and the Pauper*, *Eight Cousins*, *Rose In Bloom*, *A Connecticut Yankee in King Arthur's Court*, and *Joan of Arc* all demonstrate characters who are adolescent either in years or behavior, providing some kind of commentary on social improvements that can occur through education. Even those books that are most concerned with gender roles connect equality between the sexes in some way to education. All of these novels are capable of ideologically engaging youth readers in the assumption that social improvement is possible. And all of them have been widely enough read since their first publication that they can be said to have helped define adolescent literature in the United States as a reformist genre.

CHAPTER SIX

Historical Interlude

Authors, Authority, and Publication

"Money is the staff of life."
—LOUISA MAY ALCOTT

"I hope to see a day when I can publish in a way which shall please
my fancy best and not mind what the banking result may be—
but that time has not come yet."
—SAMUEL CLEMENS

Examining Samuel Clemens's and Louisa May Alcott's publication status provides another angle from which to examine the history of children's and adolescent literature in the United States. Comparing the two not only demonstrates an arena in which they shared similar experiences—publishing—but it also provides a sense of what authors who were publishing for juveniles in the postbellum U.S. experienced as they dealt with publishers, copyright issues, and decisions about publishing venues. Clemens and Alcott were not unusual in wanting their publications to reflect their authority, artistically and financially. The experiences they had with their publishers are similar enough to lend credibility to the conclusion that most authors of juveniles must have experienced some of the same concerns. But few of those authors ever outsold Clemens or Alcott. By the time Alcott died, her books had sold a million copies (Stern, *Louisa* 339). And a little over one hundred years after their initial publications, *Adventures of Huckleberry Finn* and *The Adventures of Tom Sawyer* had sold 25 million copies (LeMaster and Wilson 6, 12). That these authors were widely read during their lives and well past them is indisputable.

How these authors' stories were sold to the public, however, is a marketing tale that is interlaced with literary status, financial pressure, social class, and snobbery. Both debated the appropriate venue in which to publish; both were influenced by the control of strong editors or publishers; both felt pressure to place their artistic considerations second to the demands of the market; both had ambivalence about writing for children; and both objected to the inadequacy of international copyright laws. Clemens and Alcott were status-conscious throughout their lives, so it is unsurprising that many of their shared concerns about publishing centered around the status that juvenile publishing held in their culture—and in their own minds.

Publishing Venue

Three types of publishing dominated children's literature in the late nineteenth century in America, and both Clemens's and Alcott's literary productivity were affected by the availability of these venues: serial publications, subscription books, and trade books. Serial publications were among the most widespread of the venues for children's literature. More easily distributed and affordable than books, magazines and newspapers provided opportunities for many young readers to have access to fiction and nonfiction alike. Indeed, periodicals were so accessible that they contributed to the creation of story as commodity: stories could be read and easily discarded, only to be replaced by the next issue of the periodical. As a result, periodicals (for both children and adults) exploded as an industry following the Civil War. Seven hundred periodicals were circulating in the United States in 1865, while 3,300 were circulating by 1885 (Darling 10). And as Brodhead notes, the growing number of serial publications made stories available to "farmboys, soldiers, German and Irish immigrants, and men and women of a newly solidifying working class" (*Cultures* 79). The culture of reading fiction in the post–Civil War United States relied on the technologies and commerce of serial publishing.

Serials created a demand for fiction that gave Alcott and Clemens their first entrées into print, both of them having broken into the market prior to the Civil War. Alcott's first publication was a poem in *Peterson's Magazine* in 1851 (*Selected Letters* xlvi), and her first story, "The Rival Painters," was published the following year in the *Olive Branch* (xlvii). The year 1852 also marked the first known time that Clemens published outside of the newspaper his brother owned, with "The Dandy Frightening the Squatter" in the *Carpet-Bag* (Hoffman 29). Eventually, both authors would publish some of their most important work for children serially. Alcott wrote 210 "poems, sketches, stories, and serials" that would be published in periodicals over her lifetime (Stern, *From Blood* 130). Four of her eight novels for youth were published in magazines for children before they were issued as trade books: *An Old-Fashioned Girl* first appeared in *Merry's Museum* (1869), a magazine for which Alcott had served as editor from 1868 to 1870 (*Journals* 160n12) and which later was absorbed by the *Youth's Companion* (Stern, *From Blood* 135).[1] *Eight Cousins* appeared simultaneously in *Good Things* and *St. Nicholas Magazine* (1874–75); *Under the Lilacs* and *Jack and Jill* also appeared in *St. Nicholas Magazine* (1877–1878 and 1879–1880, respectively).[2] Clemens's *Tom Sawyer Abroad* first appeared in *St. Nicholas Magazine* (1893–1894) and two others of Clemens's novels for young audiences appeared in *Harper's Magazine* (then called *Harper's New Magazine*): *Personal Recollections of Joan of Arc* (1895–1896) and *Tom Sawyer, Detective* (1896). Clemens published his favorite novel, *Joan of Arc*, anonymously because he feared that readers would not expect him, a humorist, to write such a serious story (Paine 1,034).

That Clemens would refer to a serially published book as his favorite indicates the status that publishing in a literary magazine the caliber of *Harper's* could confer on an author. Clemens took great pride in *Joan of Arc*, but he had initially hoped to publish the story in book form. He wrote about *Personal Recollections of Joan of Arc* to his publisher in 1893:

> I am writing a companion to the Prince and Pauper which is half done and will make 200,000 words; and I have had the idea that if it were gotten up in handsome style, with many illustrations and put at a high enough price maybe the . . . canvassers would take it and run it with that book. Would they? It could be priced anywhere from $4 up to $10, according to how it was gotten up, I suppose.
>
> I don't want it to go into a magazine. (*LthP* 336)

To understand Clemens's ambivalence about serial publication, one must also understand the status of his usual publishing venue, the subscription book market.

The publication history of Mark Twain's first book-length narrative is well known. Based on letters Twain wrote to the *Daily Alta California*, *The Innocents Abroad* burlesques Twain's first journey to Europe in a trip that took him to the Azores, through the Mediterranean, and to the Middle East. Because the letters home proved so popular, Elisha Bliss, then secretary of the American Publishing Company, approached Clemens and invited him to transform the book into one that could be marketed by salesmen as a subscription book.[3] Books published in this manner often outsold trade books—books marketed only in bookstores—by a considerable margin. For example, *The Innocents Abroad* sold 67,000 copies in its first year (*MT-Howells Letters* 3). By the end of 1869, *Little Women*—published as a trade book—was considered a runaway best seller, having sold 38,000 copies (Stern, *Louisa* 196).[4]

The sale of most of Clemens's major works relied on the pitches of seasoned traveling salesmen who canvassed the countryside and generated prepublication sales for his books. The American Publishing Company published six of his works as subscription books: *The Innocents Abroad*; *Roughing It*; *The Gilded Age*, coauthored with Charles Dudley Warner; *Mark Twain's Sketches, New and Old* (1875); *The Adventures of Tom Sawyer*; and *A Tramp Abroad* (1880). Clemens eventually established his own publishing firm, Charles L. Webster & Company, which also employed subscription publishing methods in publishing three of his other novels that were widely read by youth: *The Prince and the Pauper*, *Adventures of Huckleberry Finn*, and *A Connecticut Yankee in King Arthur's Court*. The agents for Webster and Company had sold 40,000 copies of *Huckleberry Finn* before the book was released for distribution in February 1885—a selling figure that indicates the potential for profit that subscription books had (LeMaster and Wilson 781). Selling agents, who generally received forty percent of a book's price as their commission, showed prospective buyers a sample dummy, or a prospectus, which was bound in the same cloth as the actual book but which contained about fifty randomly selected pages of the text, the table of contents, and several illustrations (Hill, *MT&EB* 5–6). Because subscription books relied on advance sales, review copies were rarely sent to newspapers and magazines, though review copies of *Adventures of Huckleberry Finn* were broadly distributed (Hill, *MT&EB* 7, 188n9). As a result, subscription books generally failed to garner the type of critical attention and subsequent legitimacy that book reviewers generally brought to trade books.[5] Moreover, Clemens was unusual in publishing fiction by this method because subscription books were usually nonfiction: a great many of them, for example, described various soldiers' Civil War experiences. Webster and Company's most successful book was Ulysses S. Grant's memoirs. Many subscribers cared more about heft than content in the volumes they bought, so fiction was generally ill suited to that particular business practice (Hill, *MT&EB* 8–13). Axiomatically, then, Clemens sacrificed some of his literary reputation to increase the sales of his books.

As American commerce expanded, aided by railroad and industrialization, more people had access to bookstores, where trade books were sold exclusively. By 1890, the subscription book industry was in permanent decline. Signs of the subscription market's failure were evidenced by Clemens's decreasing book sales throughout the 1880s. *Adventures of Huckleberry Finn* sold well, but *The Prince and the Pauper* disappointed him with its sales (*LthP* 152). And although *A Connecticut Yankee in King Arthur's Court* sold well, it did not sell well enough to keep Webster & Company from bankruptcy (*LthP* 245). Eventually, Harper and Brothers' exclusive acquisition of Twain's writings in 1903 helped influence Twain's increasing legitimacy in the American literary canon. Harper's transformed the formerly subscription-published novels into a consistent design that was of relatively high quality. Twain's novels had finally become trade books. And that transformation led to a sort of branding of Mark Twain: his works became linked with Harper's reputation in a reciprocal process that elevated his status and the company's profits.

Likewise, Alcott's publisher, Thomas Niles, documented a disappointing experience with the decline of subscription publishing. In 1881, he proposed to have an illustrated edition of *Little Women* sold by subscription trade when its performance in trade book stores had not been successful: "We have withdrawn it entirely from the booksellers & are trying to make a success of it by subscription. Thus far we have not done much but I am hoping that the autumn will show better results" (Roberts Brothers, July 26, 1881). Sales were no better the following year, when Niles wrote to Alcott, "'The Illus. L. Women' too has been a great disappointment. I am amazed to get rid of all of the first Ed. by way of agents and printed a second Ed. of 1200 1st Dec. of wh[ich] we have only sold 100. I cant account for it & having failed by way of agents, we have brought it back again into the regular channels of trade. We make the retail price $3.50 wh[ich] is only 50 cents more than we sold the 2 vols. for" (Roberts Brothers, July 25, 1882).

As a general rule, unsold subscription books were "dumped" into trade book houses, which created oversupplies of those editions. Trade booksellers were suspicious of subscription publishers, fearing they would glut the market with their editions, and subscription publishers feared that trade sellers would "pirate" their books, selling them illegally in stores. Clemens provides a telling example of his perception of the competition between the two venues for marketing books:

> The average book-seller hardly ever orders more than 3 copies of a new book. (Do not take our word, but go and ask.) These go over the counter the first day, and he orders no more. He tells the customer he is "out," and proposes to take the customer's order. The customer doesn't care enough about it, and no sale is made. . . .
>
> Bret Harte's greatest sale was on his first book, "The Luck of Roaring Camp," when he was at the zenith of his popularity. This sale was 26,000 copies in 2 years. The price was $1.25 a copy, the royalty was 10%, or 12½ cents on each book. Result to Harte in 2 years, about $3,000!

We can sell 3 copies of *any* book where the trade can sell 1. Moreover, we always charge about a third more for a book than the trade can venture to ask for it. (*LthP* 233)[6]

Despite Clemens's sanguinity about how profitable subscription publishing could be, trade books had, nonetheless, more legitimacy than subscription books. His preferred publication venue may have been more lucrative, but it did not necessarily have a positive influence on his literary reputation in his day.

Trade book publishers were just as fierce in their competition with one another as they were with the subscription trade business. Thomas Niles, for example, excoriated another publisher for trying to lure Alcott away from Roberts Brothers:

> I ought to be very grateful, & I am sure I am grateful, that the machinations of no enterprising publisher (?) [*sic*] has been able to upset the friendly relations between us.
>
> You ask if I know Mr. Heath. No, & now I do not wish to. He has done what a respectable publisher would not be guilty of—interference between an author & that author's publisher.
>
> But I know this, that one of our best printers refused to do his printing because he was afraid of the breakers. (Roberts Brothers, Sept. 5, 1881)

Ten years prior to this contretemps, Alcott had been approached by another publisher, Charles Carroll Soule of Soule, Thomas & Winsor in St. Louis, who knew that his efforts to win her business must be kept confidential. Soule wrote, "I have been closely watching, ever since we began business in St. Louis, for some sign of an 'unpleasantness' between Roberts Brothers and yourself, with the fixed intention of falling upon you, in any such event, and talking business. But there has come to pass nothing whatever to warrant such presumption on my part." He closed the letter by telling Alcott that if she couldn't break with Roberts, she should not "boast of this offer, but lay it in the silent tomb of oblivion, as I shall" (Alcott, L. M., 1832–1888, folder 194, Nov. 6, 1871). Apparently, Alcott followed his advice and kept the invitation hidden from Niles. She may also have been motivated by Niles's occasional lapses into emotional manipulation: "But you, I am quite sure, *without ample reason*, would never desert those who both by their brains & their money have *helped* you to achieve the position you hold to day" (Roberts Brothers, Feb. 14, 1870). Alcott's loyalty to her trade book publisher was notable, and to be fair, her loyalty was justified by Niles's honorable business dealings with her. In *Jo's Boys*,

Alcott refers to her publisher—jokingly renamed "Mr. Tiber" in the novel—as "a wise pilot at the helm" (46). She writes that Niles is "one of the most successful men in the business; also generous, kind, and the soul of honor" (188); that his company "treat[s] their people like gentlemen, and pay[s] generously for faithful work" (190). Not all trade book publishers treated her as well. A. K. Loring, who published *Moods*, for example, republished and marketed the book as new in the wake of *Little Women*'s success, which frustrated both Alcott and Niles (Roberts Brothers, Nov. 8, 1870).

While trade book publishing in the U.S. was dominated by three types of publishers—general American firms, the American offices of British firms, and firms dedicated to circulating religious material—virtually all major American trade book publishers of the era were located north of the Mason-Dixon Line (Darling 14, 17). While Alcott and Clemens never published with religious publishers, they both parodied religious publishing at various points in their careers, Clemens with his notorious stories "The Story of the Bad Little Boy That Bore a Charmed Life" (1865) and "The Story of the Good Little Boy Who Did Not Prosper" (1870), and Alcott in a less satirical passage in *Little Women* in which Jo laments the tendencies of religious publishers:

> She tried a child's story, which she could easily have disposed of if she had not been mercenary enough to demand filthy lucre for it. The only person who offered enough to make it worth her while to try juvenile literature, was a worthy gentleman who felt it his mission to convert all the world to his particular belief. But much as she liked to write for children, Jo could not consent to depict all her naughty boys as being eaten by bears, or tossed by mad bulls, because they did not go to a particular Sabbath-school, nor all the good infants who did go, of course, as rewarded by every kind of bliss, from gilded gingerbread to escorts of angels, when they departed this life, with psalms or sermons on their lisping tongues. So nothing came of these trials. (281)

Twain, after reassuring the reader in his story about the bad boy that "you will find that bad little boys are nearly always called James in your Sunday-school books. It was very strange, but still it was true, that this one was called Jim" (191), describes what happens to the good little boy in the sequel: "When [Jacob] found Jim Blake stealing apples, and went under the tree to read to him about the bad little boy who fell out of a neighbor's apple tree, and broke his arm, Jim fell out of the tree too, but he fell on *him*, and broke *his* arm, and Jim wasn't hurt at all. Jacob couldn't understand that. There wasn't anything in the books like it" (376). Twain (as narrator) and the narrator of *Little Women* both register literary protests about this type of writing in stories that were marketed to the whole family and thus available to child readers. Their satire indicates their willingness to ask children to question the premises on which much religious fiction was based, though both proved themselves perfectly capable of suiting their fiction to the forms of romantic evangelism that many Americans professed.

Both authors were far more influenced, however, by the trade book industry than by religious publishers. General trade book firms included Alcott's major publisher, Roberts Brothers, and Clemens's salvation, Harper and Brothers. Nonetheless, while trade book publishing afforded authors the opportunity to earn royalties over a long period of time, magazines paid authors a flat fee before the story was published. As a result, trade book publishers could promise greater profits than magazines—but only if the book was successful. While Alcott initially chose the bird-in-the-hand path of publishing novels in magazines four times between 1869 and 1880, Clemens resisted that path until the increasing financial difficulties of his imminent bankruptcy forced him to opt for immediate payment in the 1890s. His resistance was understandable. As Alcott put it when writing to Mary Mapes Dodge about fitting chapters into a serial publication, "trying to suit the magazine hurts the story in its book form" (*Selected Letters* 223).[7]

Although both authors eventually published their serially published novels as trade books, the common wisdom of the day held that novels first published in magazines would have reduced trade sales. When the *Christian Union* began to negotiate with Alcott for serial rights to her adult novel *Work*, Niles wrote to Alcott:

> If you were not known the large circulation of "The Union" would be of great benefit to you as an advertising medium, but *everybody* knows you & it is simply absurd for the "Union" to claim that their paper is to be a benefit to us. It is your already acquired reputation which they wish to receive for *their* benefit.
>
> You have now another *lever* to use in your negotiations with this corporate band of Christian Brothers whose moral principles are quite *pale*. (Roberts Brothers, Dec. 3, 1872)

J. B. Ford, the publisher of the *Christian Union*, naturally took the opposing view of a serial publication's benefit to a trade book: "It is in some minds a question whether previous serial publication helps or harms the subsequent sale in book-forms. Both Mr. Beecher and Mrs. Stowe, and particularly the latter, have had large experience in both ways of publishing, and they decidedly think the serial helps the book. At all events the pecuniary returns from both will be larger than either separately, and that is a point worth notice" (Alcott, L. M., 1832–1888, folder 66, Aug. 5, 1871). Throughout Alcott's career, however, her trade book publisher would continue to disagree strenuously with the logic that prior publication in a magazine helped a book's sales.

No words describe Niles's position on this issue better than his own. In 1876, he wrote to Alcott:

> Still I suppose you are *bored* by magazine publishers & newspaper publishers & one thing I am sure of that an author who writes for the magazines continuously for the emolument will soon become like a lighted lamp without oil to feed the flower; what should be cream will come milk & water.
>
> How much better to have something written in the cover of a single book which brings in both fame & money, than to be buried within the covers of serials, lost-sight of, & out of mind. (Roberts Brothers, Aug. 30, 1876)

His analysis of the ephemeral nature of serial publishing has some legitimacy; none of Alcott's short stories for youth have stood the test of time as well as her novels. Niles also blamed serial sales for low trade book sales in 1878:

> Your "old" books are going off finely. We get *no* orders wh[ich] do not call for an assortment of them, but I am disappointed in sale of Lilacs—we haven't sold quite 7000 and we should have sold double that to have kept up with "Rose in Bloom."
>
> I don't understand it except on the theory that everybody read it in St. Nich. & everybody in consequence is too poor to buy. (Roberts Brothers, Dec. 13, 1878)

If Niles's analysis about the poor sales of *Under the Lilacs* is accurate, then serial sales were, indeed, driving down her book sales.

Niles was also angered by the ways that serials advertised Alcott's name in order to increase their own sales. A practice he particularly despised was the distribution to subscribers only of an insertion that contained chapters of a celebrated author's novel:

> I want to call your attention to the advertisement in "The Christian Union" giving Miss Alcotts [*sic*] beautiful story free. This dodge will probably be repeated again & we shall have a supplement to The Christian Union by and by wh[ich] will contain Miss Alcotts beautiful story complete, free to subscribers.
>
> There is no help for this, & I only wish to show you what we have got to compete with.

> If your book can be had for nothing, our beautiful illustrated Edition will
> drag heavily. (Roberts Brothers, Feb. 19, 1872)

Serials, trade books, and subscription books each had potential benefits for
Alcott and Clemens, but each publishing venue also carried liabilities with it.
Serial publishing led to profits at a fixed rate. Subscription sales could be
tremendously lucrative, but not consistently so, and subscription books were
not as respected literarily as trade books. Trade books were the most highly
valued commodity in the literary world, but—then as well as now—their publication did not guarantee authors a profit. Trade books did, however, enable
the long-term reputation of both authors, given the ephemeral nature of serial
publishing and the eventual demise of subscription publishing. And since both
authors were concerned with leaving their heirs lucrative copyrights, they ultimately valued trade book publishing over any other form of publishing. That
decision helped them to endure as children's authors, too, since youth librarians throughout the twentieth century were more likely to promote novel reading for teenagers than serials reading. Clemens and Alcott guaranteed their
legacies by securing their copyrighted novels as trade books.

Editorial Influence

As the power of commerce increased the profitability of publishing trade books,
the power of American trade book publishers over authors became more firmly
established. Alcott was especially influenced by her relationship with her publishers.[8] She dramatically edited her first novel, *Moods*, to meet the publisher's
demands. Loring advised her toward "conciseness in intruding the characters,
getting them upon the stage and into action as quickly as possible" because,
while dialogue and narrative exposition are "delightful reading when well
drawn," they are nonetheless "too often skipped by the reader to see what they
[the characters] will do next" (qtd. in Shealy, "Author-Publisher," *BRQ*, 69).
Alcott immediately regretted following her publisher's recommendation to
shorten the text by ten chapters and to eliminate much of the expository material in *Moods* (*Journals* 132). She wrote to Moncure Daniel Conway, coeditor
of the *Boston Commonwealth*, on February 18, 1865, "'Moods' is not what I
meant to have it, for I followed bad advice & took out many things which
explained my idea & made the characters more natural & consistent. I see my
mistake now" (*Selected Letters* 108). But, eager to get her first novel published—
and even more eager to earn money for her family—Alcott was willing to defer
to her publisher's advice.

When describing the author-publisher relationship in a letter on January 2, 1864, to Alf Whitman, the friend who served as one of the models for Laurie in *Little Women*, Alcott employed a distasteful metaphor: "My only excuse is that when publishers once get hold of a body they give that body no peace & keep them at work like 'negro mulatto slaves' all day & every day, & are never satisfied. James Redpath is my present overseer & a sweet time I have of it, but as money is rather a necessary of life & he hands it over with a charming ease I cleave unto him, & devote my energies to the earning of filthy lucre" (*Selected Letters* 99).

In 1869, she wrote to the same friend, "Publishers come roaring after me if I dont do my work, & money tempts my mercenary mind, so I scratch away" (*Selected Letters* 120). Alcott understood her publishers' influence in her life. That she portrayed them in such draconian terms and herself in such debased ones demonstrates some of the psychological tension she felt about money. Without her publishers' approbation, she knew she could not succeed financially.

Indeed, just as Clemens's first prosperous book was prompted by the publisher Elisha Bliss, Alcott's greatest success was motivated by another publisher, Thomas Niles of Roberts Brothers. She wrote in her journal in September 1867, "Niles, partner of Roberts, asked me to write a girls book. Said I'd try" (158). In May of 1868, she verifies again in her journal that Niles had encouraged her: "Mr. N. wants a *girls' story*, and I begin 'Little Women.' Marmee, Anna, and May all approve my plan. So I plod away, though I don't enjoy this sort of thing. Never liked girls or knew many, except my sisters; but our queer plays and experiences may prove interesting, though I doubt it" (165–66). Years later, Alcott wrote an emendation beside this entry: "Good joke" (*Journals* 166).

Alcott was also clear in her letters and journals that Niles encouraged her to write the second volume of *Little Women* (which most American readers now experience as Book II of *Little Women*). She reported that many of her readers "vowed that Laurie & Jo *should* marry" (*Selected Letters* 120), a plan she resisted. Niles, however, pressured her to have Jo at least marry someone, if not Laurie. She wrote to her uncle, "Publishers are very *perwerse* & wont let authors have thier [*sic*] way so my little women must grow up & be married off in a very stupid style" (*Selected Letters* 121–22).[9] On July 25, 1868, Niles advised her to add another chapter to *Little Women* (Roberts Brothers, July 25, 1868), and in 1869, he advised her to capitalize on the success of *Little Women* by expanding *Hospital Sketches* for republication (Roberts Brothers, April 29 and May 26, 1869). For the same reason, he urged her to write *Little Men* and to write it quickly:

I have heard for a long time . . . that you were "simmering away on 'Little Men.'" It is now a year since "Old Fash Girl" was published and it won't do to let the poker get cold before striking again.

It is my impression that a new work by author of "Little Women" if published in *May* would find the people rife for it, with a dearth of *any popular* books to *aid* it, and I feel quite certain that you could present nothing more acceptable to the little millions of admirers of "Jo" than a history of her boys. "Little Men; or the History of Jo's Boys" how is that for a taking title—or simply "Jo's Boys" wouldn't be bad. (Roberts Brothers, Jan. 17, 1871)

When Alcott's British publisher, Low of Sampson Low, Son, & Marston of London, objected to "Little Men" as a title, Niles advised Alcott not to change the title because, after all, "[Low] altered Aldrich's 'Bad Boy' to 'Not Such a Very Bad Boy'" (Roberts Brothers, March 7, 1871). Niles also encouraged Alcott's writing of *Work* and recommended that she leave that book titled with only one word, despite the advice of the editors of the *Christian Union* (Roberts Brothers, Dec. 10, 1872). Certainly, Niles's concern with titles was based in marketing strategies, but his instincts appear to have been sound.[10] Moreover, Niles was generous in praising Alcott's work, as when he told her: "I have read 'Rose' and I like it—it is much ahead of 'Eight Cousins.' That allusion to Thoreau is one of the best things you ever wrote—(after making a lead pencil, he wrote with that kind of indelible ink wh[ich] never fades)" (Roberts Brothers, Sept. 25, 1876).[11]

Jo's Boys was written at Niles's urging. He wanted the third book to complement *Little Women* and *Little Men* in book sets, so his motivation was more material than artistic:

> I hope you will be able to give us "Jo's Boys" in season to have us get it ready to canvas the market *in July* by sample. It would be ever so great an aid to the sale of the others.
>
> I find that "Hospital Sketches" is a drag on the other books *in sets* & I want to put "Jo's Boys" in its place. (Roberts Brothers, Dec. 30, 1882)

The following year, Niles was still giving her the same advice, again based on increasing sales: "All we want now to make an additional *furore* is 'Jo's Boys'. The time is right for it"; "I am very glad you are going to work, though I wish it might be in 'Jo's Boys.' That book I am sure is needed to keep up the enthusiasms & renew the demand for 'Little Men' & 'Little Women'" (Roberts Brothers, Jan. 5, 1883, and Aug. 25, 1883). In 1886, when Niles learned that Alcott was working on *Jo's Boys*, he was ecstatic and again supportive: "The news is almost too good to be true—'15 chapters of Jo's Boys done'"; "I have read the first two chapters and find them in the same happy vein as of old" (Roberts Brothers, June 19, 1886, and June 21, 1886). Although Alcott was reluctant to reassure him that she would finish the project—"I have little doubt it will be done early in July, but things are so contrary with me I can never be sure of carrying out a plan, and I don't want to fail again; so far I feel as if I could, without harm, finish off these dreadful boys"—she completed the book in July of 1886 (*Selected Letters* 298).

Niles also had good instincts in advising Alcott to avoid didacticism. When she was writing *Rose in Bloom*, he told her, "I hope we shall not be able to see the moral in Rose without looking for it hard. If you can write a book with a moral in it wh[ich] the reader does not see till he gets through & then finds that the author has 'sold' him, such a book will make a hit" (Roberts Brothers, Aug. 30, 1876). Later, he gave her advice reminiscent of Henry James's valuation of incident over exposition[12]: "Now do you know I must be candid & say that the two opening chapters disappointed me—there seemed to be too much realism in them—the *motif* of the book seemed to be told too apparently & I dont think novel readers want to know what the moral of a book is; it is something wh[ich] should be so hidden that it requires reflection after reading to discover it" (Roberts Brothers, Feb. 5, 1879). Their relationship, however, was clearly tempered by both loyalty and good-natured humor. Niles teased her frequently, as when he wrote, "If you were to knock two letters off my name instead of one, *nothing* would remain, but even then I would squeeze out something for *you*" (Roberts Brothers, Nov. 10, 1877). Her faith in him was unwavering: "*I* don't forget ten years of kindness & hope a day will come when I can in some way prove my appreciation of that which is better than money or fame" (*Selected Letters* 229).

Without the influence of Niles, *Little Women* would in all likelihood never have been written, nor would several of Alcott's other novels, notably *A Modern Mephistopheles* (1877) and *Jo's Boys*. She wrote—very likely about *Under the Lilacs*—in 1877, "I am thinking of a new book like Old Fashioned Girl, as my publisher tells me that sells better than any other of my immortal tales" (*Selected Letters* 220). Alcott considered Niles an "honest publisher" (*Journals* 166). He also served as a business consultant, purchasing stocks for her and guaranteeing that her niece and nephews would be left financially solvent after her death.[13] He was, therefore, both an important financial advisor and literary mentor in advising her about publishing venue, audience, matters of style, and business.

Serving Art or Serving Mammon?

Samuel Clemens's most important early editorial influence was his publisher Elisha Bliss, with whom he initially had a relationship not unlike Alcott's with Niles. For example, when Clemens was writing *The Innocents Abroad*, he sought Bliss's advice about his humor and how much revision would be necessary to transform the letters from newspaper columns into a book—though he was most interested in "what amount of money I might possibly make out of it" (*LthP* 21, 12–13). He also sought Bliss's business advice, specifically in relation to subscription publishing. Bliss was important to him as a creative advisor, but eventually even more important to him as a financial advisor since Clemens would not have been able to found his own publishing company had Bliss not taught him so much about the business.[14]

But Clemens was not alone in having concerns about the relationship between publishing and artistic expression. Both he and Alcott experienced conflicting emotions that emerged from the commercial nature of publishing for profit. Neither ever seemed completely comfortable serving art or serving Mammon. Their descriptions of the artist's creative impulse are typical expressions of romanticism, implying that true artists are inspired by interior motivation rather than financial pressures. Alcott certainly subscribed to the romantic belief that art springs from within an artist as an inspiration that could be separate from the artist's will. She wrote of *Moods*, "It has always seemed as if 'Moods' grew in spite of me, & that I had little to do with it except to put into words the thoughts that would not let me rest until I had" (*Journals* 133). She described her creative process as being in a "vortex" (e.g., *Journals* 213) or—as she described Jo—having "genius burn" (*Little Women* 211), a metaphor which was sometimes ironic for her, as when she wrote to Mary Mapes Dodge in 1874, "My genius refuses to burn" (*Selected Letters* 188). She valued highly those writings that she wrote for the love of writing rather than money, including her adult novels: *Moods*, *Work*, and *A Modern Mephistopheles*. But she was driven even more by the desire to be financially independent so she could support her family than by the dream of achieving Faustian greatness. "I want to realize my dream of supporting the family and being perfectly independent. Heavenly hope!" she wrote on New Year's Day of 1868, the year *Little Women* would be published (*Journals* 162). In October of the same year, in commenting on the initial success of *Little Women*, she wrote to her friend Mary E. Channing Higginson, "I should very gladly write this sort of story altogether, but, unfortunately, it does n't pay as well as rubbish, a mercenary consideration which has weight with persons who write not from the inspiration of genius but of necessity" (*Selected Letters* 118). Clearly, Alcott believed that writing for money was a different, and less noble, task than writing for "genius." As she had written to Alf Whitman in 1861, "Money is the staff of life & without one falls flat no matter how much genius he may carry" (*Selected Letters* 72).

Perhaps it was her pragmatic understanding of earning money that helped balance her romantic view of writing. She wrote to one aspiring author in 1878, "Mind grammar, spelling, and punctuation, use short words, and express as briefly as you can your meaning. . . . Read the best books, and they will improve your style. See and hear good speakers and wise people, and learn of them. . . . [I] advise any young person to keep to prose, as only once in a century is there a true poet. . . . [B]oys of nineteen cannot know much about hearts, and had better write of things they understand" (*Selected Letters* 231). Alcott also advised the young man to avoid an over-reliance on adjectives and told him that if he worked hard for twenty years, he might someday establish a reputation that would allow him to "command good pay for the same things no one would take when you were unknown" (231). Alcott's genius might have burned as she fell into a writing vortex, but at least by the time she was forty-five she understood that writing involves a craft—and the better an author is at it, the more likely she is to command her own price. Throughout her journals and letters, however, one senses the tension she felt between writing for art and writing for profit.

Clemens expressed a similar form of literary anxiety about publishing for money. In 1875, he wrote to H. O. Houghton of Hurd and Houghton Publishing: "I hope to see a day when I can publish in a way which shall please my fancy best and not mind what the banking result may be—but that time has not come yet" (*LthP* 83). Like Alcott, he distinguished publishing for profit from pursuing his literary ambitions as if it were possible for other artists—but not him, not just then—to produce art only for art's sake. He once described the writing process for *The Adventures of Tom Sawyer* to a friend, who quoted Twain thus: "He began the composition of 'Tom Sawyer' with certain of his boyish recollections in mind, writing on and on until he had utilized them all, whereupon he put his manuscript aside and ceased to think about it, except in so far as he might recall from time to time, and more or less unconsciously, other recollections of those early days. Sooner or later he would return to his work and make use of memories he had recaptured in the interval" (Brander Matthews, qtd. in Hill, *MT&EB* 102). Although Clemens described his writing process many years after the actual process, he still reflected the Wordsworthian notion that art arises out of "emotion recollected in tranquility."[15] And if Alcott considered her writing to be driven by "thoughts that would not let me rest" (*Journals* 133), Clemens described *The Adventures of Tom Sawyer*—not unsurprisingly—by using a romantic image of the story developing like the flowing of a river. He wrote to William Dean Howells about *Tom Sawyer* in 1875, "Since there is no plot to the thing, it is likely to follow its own drift, & so is as likely to drift into manhood as anywhere—I won't interpose" (87–88). Like Alcott, Clemens was willing to describe himself as a medium transcribing a story rather than as an author with agency over the narrative.

That Clemens shared Alcott's romantic belief that artists are inspired by forces beyond their control could not have eased his concern that when he wrote for a profit, he sullied his artistic integrity. This concern even drove his sense of audience. Perhaps nowhere is this more evident than in the test case of his ambivalence about writing a "book for boys": *The Adventures of Tom Sawyer*. In the matter of developing this book, Howells proved to be as influential to Clemens as Niles was when he helped Alcott develop *Little Women* as a book for girls. Howells eventually read a completed manuscript of *Tom Sawyer* and made substantive edits—including advising Clemens to delete the last chapter, which may later have become the first chapter of *Adventures of Huckleberry Finn* (*MT-Howells Letters* 111 and 112–13).

The ideas for *Tom Sawyer* emerged while Clemens was finishing the composition of *Life on the Mississippi*, which first appeared serially in the *Atlantic Monthly* during Howells's editorship. Clemens described to Howells how he was writing about his childhood (*MT-Howells Letters* 87–88). Howells responded in July of 1875, "You must be thinking well of the notion of giving us that story. I really feel very much interested in your making that your chief work; you wont have such another chance; don't waste it on a *boy*, and don't hurry the writing for the sake of making a book. Take your time, and deliberately advertise it by Atlantic publication" (90–91).[16] It is telling that Howells's first impulse was to consider writing for children "wasting" Clemens's material.

Clemens vacillated for over a year about who the intended audience for *Tom Sawyer* should be. He wrote to Howells in early July of 1875:

> I have finished the story & didn't take the chap beyond boyhood. I believe it would be fatal to do it in any shape but autobiographically. . . . I perhaps made

a mistake in not writing it in the first person. If I went on, now, & took him into manhood, he would just be like all the one-horse men in literature & the reader would conceive a hearty contempt for him. It is *not* a boy's book, at all. It will only be read by adults. It is only written for adults. . . . I wish you would promise to read the MS of Tom Sawyer some time, & see if you don't really decide that I am right in closing with him as a boy. (*MT-Howells Letters* 91–92)

Clemens's commentary reflects several significant factors in helping us establish the publishing conventions of his day. First, he is rejecting the standard *bildungsroman* plot that was proliferating in American and European publishing at the time when he says that portraying Tom Sawyer as an adult would make the character "just like all the one-horse men in literature." Indeed, the novel closes with this sentiment: "So endeth this chronicle. It being strictly a history of a boy, it must stop here; the story could not go much further without becoming the history of a man. When one writes a novel about grown people, he knows exactly where to stop—that is, with a marriage; but when he writes of juveniles, he must stop where best he can" (283). Second, Clemens's self-assessment of writing *Tom Sawyer* insists on the authority of autobiographical writing when depicting childhood. No author of created fancy he; his words imply that giving the story a fictional ending would be disastrous— as he puts it, "fatal." While Clemens is describing a work of fiction, the temptation is strong to speculate that for Clemens to write an alternate ending to his own autobiography would feel self-destructive. Finally, Clemens's July 1875 letter to Howells demonstrates his belief as he completed the manuscript that he had written for an adult audience, not a child audience.[17]

Audience

The distinction between writing for children and adults may have been literary to Clemens—or it may have been financial. In the same letter, he wrote to Howells: "I would dearly like to see it in the Atlantic, but I doubt if it would pay the publishers to buy the privilege, or me to sell it. . . . You see I take a vile, mercenary view of things—but then my household expenses are something almost ghastly" (92). As near to the publication of *Tom Sawyer* as 1871, he wrote to his brother Orion about his low opinion of publishing for juveniles: "My opinion of children's article[s] is wholly worthless, for I never saw one that I thought was worth the ink it was written with, & yet you know & I know that such literature is marvelously popular & worth heaps of money. . . . I have no love for children's literature" (qtd. in Stone 51–52). Clemens's ambivalence about the lucrative nature of children's literature may, in the end, have been what solidified his decision-making with Howells about the market for *Tom Sawyer*.

Howells and Clemens continued the discussion about the appropriate audience for *The Adventures of Tom Sawyer* over several months. On November 21, 1875, Howells wrote: "I finished reading Tom Sawyer a week ago, sitting up till one A.M., to get to the end, simply because it was impossible to leave off. It's altogether the best boy's story I ever read. It will be an immense success. But I think you ought to treat it explicitly *as* a boy's story. Grown-ups will enjoy it just as much if you do; and if you should put it forth as a study of boy character from the grown-up point of view, you'd give the wrong key to it" (110–11). Howells's remarkable about-face as to whether *Tom Sawyer* was better suited to adults or children occurred because of one simple factor: he read the manuscript. Before reading it, he thought Clemens's childhood reminiscences would be best marketed to adults. But the straightforward plot, the engaging characterization, and the narrative's relative paucity of the type of burlesque that characterized Twain's humor for adults must have convinced Howells that his initial impression was wrong.

Clemens responded with joy on November 23: "It is glorious news that you like Tom Sawyer so well. . . . Mrs. Clemens decides with you that the book should issue as a book for boys, pure & simple—& so do I. It is surely the correct idea" (112). In the same letter, Clemens parodies Bret Harte and Charles Francis Adams for using "three words where one would answer" (112). Clemens's reassertion later in the letter of what he has already stated, "It is surely the correct idea," may be a further parody of Harte's and Adams's verbosity— or it may reflect Clemens's need to assert to himself that the decision to direct *Tom Sawyer* to boys was the right one. In January of 1876, Howells advised Clemens to delete from the manuscript an example of Huck Finn swearing about the Widow Douglas and Miss Watson—"they comb me all to hell" (122)—because of market considerations: "It wont do for the children" (124). Both men demonstrate the nineteenth-century tendency to write more protectively to children than to adults.

But despite his many assertions that the book was for boys, Clemens later in 1876 began to realize that publishing in the children's market might affect his profits. In April, he wrote to Moncure Conway, his literary agent in England and also a friend of Alcott's: "You can leave out the preface; or alter it so that it will not profess to be a book for youth; or write a new preface and put your own name or initials to it.—Fix it any way you want to, if as you say, it will

be best not to put it forth as a book for youth" (*LthP* 97n2). Conway had written to Clemens, "I don't think it would be doing justice to call it a boy's book
and think it had better be left to people to form their own conclusions whether
it is for young or old" (*LthP* 97n). Surely, Clemens had sales in mind when he
wrote his response because he wrote in the same month to Conway, "I have
told Bliss to issue in the autumn and make a Boy's Holiday Book of it" (*LthP*
98). Bliss's 1876 prospectus of *Tom Sawyer* described Twain as having "the genius
requisite to render the written adventures of a boy overwhelmingly fascinat-
ing to grown up readers" (Hill, *MT&EB* 118). Even in 1876, the Christmas
market was a lucrative one for authors.[18]

No other of Clemens's books experienced quite as controversial an incep-
tion—though *Adventures of Huckleberry Finn* had a more controversial reception. With its violence, racial tension, and many intemperate characters,
Huckleberry Finn was marketed from the first for adults, as was *A Connecticut
Yankee in King Arthur's Court*. *Tom Sawyer Abroad*, however, was written for children: "It is a story for boys, of course, and I think will interest any boy between
8 years and 80" (*LthP* 314). As Clemens told his publisher, "My family (tough
people to please), like it first-rate, but they say it is for boys and girls. They won't
allow it to go into a grown-folks' magazine" (*LthP* 318–19). But Clemens quib-
bled considerably with his publisher about which magazine would be the most
lucrative for that children's story. Mary Mapes Dodge offered him $5,000 for a
50,000-word story, but *Tom Sawyer Abroad* was only 40,000, so Clemens
instructed his publisher to attempt to place it in either *Harper's Young Peoples*
magazine or in the *Atlantic Monthly*—wherever he could get the highest rate.[19]
Dodge ultimately got the story for *St. Nicholas*, but not before Clemens had pronounced judgment on how best to write for children: "I conceive that the right
way to write a story for boys is to write so that it will not only interest boys but
will also strongly interest any man *who has ever been a boy*. That immensely
enlarges the audience" (*LthP* 314).[20] In other words, the most effective way to
write for children was to write in such a way as to appeal to the broadest possible audience—so Clemens could earn the highest possible profit.

Alcott also relied on serials to sustain her financially, and she was perfectly
capable of enlarging her audience by writing what would sell most expeditiously.
Most of her contemporary readers were unaware that the bulk of her serial publications prior to *Little Women* were pseudonymously written thrillers published
under names such as "A. M. Barnard" and "Flora Fairfield." She wrote sensational tales such as "A Marble Woman" (1865) and "Behind a Mask" (1866) for
newspapers like *Frank Leslie's Illustrated Newspaper* and the *Flag of Our Union*.

Her motivation was clear; as she once told a friend, "Money is the principle object of my life just now" (*Selected Letters* 16). The profits she garnered from such stories supplemented her family income throughout the late 1850s and early 1860s. When her family needed money, Alcott wrote to please market demands.

But by the time Alcott had published the second volume of *Little Women*, she could afford to be impatient with the type of blood-and-thunder sensationalism that had been her own most lucrative writing for years. For example, Professor Bhaer describes sensation stories as "bad trash" (280). When Jo defends what she has been writing as "only silly," he responds that the stories are "poison" (280). Jo privately rereads her own manuscripts—mentally wearing Professor Bhaer's glasses so as to change her own perspective as she does so—and flagellates herself: "They *are* trash. . . . I've gone blindly on, hurting myself and other people, for the sake of money" (280). Thus, as early as 1869, Alcott displayed one tension that would characterize her career: she felt guilty if she wrote beneath what she considered her own standards to be.

More conflagrational, by far, than Jo's burning her manuscripts was Alcott's diatribe against the dime novels of Horatio Alger and Oliver Optic, the pen name of William T. Adams. In *An Old-Fashioned Girl*, Tom reads "one of those delightful books in which boys are cast away on desert islands, where every known fruit, vegetable and flower is in its prime all the year round; or lost in boundless forests, where the young heroes have thrilling adventures, kill impossible beasts, and, when the author's invention gives out, suddenly find their way home, laden with tiger skins, tame buffalos and other pleasing trophies of their prowess" (90).

In *Eight Cousins*, Aunt Jessie, in a voice that sounds much like Alcott's own, expands elaborately on her opinion of blood-and-thunder tales written for boys in overtly classist language:

> These books are as bad for the small boys as cigars for the large ones. . . . The writers of these popular stories intend to do good, I have no doubt, but it seems to me they fail because their motto is, "Be smart, and you will be rich," instead of "Be honest, and you will be happy.". . . I cannot think they will help to refine the ragamuffins, if they read them, and I'm sure they can do no good to the better class of boys, who through these books are introduced to police courts, counterfeiters' dens, gambling houses, drinking saloons, and all sorts of low life. . . . I am not satisfied with these *optical* delusions, as I call them. (199–200)

Richard L. Darling notes that "optical" was not italicized in the original printing in *St. Nicholas* in August 1875, but was in all subsequent editions (36,

254n23)—a fact that did not go unnoticed by Adams (i.e., Oliver Optic), who wrote the following month in *Oliver Optic's Magazine*:

> Ah, Louise, you are very smart, and you have become rich. Your success mocks that of the juvenile heroes you despise. Even the author of "Dick Dauntless" and "Sam Soaker," whoever he may be, would not dare to write up a heroine who rose so rapidly from poverty and obscurity to riches and fame as you did; but in view of the wholesale perversion of the truth we have pointed out, we must ask you to adopt the motto you recommend for others—"Be honest and you will be happy," instead of the one you seem to have chosen: "Be smart and you will be rich." (qtd. in Darling 38)

Alcott was not the only writer to attack Adams for his sensationalism, but she was, perhaps, one of the more hypocritical to do so.

Twain's parody of sensation fiction in *The Adventures of Tom Sawyer* captures a more comedic version of the moral ambiguity surrounding those who supplied popular fiction to an eager public. On public speaking day at Tom Sawyer's school, a "dark-complexioned, black eyed, black haired young lady" reads her own story (158). It evokes Bulwer-Lytton, opening: "Dark and tempestuous was night. Around the throne on high not a single star quivered; but the deep intonations of the heavy thunder constantly vibrated upon the ear; whilst the terrific lightning revelled in angry mood through the cloudy chambers of heaven, seeming to scorn the power exerted over its terrors by the illustrious Franklin!" (158).[21] Twain assures his readers that "this nightmare occupied some ten pages of manuscript" (159), and it does, indeed, read like some of Alcott's early blood-and-thunder stories. In Twain's version of sensationalism, however, the genre's worst offense is not its morality but how poorly it is written.

Alcott and Clemens both experienced considerable conflict about writing for children. Both were concerned about the suitability of some topics for children and self-censored, rather than either corrupt children or be criticized for doing so. Daniel Ford of the *Youth's Companion* gently suggested that Alcott edit her reference to a ball and dancing in *Silver Pitchers* (1875): "Your whole plot turns upon a 'ball' in the opening chapter, and the second chapter has such a charming presentation of dancing, that hundreds of readers of the Companion, will turn up 'pious eyes,' lest their old 'orthodox' paper, should appear to countenance what seems to them 'dangerous pleasures.'. . . Now can you give the obnoxious word a sugar coating—calling the ball a sociable or something of the sort, and give the dancing of the second chapter somewhat less prominence" (Alcott, L. M., 1832–1888, folder 61, Feb. 17, 1875). Alcott, in turn, vacillated between referring to her readers as "the dear, deluded public" in 1878 and claiming in 1879 that "years tone down one's spirit & fancy though they only deepen one's love for the little people & strengthen the desire to serve them wisely as well as cheerfully" (*Selected Letters* 229, 237).

Alcott also felt pressure—both self-imposed and suggested by friends and family—to publish a novel for adults as successful as *Little Women*. Not only was she self-denigrating about having sacrificed herself "up on the altar of juvenile literature" and being "only a literary nursery-maid who provides moral pap for the young" (*Jo's* 48, 50), but people encouraged her to write for adults in ways that implied that writing for children is an inferior task. For example, Niles urged her throughout 1876 to publish her adult novel *A Modern Mephistopheles* and "make a sensation" with it (Roberts Brothers, Sept. 23, 1876).[22] He told her, "Most of the sensible reviewers say 'Rose' is the best thing you have done since 'Little Women' and how many have said to me 'O I do wish Miss Alcott would write another book as good as 'Moods'—that was the best thing she ever wrote' and its for *this* class of people that I want a book & I feel certain that the M.M. is the book" (Roberts Brothers, Dec. 25, 1876). As he was reading the manuscript, he encouraged her with humor, "The 'MM' is getting to be fearfully interesting—what the devil is the devil up to?" (Roberts Brothers, n.d. [Jan. 1877]). She expressed her gratitude to him for his encouragement in April 1877, when the book appeared (*Selected Letters* 222). One mutual acquaintance of Niles and Alcott even speculated, to their amusement, that Julian Hawthorne, Nathaniel Hawthorne's son, was the author of *A Modern Mephistopheles* (Shealy, "Author-Publisher," Diss. 182).

The year after *A Modern Mephistopheles* appeared, Niles again approached Alcott about writing for adults: "But instead of a sequel to Lilacs, I do wish you would write a full grown novel, *just like Moods*. I see no reason why you should not corner and just such an audience as Geo. Eliot has for her novels" (Roberts Brothers, Dec. 16, 1878). In a postscript to a letter the following year, he was even more blunt: "I wish you were immortalizing yourself on a *grown up* novel" (Roberts Brothers, Sept. 17, 1879). Publisher Charles Carroll Soule had already asked the same basic question: "By the way, aren't you intending to give us (this *us* means the human family, generally), a book about grown up people? We are all hankering after it with eager eyes" (Alcott, L. M., 1832–1888, folder 194, Nov. 6, 1871).

Regardless of what their friends and editors desired of Alcott and Clemens, however, both were more concerned about maximizing their profits when they published for children than they were in writing literarily for "the dears," as Alcott was wont to describe them (*Selected Letters* 235). For both authors, maximizing their profits entailed writing for the publishing venue that would afford them the greatest revenues. But the publishing venues in which they wrote led them to work with editors who were among the most powerful literary influences in their lives. While Alcott generally had cordial relations with her publishers, Clemens did not, as his letters to his publishers indicate—but the editor of the *Atlantic*, William Dean Howells, influenced him as much as any of Alcott's publishers did her.[23] Though both prided themselves on their self-reliance, neither wrote independently of editorial influence. When it came to publishing, neither of them paddled their own canoe with any degree of consistency.

Copyright

Both Alcott and Clemens were continually frustrated by the inadequacy of American copyright law to protect their business interests. Alcott expressed her frustration over the matter as early as 1863 (Shealy, "Author-Publisher," Diss. 26); Clemens understood the potential for copyright piracy at least as early as 1868 (Powers 323). They learned early in their careers that their works could and would be pirated abroad and in Canada. Following statutes enacted by Queen Victoria in 1838 that were emended in 1842 and 1844, British copyright law required that books first be printed in England for an author's rights to be protected in the United Kingdom.[24] As Niles told Alcott in 1871, "The ablest authorities in England have decided that *any author* of a book which will advance literature, be he subject or foreign, can take out a copyright in the United Kingdom, provided the book is *first* published there and it is almost as certain that it is not necessary that the author should be present in person" (Roberts Brothers, March 7, 1871). United States Librarian of Congress A. R. Spofford notified Clemens in 1876, the year *Tom Sawyer* was published, of the same basic fact: "No the first publication in England is essential to Copyright there but previous entry here will secure you in the United States" (*LthP* 98n1). Upon receiving Spofford's telegram, Clemens wrote immediately to Conway, his agent in London, "First publication in England cannot impair my American copyright (have telegraphed Spofford and made sure on that point)" (*LthP* 98). Consequently, both Clemens and Alcott made it a practice to publish some of their later works in England: Alcott first published *Little Men* in England, and Clemens first published *The Adventures of Tom Sawyer* and *Adventures of Huckleberry Finn* there.

But publication delays of *Tom Sawyer* that amounted to months before the text was released in the United States actually facilitated the Canadian piracy of the book. Clemens's profits for the novel were seriously affected by the pirated books that had been published by Belford Brothers; it was the slowest selling of his books with the American Publishing Company (Hill, *MT&EB* 120).[25] He wrote on November 2, 1876, to his agent in London:

> Belford Bros., Canadian thieves, are flooding America with a cheap pirated edition of Tom Sawyer. I have just telegraphed Chatto to assign Canadian copyright to me, but I suppose it is too late to do any good. We cannot issue for 6 weeks yet, and by that time Belford will have sold 100,000 over the frontier and killed my book dead. This piracy will cost me $10,000, and I will spend as much more to choke off those pirates, if the thing can be done. Ask Chatto if he gave Belford Bros permission to publish. (*LthP* 106)

Chatto and Windus was Clemens's publishing house in England. When Belford responded to Chatto's inquiry, Belford assured Chatto that "we are well advised that [British copyright] gives no right in Canada" (*LthP* 106n1).

Belford Bros. had also proven to be problematic for Alcott. On July 29, 1875, they wrote to her publisher: "The new copyright law which has just passed the English House gives us a perfect right to republish Books here written by American Authors. Even though they be copyrighted in England" (Alcott, L. M., 1832–1888, folder 17). Around the time *Tom Sawyer* was published in the U.S., Clemens wrote to Conway about Canadian piracy, "Belford has taken the profits out of 'Tom Sawyer.' We find our copyright law here to be nearly worthless, and if I can make a living out of plays, I shall never write another book" (*LthP* 106–07). Given the quality of Clemens's plays, it is fortunate for posterity that he proved unable to make good on his word.

Both Alcott's and Clemens's publishers tried to stave off Canadian piracy but were unable to do so. A March 18, 1873, letter from the Canadian and Foreign Patent Offices of Charles Legge and Co. instructed Alcott's American publisher that Alcott should reside a few days in Canada to establish herself as a resident because "Low's English copyright does not cover the Dominion of Canada: in order to prevent others pirating it, it must be entered in the Office of the Minister of Agriculture at Ottawa," which could only be done by a resident of Canada or a British subject residing in Great Britain (Alcott, L. M., 1832–1888, folder 98). But because Alcott had not secured Canadian rights prior to publishing *Little Women* and *An Old-Fashioned Girl* in the U.S., "the Canada market is lost," her publisher told her (Alcott, L. M., 1832–1888, folder 127,

March 9, 1871). Clemens and his publisher James Osgood even spent time in
Montreal in 1881 to establish residency so they could establish the Canadian
copyright for *The Prince and the Pauper* (see *LthP* 141–46). Clemens described
the situation to his publisher with a particularly salacious metaphor:

> How would it do, to set up the first and last signatures in Boston, and do the
> rest in Canada? You see, what I'm after is a *preventative*; it is preferable to even
> the best of cures. Those sons of up there will steal anything they can get their
> hands on—possible suits for damages and felony would be no more restraint upon
> them, I think, than would the presence of a young lady be upon a stud-horse
> who had just found a mare unprotected by international copyright. In the one
> case, theft and piracy is the fateful doom; in the other, copulation and adultery.
> (*LthP* 144)

The mare, unprotected by international copyright, continued to be violated
until 1891 when Congress enacted the Chace Act, granting reciprocal international copyright protection to authors for the first time. Clemens was recognized as one of the public figures who urged Congress to pass the first copyright
law that prevented American publishing companies from pirating the works
of foreign authors, and that legislation also provided some protection for
Americans' work published abroad. Eventually, Clemens testified before two
Congressional committees (1886, 1906) and the House of Lords in London
(1900) about the need for copyright reform.[26] Certainly, American authors
were not helped by the protectionist actions of the American government in
1887, when Congress refused to sign the Berne Convention—the international
copyright agreement that afforded reciprocal copyrights in many European
countries. Clemens's work with Congress that led to the Chace Act of 1891
helped improve the situation. But Canadian copyright violations would continue to plague American authors until Canada conformed to England's
Imperial Copyright Act of 1911 in 1924 (Allingham 1–4).

Canadian pirates were not the only ones Clemens feared. He ended up in
court over copyrights more than once. He sued the first publisher of *The
Celebrated Jumping Frog of Calaveras County* (*MT&EB* 85–87); he sued the publisher of the San Francisco *Daily Alta California*, Frederick MacCrellish, over
the rights to the letters on which *The Innocents Abroad* was based (LeMaster
and Wilson 652); he sued publisher B. J. Such for attaching his trademarked
nom de plume to some Twain sketches that Such published because they were
in the public domain (*LthP* 77). Although that suit was successful in 1873, the
court ruled against him when he sued the Canadian publisher Belford Brothers

in 1887 on the same basis (LeMaster and Wilson 183). Clemens was capable of considerable invective when he believed his copyrights had been infringed. He wrote on June 8, 1875, to William F. Gill, owner of William F. Gill & Co. Publishing Co., who was producing the Treasure Trove series:

> It is perhaps no more my publisher than it is myself that objects to the insertion of my matter in outside books.
>
> I think that nothing of mine has ever so appeared (except in one case) without my permission being first asked and obtained. . . .
>
> It was hardly right of you to *announce* me and *THEN* propose to ask my permission. But I gather from your letter that your justification for this was that you felt free to take possession of any uncopyrighted matter of mine which might be lying around, and you meant to ask permission only in the case of copyrighted matter. There was another publisher who allowed that queer sort of morality to fool him. He discovered, in a United States Court, to his serious pecuniary cost, that my sole ownership of my matter is perfect and impregnable—I mean *all* of my matter—every single page I ever wrote.
>
> Now in giving you fair warning that if a single line of mine appears in one of your books I will assuredly stop that book with an injunction, I beg you to believe me when I say that I do not do this in any fractious or unamiable spirit toward you or your editor, but solely and only because I think it injurious to me to come prominently into print any oftener than I am professionally *obliged* to do. (*LthP* 88–89)

Clemens signs the letter "Yours, in all kindness, Saml. L. Clemens" (89). Hamlin Hill notes—ironically—that Gill may, indeed, have had Clemens's prior permission to publish the offending piece, "An Encounter with an Interviewer," in his 1874 edition of *Lotos Leaves* (*LthP* 88n1).

In 1874, Alcott was also squabbling with editors about copyrights—this time, about whether Alcott or Charles Scribner's Sons, who published *Eight Cousins* in their journal, *St. Nicholas*, owned the overseas serial rights to the book:

> If the copyright matter annoys publishers it certainly bewilders authors & leaves them in very defenceless positions at times, for there seems to be no law to guide or protect them. . . .
>
> It is certainly for my own interest to keep faith with American publishers as I find them far more generous, active & obliging than English ones. If it were not for protecting the interests of Roberts Bros. I should prefer to lose the little

John Bull pays me than to be worried by delay, small returns & the very peculiar way in which business is done there. (*Selected Letters* 186)

Alcott shared Clemens's frustration with copyright laws affecting her profits.
Jo's Boys dramatizes the prioritization of copyright in Alcott's thinking when
Jo quips that she considers the nuisance of autograph hounds "a more vital
subject than international copyright; for time is money" (49).[27] Copyright
encroachments and autograph hounds are odious for the same reason: they
cost Alcott money.

That copyright law and perceived violations of it created tension between
American and British publishers is captured exquisitely by the snide tone in
one of Niles's letters to Alcott. The letter was written in 1873, the year after
Clemens had contracted with Routledge to publish the British version of
Roughing It:

> One of your London publishers, George Routledge, with his wife, called today.
> He wanted "Work" and of course he could not have it. He seemed to be some-
> what disappointed & wished to know how you published there. I said you secured
> a copyright & he wanted to know how you could do that without going to
> England. I explained to him that there was a conflict of opinion among the Lord
> Chief Justices & that one of them had decided that *any body* could secure a copy-
> right in England for a book *first published* there.
>
> Yes, he said that was so, & altho there was doubt about the legality of such a
> copyright, he should not undertake to interfere with any publisher who claimed
> a copyright under this decision. I *hit* him rather hard, said to him, so you have
> been pirating "Little Women" yes, rejoined Madame, trying to return some of
> your compliments. (Roberts Brothers, May 5, 1873)

Niles shared Alcott's bitterness about the violation of her copyrights.

Conclusion

Besides Harriet Beecher Stowe, Twain and Alcott were undoubtedly the two
most prominent authors publishing for youth in the 1870s and 1880s. Both
wanted to believe in their own authority, as authors, as copyright holders, and
even as the marketing agents best suited to determine the audience for their
writing. They shared their authority willingly with colleagues whose editorial
skills they trusted, and they shared their authority unwillingly with those who
pirated their copyrights. Their failures and successes serve to demonstrate what
other authors writing for youth were experiencing in the same decades.

Publishing practices in the nineteenth century were driven by copyright issues. And strong editors influenced authors to write for market considerations. The perception of the juvenile market as being less lucrative than the adult market was widely held, as Clemens's reluctance to publish in the field and Alcott's friends encouraging her to publish for adults demonstrate. But the perception was a prejudice that was perhaps unfounded, given how great the sales of Twain's and Alcott's books and serial publications were. Their books proved to be lucrative because they struck a chord with Victorians (both adult and child readers) who believed in social progress and who appreciated the reform-minded values that permeated the novels. Clemens's didacticism was often more veiled than Alcott's, but their novels for youth sold well because the reading public shared with the authors the romantic evangelical heritage that fed the social optimism of the early Progressive era.

Stowe's assessment of the importance of Alcott's early novels demonstrates that *zeitgeist* well. Stowe wrote to Alcott that after reading one of the collections of Alcott's short stories published in 1872:

> I was increasingly convinced that God has appointed you to a beautiful mission & is blessing you with it.
>
> In my many fears for my country & in these days where so much seductive & Dangerous literature is pushed forward, the success of your domestic works has been to me most consoling. It shows that after all our people are *all right*, & that they love the right kind of thing. (Alcott Family, Additional Papers, folder 154, Jan. 2, 1872)

The correspondence was a private statement, not a public proclamation, which left Stowe free to overgeneralize with impunity that "all our people are *all right*." Alcott was aware of the morality involved in being an "object of production" that occurred because of her experiences as a popular writer (Reynolds 408). But she could ameliorate her sense of writing for a profit by assuring herself that what she was writing had a moral intention.

That Stowe, then the best-selling author in the United States, would tell Alcott she was on a divine mission from God to promote the reform ideologies that Stowe considered "the right kind of thing," while also acknowledging Alcott's success in the marketplace, demonstrates both authors' awareness that morality was a commodity in the Gilded Age. Clemens—whose book of that title named the age—shared the same consciousness. Family pressures drove Clemens and Alcott to publish as profitably as they could, which is why they listened to the advice of the editors and publishers they trusted and why they concerned themselves with matters of copyright, publishing venue, and audience. Virtually any successful author shares the same concerns. But Clemens's and Alcott's gift was to capitalize self-consciously on the religious ethos of the day in creating juvenile novels whose reform-minded protagonists would appeal to the widest possible reading audience. Many subsequent authors for youth have profited from the legacy of capitalizing on a reform ethos, a legacy that Clemens's and Alcott's publishing careers entrenched in American children's literature.

CHAPTER SEVEN

Adolescent Reform Novels
The Legacy of Twain and Alcott

"The mark of the immature man is that he wants to die nobly for a cause,
while the mark of the mature man is that he wants to live humbly for one."
—SALINGER, *The Catcher in the Rye*

"We are together . . . because we have to learn to live for each other."
—HAMILTON, *The Planet of Junior Brown*

U p to this point, I have discussed novels that might easily be identified as adolescent reform novels. Novels that admit the possibility of reform tend to have hopeful ideologies. Many of Alcott's and Twain's novels for youth imply that social change is possible: *Eight Cousins*, *Rose in Bloom*, and *The Prince and the Pauper* are the most notable examples. The legacies of these novels are a body of literature for youth with an ideological investment in reform. Whether the reform ideology in a text concerns itself with gender or race or politics or any other social issue, novels for adolescents written in the traditions established by Alcott and Twain communicate that adolescents can make a social difference. That is, if Rose Campbell or Edward Tudor can become more educated and thus more sensitive to the needs of the poor, so can the reader—and so can the members of the society about whom the text is commenting. In the case of both Alcott and Twain, the reform impulse evolves from their romantic evangelical faith in education as a means of reform, and that impulse was reinforced by their novels' popularity. The narrative and ideological patterns that Twain and Alcott developed appear almost formulaically in the adolescent literature that the two have influenced.

Adolescent reform novels share several characteristics. The protagonist is an ethical character who transcends his or her society by some form of self-reliance. He or she lives in a society that is demonstrably less ethical than s/he. That society's need to improve its values is made evident either by directly depicted flaws in the culture or by the character being falsely repressed by it. If the protagonist experiences growth—and s/he usually does—that growth provides a commentary as to how the society itself might also "grow" (i.e., improve). And the character's growth is a sign that the society can, indeed, potentially change. The protagonist grows as a means of communicating the hope for social change. Ultimately, these texts articulate direct agendas of social justice: the growth that the characters in the story experience leads to at least one or more person's ability to live in the world more justly.

These texts share a romantic faith in the ability of youth to improve the future. The message to readers is, invariably, "with self-improvement, you can improve the world." Twenty-first-century critics take it as a given that novels for youth often rely on adolescents' growth and imply hope in the future. What we often fail to recognize, however, is how frequently these texts create a parallel between the individual's need to grow and the society's need to improve itself. In focusing on the growth of an individual character, we often miss the metaphorical use to which the individual's growth has been put. But the social agenda advocating reform appears in twenty-first-century novels for youth as consistently as it did in novels for youth in the late nineteenth century. In this chapter, I will identify some novels that fit the pattern of the adolescent reform novel, especially in the ways that the genre appears to have been influenced by Twain and Alcott. I will also contrast the novels in that legacy to novels that operate in different paradigms, and I will conclude with an argument about the importance of Twain and Alcott's combined legacy in the history of American literature.

Huck Finn's Progeny

While I do not agree with Hemingway's pronouncement that all American literature descends from *Adventures of Huckleberry Finn*, I certainly do think the novel has been a major influence on American adolescent literature.[1] As Eliot observed in 1950, *Huckleberry Finn* is the first book written entirely in a vernacular style (323). Fishkin further develops that point in noting that Twain was the first to have a first-person vernacular narrator who was also an adolescent (*Was* 3). The narrator's irony was also precedent-setting because Huck was the first narrator whose youth allowed him to create dramatic irony with his innocently inaccurate proclamations. Moreover, Twain established the American pattern of the *bildungsroman* as a picaresque: follow a boy on a trip, and you'll follow him as he grows. These narrative elements—the ironic, vernacular, first-person narrator who is on a journey—are apparent in the adolescent novels that are most often compared to *Huckleberry Finn*.

Sarah Herz and Donald R. Gallo note the parallels between *Huckleberry Finn* and a number of other novels, including Chris Crutcher's *The Crazy Horse*

Electric Game (1987), *Chinese Handcuffs* (1989), and *Staying Fat for Sarah Byrnes* (1993); Gary Paulsen's *Hatchet* (1987), *The River* (1991), and *The Island* (1988); Avi's *The True Confessions of Charlotte Doyle* (1990); Francesca Lia Block's *Weetzie Bat* (1989); Dennis Covington's *Lizard* (1991); Sue Ellen Bridgers *Permanent Connections* (1987); Katherine Paterson's *Lyddie* (1991); and Virginia Euwer Wolff's *Make Lemonade* (1993). The connection Herz and Gallo make between these young adult novels and *Huckleberry Finn* involves the protagonist's isolation as he or she faces exploitation at the hands of corrupt adults or confronts the hostility of an intolerant society (28–30).[2]

Holden Caulfield of J. D. Salinger's *Catcher in the Rye* has been compared to Huck so often that even CliffsNotes informs its readers of the parallel.[3] Initially, Holden's journey seems as aimless as Huck's, but the reader eventually understands that Holden is trying to reconcile himself to his brother Allie's death. Holden's narrative voice is as ironic as Huck's: both are adolescents whose maturity the reader can call into question. Huck's mentor is Jim; Holden's is his former teacher Mr. Antolini, who tells him that it is better to "live humbly" for a cause than to "die nobly" for it (188). But Holden does not really have a cause, other than perhaps rejecting his parents' shallow values, also the conformist values of post–World War II America. Salinger's novel is an apt metaphor for the 1950s, the decade it was published, but readers can become impatient with Holden's self-absorption. Unlike Huck, who is trying to save someone else—and who, in the process, creates a social commentary on U.S. race relations—Holden often seems as if he is only trying to save himself. His narcissism creates a critique of postwar American culture, especially of its superficiality (i.e., its "phoniness"). But the irony lies in Holden's inability to see that he is as implicated in the superficiality created by consumer culture as is everyone he criticizes: he buys records, wants to skate at Rockefeller Center, and is a snob about other people's luggage. Salinger's novel is a picaresque with an ironic, first-person narrator who speaks the vernacular. But its greatest similarity with *Adventures of Huckleberry Finn* is its reliance on a well-meaning and basically decent adolescent to depict the flaws, not in the adolescent, but in the culture in which he lives.

Harper Lee does the same thing in *To Kill a Mockingbird*. Scout, although female, is a naïve, first-person, and very androgynous narrator whose voice is often ironic, as when she describes her father: "Atticus was feeble: he was nearly fifty" (89). Lee relies on the dramatic irony of an innocent narrator not only to create humor, but also to build the tension surrounding Tom Robinson's being accused of raping a white woman. At least initially, it is not clear that

Scout understands the implications of the accusation, though the reader does. And while Scout grows to be more tolerant of otherness, marked in the text by her acceptance of her autistic neighbor Boo Radley, she remains throughout the novel an articulate and likeable character whose worst flaw is living in an unjust culture. Her guileless observations about southern culture and her defense of justice create the novel's two closest parallels to Huck Finn.

The Outsiders by S. E. Hinton (1967) also relies on a first-person adolescent narrator, Ponyboy Curtis, who speaks with the southern stylings of Tulsa, Oklahoma.[4] Like Holden and Huck, Ponyboy runs away. His best friend, Johnny Cade, is a boy of color whom he tries to rescue from an abusive home situation. The text hints vaguely that Johnny is at least part Native American: "He had big black eyes in a dark tanned face; his hair was jet-black" (14). Playing on stereotypes of Native Americans, the text intimates that his father beats him and his mother is an alcoholic. His family is poorer than Ponyboy's— even though Ponyboy's parents have both been killed in a car accident. Ponyboy and Johnny are idealistic boys who want nothing more than to rid the world of class difference. Unable to do that, they at least save some children from a church fire. Johnny dies because he has been a savior to them. (My students often note that his initials are "J. C.") Johnny's completely unironic advice to Ponyboy comes from Robert Frost's poetry: "Stay gold, Ponyboy. Stay gold" (130). By this, he means to advise his best friend to retain his innocence, as Huckleberry Finn has, even in the face of lynchings and murderous family feuds and Colonel Sherburn's cold-blooded murder of Boggs. Ponyboy and his friends are outsiders to the culture their story critiques, just as Huck and Holden are outsiders to theirs.

Jo March's Progeny

If Twain is cited for vernacular first-person narrators, the picaresque, irony, and male bonding, Alcott is the author credited with creating both the quintessential sister novel about female community and the prototypical *künstlerroman* of the female writer. She might also well be credited with the creation of the androgynous female protagonist. Elaine Showalter calls *Little Women* the "American Female Myth" (42–64) and describes how Alcott influenced writers such as Gertrude Stein, Adrienne Rich, Cynthia Ozick (42), Joyce Carol Oates (62), and Simone de Beauvoir (64).[5] Peter Stoneley considers Alcott the "first generation" author who inspired *Rebecca of Sunnybrook Farm* (1903) as a book for girls, and, through that novel, *Anne of Green Gables* (1908) and *Pollyanna* (1913) (*Consumerism* 61–62). Barbara Sicherman argues that the book's influence crosses cultural lines. She identifies social worker Jane Addams's passion for the book (245); economist and writer Charlotte Perkins Gilman and writer M. Carey Thomas also admired it (256).[6] African American reformers Mary Church Terrell and Ida B. Wells were influenced by Alcott; African American writer Ann Petry identified *Little Women* as the first novel she read by herself (260).[7] Jewish American immigrants read the novel "as a vehicle for assimilation" (Sicherman 263).[8] Carolyn Heilbrun speculates about the feminist influence of *Little Women* on American women artists in the 1920s, including Gertrude Stein, Natalie Barney, Janet Flanner, Alice B. Toklas, and Sylvia Beach (25).[9] Showalter demonstrates the tension at work in the novel between "feminine identity and artistic freedom" (43). She reads the novel as a feminist work for the way it depicts the possibility of female creativity. Any novel that has influenced this many strong women has assuredly earned its place in the canon of feminist literary history. Contemporary novelist Susan Cheever admitted in 2006, "I can see how profoundly the book influenced me—as a woman, but even more than that as a writer. . . . *Little Women* gave my generation of women permission to write about our daily lives" (191–92).[10]

Jean Webster, author of *Daddy-Long-Legs* (1912), is one of the early examples of a writer whom Alcott inspired. Webster, coincidentally enough, was Mark Twain's great-niece. She had a picture of him hanging over her desk but kept a social distance from him, perhaps because she resented how he treated her father, Charles Webster, when he was Twain's publisher, or perhaps because she did not want to appear to be riding on his literary coattails (LeMaster and Wilson 781). But the *künstlerroman* pattern that traces the protagonist's development as a writer in *Daddy-Long-Legs* bears a much closer similarity to *Little Women* than to anything Twain wrote. For example, Judy's first success as an author occurs after a kind-hearted publisher tells her to quit writing improbable fiction about things she doesn't understand and instead to wait to finish college and write about what she knows. Judy later agrees: "You are most convincing when you write about the things you know" (167–68). The advice parallels Jo March's success that comes from writing a domestic story about what she knows after Marmee suggests that she "write something for us, and never mind the rest of the world" (339). Both authors learn from their failures and then write simple tales based on their own experience, which are published to public acclaim. During her formation as a writer, Judy has had two roommates who provide her with both the support and antagonism that Jo's sisters provide her. The sense of female community she develops because of them also inspires her political activism. Both Alcott and Webster are direct about "discussing Women's Rights," too (*Little Women* 213). Among other commentaries on suffrage, Judy thinks she would make "an admirable voter" if women had the right to vote (*Daddy-Long-Legs* 127). Most significantly, Judy praises *Little Women* as a book that most girls have been "brought up on"; Judy thinks of herself as "queer"—one of Jo's favorite terms—because she hasn't read it (30).

Laura Ingalls Wilder appears to have been influenced by Louisa May Alcott as well. In fact, I noticed the similarity between *Little Women* and the "Little House" books when I was a preadolescent. Both books are about four sisters; the second sister in each is a tomboy—that is, androgynous. Both Laura and Jo grow up to be writers in semiautobiographical narratives. But Laura bears more than these superficial resemblances to Jo. She is—like Jo—an independent and strong woman whose need to curb her temper says more about the culture in which she lives than about her character.[11] Laura's mother often silences her, once even reminding her to be like Shakespeare's Cordelia: "Her voice was ever gentle, low, and soft, an excellent thing in woman" (*Little Town* 97).[12] Furthermore, Anita Clair Fellman explains that the Little House books say more about the grown Wilder's libertarianism than about any actual history of pioneer life in America. When Wilder wrote fiction, she modified what actually happened to her to convince her readership that self-reliance was essential to a strong America, a country she believed was about to be weakened by the excessive reliance on the New Deal created by the Depression (Fellman 107–14). Laura's independence is tied to her development as an artist, though the *künstlerroman* evolves largely outside of the plot, for the reader knows it is the adult Laura who has turned into an author. As part of that process, she grows into some of the same habits of self-repression that Jo March develops, notably in curbing her temper and her tongue around her blind sister, Mary.

Betty Smith's *A Tree Grows in Brooklyn* also follows a *künstlerroman* pattern. The four sisters in this book are Francie's mother and her three sisters, around whom much of the story revolves. Like Jo and Laura Ingalls, Francie is poor, and her writing proves to be one path out of her poverty—even though her eighth grade teacher denigrates her writing for being "sordid" (277). Francie has only written about what she knows: life in the ghetto. Unlike Alcott, who believes that some poverty can be ennobling, and unlike Wilder, who believes that poverty provides people with the hard work that makes Americans great, Smith is unstinting in her criticism of the poverty that American immigrants suffer. In her novel is no depiction of genteel little women who make do by turning their dresses. It contains no depiction of hardworking and virtuous laborers whose pride is born of their self-reliance. In *A Tree Grows in Brooklyn*, poverty is dirty and humiliating and leaves children vulnerable to depravity. Francie is too outspoken, too honest, too strong-minded for the culture in which she lives, but her voice is that of a reformer who understands that living conditions for the poor need to be improved. She does not need to grow as much as America does.

Louise Fitzhugh's *Harriet the Spy* (1964) is also about a loner in New York. Harriet is not a spy so she can learn about espionage, but so she can be a writer when she grows up—she spies on people so she has things to write about in her notebook. She is irascible, intelligent, and even more androgynous than Jo March.[13] She does need to learn to develop empathy, so her personal growth is perhaps more necessary than Laura Ingalls's or Jo March's. But her story holds the same social critique as theirs. She is punished for her androgyny and—at least temporarily—expected to wear dresses and attend dance class. The book is controversial for the same reason that *Huckleberry Finn* was condemned in the 1880s: the climax depends on the protagonist making a moral decision to lie. When Harriet's classmates read her notebooks and discover that Harriet has written unpleasant things about them, Harriet's former nanny advises the child to lie to her peers.[14] The girl does, demonstrating an uncomfortable social truth that *Huckleberry Finn* also demonstrates: sometimes people must lie to get what they want. Fitzhugh's was one of the first overtly feminist *künstlerromane* written for children. Her ideological intent in the book is direct and incisive.

The Catcher in the Rye, To Kill a Mockingbird, and *The Outsiders* are three of the most noteworthy adolescent novels influenced by *Adventures of Huckleberry Finn*. The same can be said of *Daddy-Long-Legs, A Tree Grows in Brooklyn*, the Little House books, and *Harriet the Spy* in relation to *Little Women*. Alcott and Twain were participating in a *zeitgeist* that was profitable for them, just as the authors of these twentieth-century novels were. They have all floated in an intellectual current that flows through children's literature because Americans are still idealistic enough to want to read stories about uncorrupted youth with reform agendas. Perhaps, too, adults have a vested interest in teaching youth that it is their job to improve a world that adults have not made much progress in bettering.

Adolescent Reform Novels

The most enduring legacy of Twain and Alcott is their adolescent characters who serve as metaphors for the need for social change. Even in novels devoid of first-person narrators or male bonding or sororal harmony or female artistic development, the political awareness of adolescent narrators advocating reform is so entrenched a pattern in American young adult novels that the tradition largely goes unobserved. Even more remarkable, these ideologies sometimes work counter to the prevailing trends in the literature. Children's literature is often, by its nature, a conservative genre that reinforces the status quo to assure children that their worlds are safe: Mommy and Daddy will love you no matter what; your home is wherever you are loved; your hopes and dreams can come true; all children have good traits. Adolescent literature, on the other hand, often purports to be radical, but still usually communicates to adolescent readers a repressive ideology that teenagers need to overcome their immaturity and grow out of their subject positions as adolescents to become adults.[15]

Despite the repressive tendency of young adult novels, narratives that follow in the Twain and Alcott legacy often articulate progressive ideologies about gender or race or politics. Two criteria mark the legatees of Twain and Alcott: the texts directly articulate a progressive ideology, and the protagonists' idealism contrasts with their cultures' corruption. By narrative implication, the protagonists in these novels are usually superior to the cultures in which they live, which is how they ultimately emerge as metaphors for the need for social change. These texts imply that if only all Americans were as noble as Scout or Ponyboy or Laura Ingalls, we would live in a more perfect world.

Race

Given that both Twain and Alcott were concerned about conditions for African Americans at various points in their careers, it seems appropriate that they may have inspired other authorial voices to write about justice and race. Virginia Hamilton's *The Planet of Junior Brown*, for example, is about imbalance in the universe. Buddy Clark is a homeless boy who meanders on a journey through the streets of New York City perceiving injustice as imbalance. Although the novel has no first-person narrator, it depicts a friendship that is highly evocative of Huck and Jim's friendship. Buddy befriends an overweight artist named Junior Brown. Junior's mother is repressive and hostile to her son's artistic expressions, so Buddy rescues *his* buddy, Junior Brown, in much the same way that Huck rescues Jim. Buddy hides Junior, first at school, where they construct a solar system with a huge tenth planet designed to balance the other nine planets. Buddy names this balancing planet after Junior. Later, the boys must hide in an abandoned building where Buddy and a community of homeless boys have learned to "live for each other" in what they call the "planet of Tomorrow Billy" (217, 74). The boys are socially invisible and able to live in their counterculture because they are black in a city—New York—that ignores impoverished people of color. Buddy is self-reliant and a brilliant mathematician. He is a mature adolescent who does not need to grow as much as the bigoted culture around him does. Junior is an artistic genius, sensitive to the point of being empathic. He is driven to the brink of insanity by his mother and his piano teacher, who has not come to terms with her own racial identity. Hamilton depicts New York as a city that does not care for its poor or its children, especially if they are black. It is a city that does not even see black people, except to fear them. Buddy admits that Junior's mother is "halfway right" in fearing that "they gonna lynch you if you go downtown too far" (32). Hamilton's ideology is direct and her protagonists are greater than the culture in which they live. My students often notice the parallels between this novel and *Adventures of Huckleberry Finn*: as two runaways undergo a bonding process, they help one another and other people.

Laurence Yep's *Dragonwings* (1975) is about Chinese immigrants to America. Like *The Planet of Junior Brown*, this book has two protagonists: Windrider, a father whose integrity parallels Jim's on the raft, and his son, Moonshadow, who comments on the corruption of the culture around him. Moonshadow's observational narrative makes him sound not unlike Huck: he narrates that which he observes with some degree of dramatic irony.[16] Windrider learns in the course of the novel to accept the limitations of being human; Moonshadow's story is an assimilation story that includes a realistic depiction of racism in San Francisco at the beginning of the twentieth century. Moonshadow is bullied by white children who call him names and throw rotten vegetables at him; white men hang Chinese men by their hair from lampposts. During the San Francisco earthquake, the Chinese are evicted from the refugee camp and white businessmen try to use the earthquake as an excuse to steal their property. But when the leader of Windrider's company refers to all white men as greedy, Windrider remarks that "that's the way it is with most men" (193). Moreover, white people are referred to as "demons" throughout the novel. Moonshadow is superior to the racist white children who taunt him; Windrider is superior to almost all the people in the novel, American or Chinese. He even concludes the novel believing that it is his destiny to "raise a brood of superior women and men," and the reader has no doubt that he will be able to because of his intelligence, his integrity, and his profound spirituality (242). While the narrative purports to deplore racism of any type, the book still suffers from the same inherent flaw that troubles *Huckleberry Finn*: at the end of the day, the narrator still believes that his race is superior to any other, even though the overt ideology is antiracist.

Maleeka Madison is the narrator of Sharon Flake's *The Skin I'm In* (1998).
Her father died three years earlier, so she wears ill-wrought clothes that her
mother sews compulsively to compensate for her grief. Because she is often
ridiculed by her peers, Maleeka is self-conscious about having darker skin than
most of the other African American students at her school. And she is a writer
who learns to reconcile herself to difference by finding strength in the creation
of fiction. Maleeka writes a slave narrative about a girl on a slave ship. She
rearranges the letters of her own name to give the character who becomes her
alter ego a similar name, Akeelma. Through Akeelma, Maleeka learns to stand
up to the bullies at her school and to take pride in her intelligence. (Besides
being a gifted writer, Maleeka is also a math whiz, like Buddy Clark in *The
Planet of Junior Brown*.) Maleeka's best friend tells her early in the story, "It's
not about color. . . . It's how you feel about who you are that counts" (40). But
only after Maleeka has shorn her head in a scene reminiscent of Jo's cutting
her "curly crop" (*Little Women* 176) is Maleeka able to develop enough poise
to tell a teacher who has a birth defect of discolored pigmentation on her face,
"Some of us is the wrong color. Some is the wrong size or got the wrong face.
But that don't make us wrong people, now does it?" (119). Like Jo March,
Maleeka has very little self-confidence. Once she gains some, she is able to
perceive herself as the strong and articulate writer that the reader has understood her to be all along, and she models an ideology that rejects racism, even
intraracial racism.

Few series in fiction for youth are more directly political than Mildred D.
Taylor's books about Cassie Logan and her family (which includes her three siblings). These novels imply that race is a matter of civil rights, while gender equality is a personal right. In *Roll of Thunder, Hear My Cry* (1976), Cassie protests
racism and learns to believe in herself despite the way racist white people might
treat her. In *Let the Circle Be Unbroken* (1981), she insists on the integrity of her
interior voice, even when her older brother repeatedly attempts to silence her.
He uses his fear of racist repercussions to silence her, but Cassie learns to fight
for civil rights in ways that do not compromise her safety. In *The Road to Memphis*
(1990), Cassie finds self-confidence and pursues her education. But as in all of
Taylor's novels, white male aggression against people of color is the catalyst for
the plot, which is driven by Cassie's journey toward independence.

Cassie's primary defense is her voice. She is articulate and intelligent and
considers herself the equal of her three brothers. She particularly values stories
and storytelling as a means of self-expression. For example, in *Song of the Trees*
(1975), she grieves that "the song of the trees" has been silenced when white

loggers illegally raid her parents' timber farm. The rape of the land becomes frighteningly close to a literal rape in *The Road to Memphis*, when the aggression of white males against her becomes sexualized. She's a mixture of "a sassy little girl and a most outspoken woman" (252), and by the end of the series she plans to become a lawyer because "white folks are always falling back on the law. Maybe if colored folks knew the law as well as they did, we could do something about it" (244). Taylor's ideological intent is as direct about race as it is about gender. Cassie is far more self-conscious about reform than Huck or Jim or Jo—but she bears similarities to all three.

Gender

Cynthia Voigt's Tillerman series also includes a series of novels with a social conscience: *Homecoming* (1981), *Dicey's Song* (1982), *A Solitary Blue* (1983), *The Runner* (1985), *Come a Stranger* (1986), and *Seventeen Against the Dealer* (1989). In the first book in the series, four children—two sisters and two brothers—are on a journey that takes them not down a river, but across the coast of Connecticut and south along the eastern seaboard to their grandmother's house in Maryland. Their mother has abandoned them, and eventually they convince their grandmother to adopt them. The protagonist, Dicey, is the oldest—a Jo-like, androgynous girl who pretends to be a boy because "it's safer to be a boy than a girl. . . . People leave boys alone more" (*Homecoming* 48). The grandmother understands Dicey's independence because she was herself an abused wife who watched her husband's anger drive their children from their home. The series' concern with otherness includes both gender and race: an African American girl in a later novel acknowledges the suffragettes and those who ran the Underground Railroad as individuals in conflict with their society (*Dicey's* 25). The series also addresses injustices surrounding the Vietnam War, class, and even age: "The whole world was arranged for people who had money—for *adults* who had money. The whole world was arranged against kids" (*Homecoming* 61). As one of the teenagers they meet on their journey tells them, children don't have rights "because parents own them. . . . Your parents can beat you, steal your money, decide not to take you to a doctor—anything they want" (62). Indeed, in *Homecoming* the children are patronized by a cousin, forced into child labor by a farmer who refuses to pay them, and live in fear of molestation and starvation in ways that parallel the various forms of bondage that Huck and Jim experience while they are traveling downriver.

 Dicey's Song adopts a *künstlerroman* quality that is, like *Little Women*, the story of two developing artists, Dicey and her blonde and fragile younger sister

Maybelle, who is evocative of Amy March. Maybelle is a singer whose music compensates for her learning disabilities. Dicey is a writer, like Jo. She writes an essay about their mother's increasing insanity that is so poignant that the teacher believes she plagiarized it, a scene that bears some resemblance to Francie Nolan's humiliation at her teacher calling her stories "sordid" in *A Tree Grows in Brooklyn*. Eventually, Dicey shifts her artistic energy from writing to boat-building, but she is clearly a strong female who has more sense than many of the people in her world, and her artistic calling gives her a purpose to live. Because she builds boats, however, she faces hostility for being a woman in a man's trade. She calls a coworker sexist and sarcastically tells a patronizing male customer that she makes only pink boats. One conflict she must resolve is rec-ognizing that she can be both a boatbuilder and a bride. She tells her coworker, "I just don't want to be any man's woman" (*Seventeen* 44). But the man she loves eventually tells her, "You have no right to promise me things I never ask for. . . . There's no need for you to choose" (*Seventeen* 177). Voigt's feminist agenda throughout the series is of the type that calls for women to be strong and true to themselves, whether they marry or not. Dicey's implied success at both love and a career parallels the Jo of *Jo's Boys*.

Jennifer Donnelly is more direct about addressing the issues that confronted Twain and Alcott than any other novelist discussed in this chapter. *A Northern Light* is a *künstlerroman* set in the early twentieth century about a young writer, Mattie Gokey, who faces the same choice between work and art that Dicey Tillerman believes she faces. Mattie works in the hotel where Grace Brown—the murdered girl from the news story on which Dreiser based *An American Tragedy* (1925)—has been staying. This retelling of *An American Tragedy* artic-ulates many questions about how Grace must have felt when her fiancé, know-ing she was pregnant, intentionally drowned her. Mattie struggles with Grace's story—and her own—as well as the stories of the women whose lives surround her. She asks, "How exactly do you stand up like a man when you're a girl?" (33). The answer in Grace Brown's case is clear: she does not stand up, and she dies as a result. In a complementary subplot, Mattie observes her best friend experiencing the unromantic reality of marriage that Marilyn French once dubbed "[baby]shit and string beans" (67). Mattie also witnesses her neighbor being repeatedly impregnated and kept in abject poverty by the adulterous attentions of a married man in their neighborhood. That woman, at least, is aided out of her abjection by the sisterhood that comes through friendship with another woman. But the artist Mattie most admires, a poet named Emily Baxter, is hounded by an abusive husband and can only transcend the situation by hiding from him and writing more. When Baxter tells Mattie to use her voice as a writer, Mattie thinks, "Just look where your voice got you. . . . And look where Grace Brown's got her" (362). Mattie's boyfriend, Royal, can't understand why anyone would want to waste time on writing or reading. Eventually, Mattie breaks off their engagement and journeys to college in New York because she realizes Royal is stifling her voice.

Before she goes, however, she has contemplated seriously what it means to be a writer. She admires Mark Twain for his honesty. Emily Baxter tells her that "Mark Twain had a pitch-perfect ear for the vernacular of the Mississippi River and that this talent of his changed writing forever by allowing a wild truant boy to sound like a wild, truant boy, and an ignorant drunk to sound like an ignorant drunk" (180). Mattie concludes:

> It seems to me that there are books that tell stories, and then there are books that tell truths. . . . The first kind, they show you life like you want it to be. With villains getting what they deserve and the hero seeing what a fool he's been and marrying the heroine and happy endings and all that. Like *Sense and Sensibility* or *Persuasion*. But the second kind, they show you life more like it is. Like in *Huckleberry Finn* where Huck's pa is a no-good drunk and Jim suffers so. The first kind makes you cheerful and contented, but the second kind shakes you up. (201–02)

Mattie then lists Charles Dickens and Louisa May Alcott and Jane Austen in the first category: "Why do writers make things sugary when life isn't that way?" (202).

But Mattie cannot escape from what Harold Bloom might refer to as Donnelly's "anxiety of influence."[17] Mattie's mother read *Little Women* to her when she was a child, and "she used to tell me that I wrote real nice, as nice as . . . Louisa May Alcott, even" (210). One of Mattie's sisters, named Lou, is a tomboy who cuts her hair. Their sister Beth contracts an almost fatal illness: "Beth, whose voice was only a whimper now. Whose small, busy hands had fluttered like doves against me as I'd washed her" (289). The four sisters in the family even have an aunt named Josie, as if the connection between Mattie's family and Jo's has not already been made clear enough. Eventually, Mattie wonders why writers like Emily Dickinson and Louisa May Alcott never married. She realizes Emily Dickinson never would have written poetry, had she had "two howling babies, a husband bent on jamming another one into her, a house to run, a garden to tend, three cows to milk, twenty chickens to feed, and four hired hands to cook for. . . . I knew why they didn't marry. Emily and Jane and Louisa. I knew and it scared me" (274). Mattie doesn't want to choose between marriage and writing; she comments that "Mark Twain didn't have to" (274).

Mattie is motivated to pursue her education because of the examples she has in the poet Emily Baxter and her closest male friend, Weaver Smith. Weaver is an African American who is almost lynched; angry racists burn his mother's house down and steal his college money. Mattie urges him to go to college because she doesn't want him to waste his potential, which cements her own decision to go. Before she leaves, she gives him some of her college money to ensure that they both pursue their dreams. Then, instead of lighting out to the territory, they both light out for New York to get an education.

In *Jacob Have I Loved* (1980), by Katherine Paterson, the Jo prototype and the Amy prototype are paired as twins named Louise and Caroline. In this book, Louise's Apollyon, jealousy, overwhelms her; she cannot perceive that her blonde, blue-eyed, artistic sister is not a threat to her. Louise is androgynous and drawn to male occupations—crabbing and medicine. Caroline, like Amy, wins all the prizes: the education of her choice, artistic success, and the husband that both girls have considered marrying. But Louise, like Jo, ultimately transcends her antipathy for her sister. She does this by rejecting her anger. That of her anger which has not been motivated by her sister has been motivated by her gender: "Males, I thought, always have a chance to live no matter how short their lives, but females, ordinary, ungifted ones, just get soft and die" (162). Louise is talking about crabs, but her metaphorical self-reference is obvious. When a friend tells her, "You were never meant to be a woman on this island. A man, perhaps. Never a woman" (192), she decides to leave the culture that is repressing her and seek her fortune elsewhere. Although she is denied entry into medical school because of her gender, she decides that "if you can't catch crabs where you are, you move your pots" (204). She becomes a nurse-midwife with a rewarding practice and, like Dicey Tillerman and Jo March, is able to balance her career with her marriage.

Politics

American novels for youth take a variety of political stances on issues like race, gender, and sexuality. Such novels as Francesca Lia Block's *Weetzie Bat* (1989) and *Baby Be-Bop* (1995) celebrate sexual choice and tolerance, as does Jacqueline Woodson's *From the Notebooks of Melanin Sun* (1995) in a novel that also addresses racial difference. Stephen Chbosky's *The Perks of Being a Wallflower* (1999) poignantly depicts the power issues and residual pain involved in abusive sexual relationships. The eponymous protagonist of Rosa Guy's *Edith Jackson* (1978) is a poster child for abortion rights. Nancy Garden's *Annie on My Mind* (1982) and *Good Moon Rising* (1996) celebrate lesbian love. These are only a handful of the books that address openly the politicalization of sexuality. Most of them are consciously reform novels; their likeable protagonists articulate ideologies of tolerance directly for the youth reader to understand. Interested readers can also find novels with ideological agendas about environmentalism, religion, pacifism, consumerism, and virtually every sociopolitical cause that interests Americans. And despite the common misconception that youth are apolitical, these novels sell, just as they did in Twain's and Alcott's day.

Novels that address government politics tend to be even more openly ideological than most reform novels, even when authors employ metaphors to make their message less direct. For example, in *Before We Were Free* (2002), Julia Alvarez writes the story of an adolescent girl, Anita, living in the Dominican Republic during the revolution that toppled the dictator General Trujillo in 1961. Alvarez acknowledges that she is writing in the Latin American tradition of the *testimonio*, a testimony of what has happened that is written to memorialize those who died fighting for freedom. The testimonio is hardly a product of romantic evangelism, but it shares with that nineteenth-century religious movement a concern for social justice. Alvarez is also writing within the American tradition that celebrates the individual. For example, Anita's father calls educating each individual citizen "the key" to democracy, so education is, in this novel, again portrayed as a panacea (37, 58). Anita is a first-person narrator whose innocence sometimes creates dramatic irony, as when she expects the first snowflakes she sees to look like doilies or when she believes that the woman revolutionaries her father calls "the butterflies" have been killed in a car accident, though the reader suspects what the text later confirms—that they have been murdered by the fascist regime (18). Anita is also a writer who comes to terms with her art by keeping a diary while she is in hiding with her mother. In the face of the growing horrors, including her father and brother being imprisoned by the secret police who eventually kill them, Anita grows more and more silent, though her family once nicknamed her *Cotorrita*, or "little parrot," because she talked so much. Once she begins to write about her pain, however, she recovers her speaking voice and her sense of self: "When I write in [my diary], I feel as if I've got a set of wings, and I'm flying over my life and looking down and thinking, Anita, it's not as bad as you think" (124). Anita's entire family consists of honorable people, and Alvarez depicts a nation with many such people. As one member of this nation, Anita is unequivocally portrayed as a metaphor for freedom. Anita's father and her nanny both tell her that she can fly (66, 113), and images of butterflies, moths, kites, and birds soar through the narrative. Anita acknowledges the meaning of the flight metaphors when she proclaims the book's ideology: "I guess I finally understand what [my nanny] and Papi meant by wanting me to fly. It was like the metaphors [my teacher] was always talking about. To be free inside, like an uncaged bird. Then nothing, not even a dictatorship, can take away your liberty" (160). Anita, her family, and the other revolutionaries are superior to Trujillo's supporters, creating the sense that people can grow to become reform-minded liberators who resist injustice and repression.

I Am the Cheese (1977) is Robert Cormier's paranoid post–Vietnam War disquisition on why no one should trust the government. Adam Farmer is a fourteen-year-old who bicycles around the grounds of a mental institution, believing he is bicycling on a journey to save himself from the government agent who knows his true identity. Adam's family was part of the witness-protection plan; eventually, his parents were killed because the government agent who was charged with protecting them betrayed them. Another agent keeps Adam imprisoned and drugged at the mental institution, hoping that Adam will tell him one last piece of information that is vital to the government. Adam's life depends on his keeping to himself whether or not he knows any additional information. Like Huck, Adam is on a journey. Like Huck, he learns he is an orphan at the end of the novel—though unlike Huck, he is doomed to repeat his novel in circular form and have that realization again annually. Like Huck, Adam's voice is first person and ironic; the reader must learn that not everything Adam says is true. But most important, like Huck, Adam's youth positions him as an agent of innocence in a society corrupted by fear, aggression, and the politics of power.

Josh, the narrator of Janet Tashjian's *The Gospel According to Larry* (2001), acknowledges his direct debt to the traditions of romantic evangelism on the first page of the novel, when he typifies Thoreau's politics: "Nature is good, materialism is bad" (7). He quotes Thoreau to inspire others to social activism: "For every walk is a sort of crusade" and "He who sits still in a house all the time may be the greatest vagrant of all" (qtd. 108). Like Thoreau, Josh regards Christ's life as important because he was a good role model: Josh quotes scripture and Thoreau as examples of how meaningful lives should be lived. Josh uses a Web site to convince other American consumers to protest consumerism and advertising. The overwhelming response to his site communicates

Americans' readiness to stop being exploited by business. Using his alter ego, Larry, Josh writes on his Web site:

Change the world?
Did.
Are.
Can. (129)

In an ironic narrative backlash, however, Josh becomes consumed by his alter ego. The fame is too much for him, and he realizes that he is selling out to the media and becoming himself commodified. Josh does not perceive himself as a messiah, though others do. To escape this untenable life, he stages his own death, and he claims Tom Sawyer as his inspiration: "When I was little, I adored *Tom Sawyer*. I read and reread the part about Tom and Huck attending their own funeral—listening in while everyone sang their praises, the looks of surprise on Becky's and Aunt Polly's faces when the minister spotted Tom and Huck upstairs. Dying yet not dying" (178). He calls his fake suicide "Project Tom Sawyer just for laughs" (178)—although the book lover Josh seems to be remembering the movie version better than the book, since the boys don't hide in the gallery but walk in down the aisle in the book. Josh's plan for what he calls a "pseudocide" carries with it all the spectacle of Tom Sawyer's funeral, but the faked suicide is actually much closer to Huck Finn's staging his own death to escape his untenable life with Pap than to Tom Sawyer's showy grab for attention. Josh genuinely wants people to believe he is dead, just as Huck does: "My death became the act I'd been rehearsing for my whole life" (183). He protests that he is no messiah, but the biblical references he quotes about the resurrection cast that into doubt. The reader is meant to internalize his refrain: "Be the hero of your own life" (187). His final prayer is "just an old-fashioned is-anybody-out-there kind of prayer," and he concludes that there is: "It's me" (215). He decides that instead of trying to improve the whole world, he will improve the world by improving himself. This sentiment is very Thoreauvian, as he acknowledges in his conclusion. Josh is a loner, an ironic, first-person narrator with a reform agenda that includes teaching youth to be self-reliant. His story might well resonate with both Twain and Alcott.

Adolescence in American Literature

It would be a mistake to say that all American adolescent novels are descended from Twain and Alcott. Any cursory glance at a list of young adult novels will include books that are motivated by different trends than those occurring in the adolescent reform novel. For example, one profitable branch of adolescent literature has been novels that focus intensely on an adolescent's emotional maturation. These books often center around one emotion: grief or fear or longing or love. Such novels play a pivotal role in defining the canon of adolescent literature, and they are an integral part of what adolescents read and enjoy. But books that focus on emotional maturation and have little or no reform ideology cannot claim to be working in the same intellectual tradition that influenced Alcott and Twain to rely on adolescents as metaphors for the need for social change.

While fantasy novels set on Earth lend themselves easily to social concerns, they do not always seem to participate directly in the narrative patterns that link adolescent reform novels to Twain and Alcott. The Charlie Bone and the Lemony Snicket books direct the reader's attention to class difference. Harry Potter is also concerned about otherness: his and Hermione's advocacy for "Mudbloods" is a none-too-subtle code for youth to confront the racism, classism, and anti-Semitism at work in their own schools. But with neither first-person ironic narrators nor the sisterhoods that inspire *künstlerromane*, these novels do not seem to be obvious heirs of Twain and Alcott. Fantasy novels set in other worlds are often, like Harry Potter's story, metaphorical in their description of social ills. Anne McCaffrey's *Dragonflight* (1968) and Robin McKinley's *The Hero and the Crown* (1985) and Ursula K. Le Guin's *Tehanu* (1990) are feminist critiques of traditional gender roles set in other worlds. But the otherworldliness of fantasy set in alternative worlds often moves the narrative out of the direct confrontation with ideology that marks the more immediate heirs to romantic evangelism. It's hard to imagine Eragon or Taran, Wanderer, making an impassioned speech about social justice in contemporary America. Were they to do so, they'd violate the verisimilitude of their own narratives.

On the other hand, much of the so-called chick lit currently being published has evolved from the same strand of romanticism that inspired Alcott's domestic dramas. These books about the individual focus on the interior life of the major characters and how they interact with other people.[18] For example, most of Judy Blume's novels are about the problems adolescents must overcome in order to mature. The female-bonding stories currently proliferating usually validate friendship but avoid in-depth analysis of social issues: Cynthia Voigt's *Bad Girls* series and Ann Brashares's *Sisterhood of the Traveling Pants* (2001) and Megan McCafferty's *Sloppy Firsts* (2001) are examples. The same can be said of the anti-female-bonding series *The Gossip Girl* (2002), by

Cecily von Ziegesar. While these books often mention social issues, such as drug and alcohol abuse, the adolescent characters in them need so badly to grow up that they don't seem like metaphors for much of anything.

Nihilistic books that refute the possibility of reform seem like the antithesis of Twain's and Alcott's novels for youth—although they may well be influenced by the dark tones of such novels as *Pudd'nhead Wilson* and *The Mysterious Stranger*. For example, Gordon Korman's retelling of *The Great Gatsby* (1925) in *Jake, Reinvented* (2003) has an ending that is even more despairing than its prototype. In Woodson's *If You Come Softly* (1998), a black youth is gunned down by New York cops who mistake him for a criminal, leaving his girlfriend—who is white and Jewish—grieving the rigidity of social class and race. Gail Giles's *Shattering Glass* (2002) depicts the senseless murder of one boy by a group of boys who stand over his shattered body in the final line of the novel, completely frozen and powerless: "We stood silent and unmoving" (215). The novel is a chilling critique of the emotional barrenness that hypermasculinity coupled with class consciousness creates.[19] These are novels about adolescents who struggle to enact change and, in their failure, imply that change is impossible.

Many of the canonical pieces of American literature, however, involve adolescents or young adults struggling to understand their role in society in ways that imply that change is at least desirable. *Adventures of Huckleberry Finn* is the most notable example; *The Great Gatsby* is another. So is *The Sound and the Fury* (1929) and *The Grapes of Wrath* (1939) and *The Glass Menagerie* (1945) and *The Member of the Wedding* (1951) and *Invisible Man* (1952) and *Go Tell It on the Mountain* (1953) and *The Miracle Worker* (1957) and *Catch-22* (1961) and *The Bluest Eye* (1970) and *My Name is Asher Lev* (1972) and *The Color Purple* (1982) and *The House on Mango Street* (1984) and *The Beet Queen* (1986) and *The Joy Luck Club* (1989) and, of course, *Little Women*. While critics often focus on how these narratives have coming-of-age as a common theme, they also have in common either explicit or implicit ideologies that advocate some form of social reform. Reform-oriented literature in the United States often relies on a youthful protagonist as the embodiment of an author's idealism. Not all of the literature about adolescence descends from Huck and Jo, but much of it that is idealistic and reformist belongs to traditions that have been influenced by the strain of romantic evangelism that permeates American literature.

Historically, however, college-level survey courses in American literature have not included literature that was published for a youth audience. But to ignore novels written for adolescents simply because they are written for youth is to ignore one of the greatest traditions of American literature. Because children and adolescents are culturally disempowered, the mistake of ignoring their books is a common one. Youth is the one disfranchised group in which all of us—every single adult in the world—has once belonged. Dismissing youth literature because it is the literature of a disfranchised group is not unlike twentieth-century New Criticism dismissing African American literature. Or women's literature. Or any other form of minority literature. Many of us came of age studying canons that excluded the voices of the other. And now most of us recognize the richness that has come from expanding our understanding of literature. Young adult novels—whether or not they have been influenced by Twain and Alcott—are all part of the river of tradition that T. S. Eliot describes in "Tradition and the Individual Talent" (1950). Adolescent literature is simply one literary category of many in the world—no more, no less. In this country, however, we ignore it at the risk of failing to understand the complexity and interrelatedness of our own literature.

AFTERWORD

Two forces propelled me to undertake this project: my concern that critics of youth literature spuriously separate Mark Twain's and Louisa May Alcott's writings as existing in the separate spheres of boys' and girls' stories, and my belief that the history of ideas influenced the two authors in similar ways that are still being rehearsed in twenty-first-century adolescent literature. In 1995, when I first taught a seminar on Twain and Alcott, my departmental colleagues questioned why I would teach the two together, but by 2004, I knew similar courses were being taught at other universities.[1] Although Twain's children's books are often taught as "books for boys" and Alcott has too often been pigeonholed as a women's writer, that form of segregation was less distinct when the two were first publishing their novels at a time when youth readers were likely to read whatever materials were made available to them (Mintz 186; Clark, *Kiddie Lit* 48–76). The gender-based distinction between the two writers strikes me as unnecessary because they are both so focused on issues of growth and social reform.

Clemens and Alcott shared similarities in their lives that history has often erased. They may have perceived themselves as growing up in different classes and different regions, but like most writers of their era, they were affected by the turmoil of the Civil War and the dependency of their families throughout their lives. They also participated in intellectual movements that called attention to issues of social justice: emancipation, universal suffrage, health reform, and emerging labor laws. Both authors came to their understanding of human potential through the common influences of Jonathan Edwards and Ralph Waldo Emerson, who directly or indirectly inspired them to revere nature, and, in Emerson's case, taught them to value the potentiality of childhood. Both authors thus wrote about childhood as a way of talking about the human potential for growth, for change, for improvement, for reform. Whether they are describing characters who need to grow or actually *do* grow matters less than their use of youth as a site for mutability and the possibility of change creating hope. In Twain's and Alcott's novels for youth, adolescent protagonists communicate repeatedly that the young can make a difference in improving the world for others. While many nineteenth-century American authors wrote about children and about social change, none relied on the plasticity of adolescence as a platform for advocating social change with novels as compelling as Twain's and Alcott's.

Twain and Alcott also shared a concern that writing for (or about) youth lacked the legitimacy that writing for adults would give them as authors. The financial pressure their families put on them sometimes compromised their own work ethics—but that same pressure also led them to want to capitalize their profits by securing the income for their work and protecting their copyrights. They wanted their heirs to inherit a bountiful legacy, so they wrote books that they knew would sell—books that appealed to the reading public's contemporary reform sentiments.

As a result, their legacy is far greater than the profitable estates they eventually left those heirs. Twain and Alcott were two nineteenth-century contributors to the establishment of juvenile writing as a lucrative publishing enterprise—but even more, they legitimized the field, making it seem more literary by connecting their work to the various reform movements of the day. Ever after, American writers for youth have assumed as a common practice the inclusion of reform ideologies in their narratives. That Twain and Alcott shared a faith that youth were more capable of enacting reform than adults is noteworthy, but even more noteworthy is their influence on the generations of authors who have followed in their footsteps. Twain's and Alcott's popularity made socially aware writing for youth the norm, not the exception. Such writing is still the norm because so many generations of adolescents have been trained to read about the connection between adolescent growth and enacting social change.

In that sense, many authors of youth literature are perpetuating the legacy that Twain and Alcott capitalized on in creating successful juveniles. When we make that literary heritage clear to youth readers, we help them better understand both history and literature. And, in the process, we create the opportunity for them—and for ourselves as critics—to interpret adolescent literature as integral to American intellectual traditions.

NOTES

INTRODUCTION

1. For the standard analysis of libertarian ideology in the Little House books, see Fellman (101–16).

2. For an analysis of the gender division between the two authors as a factor in the twentieth-century academic denigration of children's literature, see Clark, *Kiddie Lit* (1–16, 77–127). See also John Crowley for a comparison of *Little Women* to the genre of the boy book (384–99). Crowley concludes that the ending of *Little Women* is circumscribed by gender conventions available to girl characters, but he uses Huck Finn's freedom to emphasize Jo March's limitations (399).

3. See Townsend (67) and Hunt (52–57).

4. See *Mark Twain and the Feminization of Culture* for Stoneley's initial argument about the relationship between consumer culture and gender; see *Consumerism and American Girls' Literature* for his analysis of the way that many women writers, including Alcott, relied on adolescent fiction to interpellate readers into girlhood as the site of an increased American consumerism.

5. For those who think *Adventures of Huckleberry Finn* was not written for a youth audience, *The Prince and the Pauper*, with its commentary on social class, penal reform, and education reform, can provide a more comfortable example of Twain writing social consciousness into a novel for the young.

6. I have, however, found at least one critic who excoriates Alcott for "the transformation of women's fiction into girls' fiction": Nina Baym (296). In her early feminist work, Baym can never quite forgive Alcott for writing juveniles—and she certainly can't see that Alcott's novels had important historical ramifications for the feminist social consciousness that emerged in children's literature in the nineteenth century.

7. The *Christian Union* refused to list Alcott's work among its list of Christian works for children because, according to a letter from her infuriated publisher, her novels were "wanting in *orthodoxy* & must be taboo from orthodox S.[unday] Schools" (Shealy, "Author-Publisher, Diss. 234; italics in the original). See also the critique from the *Ladies Repository* ("From" 549).

8. Historian Steven Mintz captures the subversiveness of Pap's appearance in a novel for youth when he aptly describes Pap as an "abusive drunkard who beat his son for learning to read" (1).

9. Dates of publication included here indicate the date when the work was first published as a novel, rather than when it was first published serially. Publication dates for those that were first serialized appear in Chapter 6.

10. I admire Ron Powers for addressing the problem with a parodic notice: "PER-SONS failing to understand why I refer to my subject as 'Sammy' in his childhood will be prosecuted; persons failing to understand why I call him 'Sam' and 'Clemens' in dealing with his personal life thereafter will be banished; persons failing to understand why I use 'Mark Twain' when speaking of him as an author will be shot. BY ORDER OF THE BIOGRAPHER, PER S.L.C.M.T., CHIEF OF ORDNANCE" (ix).

1. THE FANTASY OF SELF-RELIANCE

1. Edward Waldo Emerson (1844–1930) appears with some regularity in Alcott's letters to her friend Alf Whitman (*Selected Letters* 50, 64, 66, 70, 76). In 1872, Alcott wrote reassuring a reader that the character Tom in *An Old-Fashioned Girl* was not modeled on Edward Emerson. Her letter implies that the imputation that Tom Shaw was patterned after Edward Emerson was a common assumption at the time: " 'Tom' is no more Edward Emerson than 'Laurie' is Julian Hawthorne. [. . .] Never believe anything 'they' say, or anything you see in the papers. Its [*sic*] never true" (*Selected Letters* 167–68).

2. Clark assesses the historical authenticity of this quotation in *Kiddie Lit*, noting that the first discoverable instance of the quotation being attributed to Alcott is in an unreliable literary gossip, *The Mauve Decade*, published by Thomas Beer in 1926 (84).

3. Mark Twain's farcical letters to the editors of the *Missouri Democrat* on "Female Suffrage" in 1867 include Mark Twain's statement that women should not be allowed to vote because they would vote themselves huge salaries to hold offices such as "state milliner" and would assassinate each other's "private moral character" instead of each other's political records, as men do (11). The completely fictional "Mrs. Mark Twain" writes the first attack on Twain's sexism, in which she calls her "husband" a "flippant ass" (12); the next letter of protest calls Mark Twain an "atrocious scoundrel" (13). The sequence of letters eventually makes the point that even though women are far more intelligent than men, their going to the polls would sully their purity. For more on Clemens's conflicted attitudes toward suffrage, see chapter 5.

4. Jeffrey Steinbrink, Andrew Hoffman, and John C. Gerber are among the critics who attempt, like Justin Kaplan, to distinguish Clemens from Twain.

5. Theorists of Twain's duality abound. Forrest Robinson refers to Mark Twain as "fiction . . . a varied cast of characters" (14) and describes Clemens, the man who created those characters, as a person driven by guilt (19). James D. Wilson in "Religious and Esthetic Vision in Mark Twain's Early Career" and Stanley Brodwin in "Mark Twain's Theology" and "The Theology of Mark Twain" assert that spiritual struggles are the source of Clemens's psychological tension. The biographers who focus on the latter portion of his life, such as Hamlin Hill in *God's Fool* and John Cooley in *Mark Twain's Aquarium*, identify Clemens's frustrated idealism as the source of his greatest emotional

pain (Hill xxvii, Cooley xx–xxi). One of his publisher's sons thought he might as well have titled his biography of Clemens *Mark Twain vs. Mark Twain*: "What came to him from the inside was as real as what came from the outside" (Webster 398–99). The man who made that assertion, Samuel Webster, was the son of Clemens's niece.

6. See, for example, Bedell's analysis of Bronson Alcott's description of Louisa and her mother: "Two devils, as yet, I am not quite divine enough to vanquish—the mother fiend and her daughter" (qtd. in *Alcotts* 244).

7. Charles Strickland attributes the "contradictions" in Alcott's spirit to the power struggles that occurred between Louisa's ascetic father and her emotionally forthcoming mother (29–36). Zwinger characterizes Bronson and Louisa's relationship as "resembl[ing] nothing so much as a true romance courtship" that she believes is rehearsed again on the pages of *Little Women* (71). The editors of Alcott's letters and journals explain Alcott's self-description of herself as a "moody girl" by noting that her moodiness was a result of her natural energy being repressed by Victorian mores (Alcott, *Journals* 6). Elbert describes Alcott's "strange feelings" as emerging from her recognition that sexual power must be controlled in both men and women, a recognition that was tied to her emerging feminist belief in equality between the sexes (85–89, 156–64). Madeleine Stern depicts Alcott as influenced by both her love of the lurid and the influence of transcendentalism (*LMA: From Blood* 253–65).

8. Saxton is especially harsh in her criticism of Alcott's mother for inspiring her with guilt so great that Alcott eventually needed to apotheosize the woman into Marmee (13).

9. Alcott reflected her father's opinion of himself while she simultaneously demonstrated her ambivalence about San Francisco and westerners, such as Clemens, when she discouraged her father from a lecture tour in San Francisco in 1870. She said his being in San Francisco would be like having a "saint in a barroom" (*Selected Letters* 152).

10. "A True Story," published in November 1874, was Clemens's first *Atlantic* publication.

11. See Sarah Elbert's "Introduction" to Alcott's *Louisa May Alcott: On Race, Sex, and Slavery* (ix–lx).

12. Mark Taply is an optimistic character in *Martin Chuzzlewit*.

13. Elbert connects the Spaniard to Alcott's racial anxiety, specifically linking the anxiety to Alcott's perception of herself as having a dark complexion and being, therefore, more passionate than her Teutonic father (157).

14. For example, she wrote in her journal in 1874, "Got no sleep without morphine" (192). See also Stern, *Louisa* (196, 205, 239).

15. Powers is particularly antifeminist in describing the work of those, such as Harris, who have speculated on the influence of women on Twain's writing process. Powers sardonically describes Mary Fairbanks, whom Clemens met on the *Quaker City*, Clemens's mother, and his wife as "a three-headed hellhag who, under the Freudian template of Mark Twain interpretation, leeched the writer's precious raw Western genius, turning him into a literary girlie-man" (219). I am more interested in the ways

that Clemens and Alcott were similarly influenced to restraint in their writing by family members than I am in identifying that influence as a matter of gender influence.

16. Brewer's *Dictionary of Phrase and Fable* (1898) attributes the original use of the phrase to Abraham Lincoln.

17. See James L. Johnson's *Mark Twain and the Limits of Power: Emerson's God in Ruins* for Twain's intellectual responses to Emerson; for Emerson's influence on Alcott, see Elbert's *A Hunger for Home: Louisa May Alcott's Place in American Culture* and Estes and Lant, "Dismembering the Text: The Horror of Louisa May Alcott's *Little Women*" and Daniel Shealy, "Singing Mignon's Song: The Friendship of Ralph Waldo Emerson and Louisa May Alcott."

18. Emerson had his own share of dependents, including, at times, the entire Alcott family. Emerson began his financial support of the Alcotts in 1840, the year before he published "Self-Reliance" in *Essays* (1841).

19. Stowe (1811–1896) was one of the top-selling juvenile authors of the nineteenth century, especially if one classifies as children's literature the book *Uncle Tom's Cabin* (1852), which Mott estimates had sold three million copies by the middle of the twentieth century in the United States alone (118). Lilly Warner was the sister-in-law of Charles Dudley Warner (1829–1900), who coauthored *The Gilded Age* with Twain. Lilly was one of the original contributors to *St. Nicholas Magazine*, which her close friend, Mary Mapes Dodge (1831–1905), edited.

20. Aldrich (1836–1907) also had import in Clemens's life as the editor of the *Atlantic Monthly* who followed Howells, serving in that capacity from 1881–1890.

21. Hawthorne bought the house next door to Orchard House, Hillside, from Bronson Alcott, where he and his family had lived prior to the Hawthornes living there. Hawthorne changed the name of the house to Wayside. In 1858, the Alcotts rented the house from the Hawthornes while they were overseas. Eventually, Margaret Sidney, author of *Five Little Peppers and How They Grew* (1880) also lived in Wayside—and she eventually owned Orchard House, where Alcott wrote *Little Women*—but it would be more accurate to say that Alcott inspired Sidney than the other way around.

22. See also John Seelye's *Mark Twain in the Movies* for a photographic essay that includes pictures of Twain holding Angel Fish on his lap (126, 175), hugging them (100), swimming with them (173), and them leaning against him (95) or putting their heads in his lap (175).

23. For a more developed analysis of the possibilities of Alcott's lesbianism, see Trites, "Queer Performances."

24. Daniel Ricketson (1813–1898) was a contemplative Quaker and poet who lived in New Bedford and who valued highly his friendships with Thoreau, Emerson, Bronson Alcott, and Ellery Channing (Ricketson 3–7). In 1865, Ricketson praised Alcott's *Moods* to Bronson: "I am glad thus to learn that your daughter is herein a public educator for good" (193).

25. The second repetition of the word "wife" might have been intended to be "life," since the phrase "loyal through all her life" makes more sense.

26. Although Louise Chandler Moulton (1835–1908) was one of Alcott's earlier biographers, writing a chapter on her in *Our Famous Women* (1883), apparently Alcott did not always think of Moulton with the highest of praise. One of the many crossed-out deletions in Alcott's letters was her description in 1876 of Moulton as "fat and coquettish" (*Selected Letters* 214). Moulton was the Boston literary correspondent for the *New York Tribune*. Clemens also knew her. For an example of Clemens's correspondence with Moulton in 1874, see his *Selected Letters* (6.33).

27. In the same essay, published posthumously, Twain poses as Satan, amazed at humans' stupidity: "First of all, I recall to your attention the extraordinary fact with which I begin. To-wit, that the human being, like the immortals, naturally places sexual intercourse far and away above all other joys—yet he has left it out of his heaven!" ("Letters from the Earth" 887).

28. In a largely speculative thesis, Andrew Hoffman asserts that Clemens may also have experimented with homosexuality (77–91).

29. Frank Luther Mott defines a best seller as having had "a total sale equal to one per cent of the population of continental United States . . . for the decade in which it was published" (303). By this measure, both *Little Women* and *The Innocents Abroad* were among the twenty-six best sellers in the 1860s (308–09).

30. In most editions, however, the ghost of Annabel's first name reappears when Uncle Alec erroneously refers to her as "Ariadne Blish" one time in chapter 14 (154).

31. Hemingway also observed that American women writers quit writing because they "become leaders"; they are "Joan of Arc without the fighting" (23). Given Alcott's dedication to the suffrage and temperance movements later in her life, she seems to fit his description, though it seems unlikely that he was talking about her.

2. THE METAPHOR OF THE ADOLESCENT REFORMER

1. Readers will find more about the historical context of romantic evangelism in the interlude that follows this chapter.

2. In *Beneath the American Renaissance*, Reynolds provides a compelling commentary about how religious ideologies influenced the interaction between popular writing and such major writers as Emerson, Melville, Hawthorne, Dickinson, and Whitman.

3. Jane Tompkins calls *Uncle Tom's Cabin* "the *summa theologica* of nineteenth-century America's religion of domesticity, a brilliant redaction of the culture's favorite story about itself—the story of salvation through motherly love" (125).

4. Eiselein complicates the nuances of Civil-War era humanitarian reform by identifying the panoply of motivations that led individuals to work for social change: religious duty, efficiency, patriotism, and self-improvement. He distinguishes those motivated by scientific and philanthropic motivations from those motivated by sentiment and Romanticism, but he observes the ways that these motivations interacted

with and affected each other (87). Eiselein's sense of the complexity of humanitarian reform is applicable here; for example, he describes the variety of factors that motivated Alcott's humanitarian impulses during the Civil War (85, 98–101). Clemens's motivations for reform were similarly complex.

5. The term "youth" also eliminates the distinction between children's literature and adolescent literature that twenty-first-century literary criticism assumes. Neither Clemens nor Alcott would have distinguished literature for children from literature for adolescents.

6. In a letter dated May 9, 1873, Daniel Ford, the editor of the *Youth's Companion*, impressed upon Alcott how important it was for her to remember the appropriate ages for the readership his journal defined as "youth": "Please remember that the Companion seeks mainly to interest *young folk—from 12 to 25* years old!" (Alcott, L.M., 1832–88, folder 64). Ford underscored three times the words "from 12 to 25."

7. See also Budd, *MT: Social Philosopher* (93–107); DeVoto (73–77); Hoffman (6, 35–38); Sanborn (28–30); D. L. Smith, "Black Critics" (116–27).

8. See also Twain's "Disgraceful Persecution of a Boy" (1870): "By watching his elders, the boy found out that a Chinaman had no rights that any man was bound to respect; that he had no sorrows that any man was bound to pity; that neither his life nor his liberty was worth the purchase of a penny when a white man needed a scapegoat; that nobody loved Chinamen, nobody befriended them, nobody spared them suffering when it was convenient to inflict it; everybody, individuals, communities, the majesty of the State itself, joined in hating, abusing, and persecuting these humble strangers" (380–81).

9. Warner McGuinn, the Yale Law School alumnus whom Clemens supported, was later one of Thurgood Marshall's mentors, which Phipps argues demonstrates the long-term impact of Clemens's generosity to American civil rights (Phipps 163–64).

10. Those influences included the African Americans from Clemens's childhood who taught Clemens the oral tradition and a black child named "Sociable Jimmy," who inspired him in his adulthood. Fishkin traces how Sociable Jimmy's linguistics have a demonstrable influence on Huck's speech patterns (*Was* 14–47).

11. Nonetheless, John H. Wallace, perhaps more than any other critic, has excoriated it for being "the most grotesque example of racist trash ever written" (16). He condemns the novel's use of the term "nigger" as something that objectifies black readers, especially those in high school. Although Peaches Henry recommends *Huckleberry Finn* teaching racial issues on the high-school level precisely because of its complexity, she nonetheless observes that Huck's decision to help Jim is no indication that he has become an abolitionist; his loyalty is to one friend, not to a principle of emancipation (32). Frederick Woodard and Donnarae MacCann condemn Jim's characterization as "imbued with the white supremacy myth of the time" (141). In "Huck, Jim, and American Racial Discourse," David Lionel Smith further complicates the issue of whether or not the novel is racist, concluding that Twain relies on stereotypes to "undermine rather than revalidate the dominant racial discourse" ("Huck" 108).

12. Robert E. Weir and Fishkin both believe that Twain rejected Social Darwinism—which guaranteed against social mobility—largely because of the way it conflicted with his sense of the Protestant work ethic—which guaranteed social mobility (Weir 205; Fishkin "MT and Race" 129–30). Twain's ambivalence about evolution and its relationship to Social Darwinism becomes clear in a passage in *A Connecticut Yankee*:

> Training—training is everything; training is all there is *to* a person. We speak of nature; it is folly; there is no such thing as nature; what we call by that misleading name is merely heredity and training. We have no thoughts of our own, no opinions of our own; they are transmitted to us, trained into us. All that is original in us, and therefore fairly creditable or discreditable to us, can be covered up and hidden by the point of a cambric needle, all the rest being atoms contributed by, and inherited from, a procession of ancestors that stretches back a billion years to the Adam-clam or grasshopper or monkey from whom our race has been so tediously and ostentatiously and unprofitably developed. (208)

Twain also expresses ambivalence about Social Darwinism in *Pudd'nhead Wilson* and *Joan of Arc*, which I discuss in chapter 5.

13. Louis J. Budd interprets the ending as Twain's social critique of Jim Crow laws in the deep South (*MT: Social Philosopher* 102–05). Steven Mailloux perceives the novel, and especially its ending, as a rhetorical tour de force in which Twain manipulates the reader to accept "ideological critiques of white supremacy" (117). Cecil Moffitt describes the final chapters as reflecting Clemens's sense of national guilt during Reconstruction (280–83). Charles H. Nilon demonstrates how Tom Sawyer's treatment of Jim parallels the U.S. government's treatment of blacks in the South during Reconstruction (62–76). Fritz Oehlschlaeger considers the ending "chilling" because Jim "becomes again the stereotyped, minstrel-show 'nigger' of the first section" (117). Gilbert Rubinstein analyzes the ending as a moral triumph of "realism" over the sentimentalism of slave-holding society (72–76). Neil Schmitz laments the impotence with which the ending depicts freed slaves (125–35).

14. Hemingway claims, "If you read it you must stop where the Nigger Jim is stolen from the boys. That is the real end. The rest is just cheating" (22). With that passage, Hemingway displays the racism common to twentieth-century critics: he refers to Jim by a name by which he is never once called in the novel.

15. Huck is unmotivated to go to heaven in chapter 1 because he doesn't want to spend eternity listening to Miss Watson nag him, but the statement is significant for its foreshadowing of Huck's later decision to go to hell and for its indication of Huck's awareness that deciding not to try to earn a place in heaven is a matter of violating social propriety.

16. In that passage, Huck remembers incorrectly that Jim calls him his best friend after Huck saves the runaway from potential capture: "At last I struck the time I saved him by telling the men we had small-pox aboard, and he was so grateful, and said I was the best friend old Jim ever had in the world, and the *only* one he's got now" (273).

In point of fact, Jim called Huck his best friend earlier, which is what causes Huck to lie to the raftsmen in the first place.

17. Stone considers Huck to be Twain's "ironic masterpiece" (275). See also Cadden (146–47).

18. Henry Nash Smith, Leo Marx, and Martha Banta conclude that Huck has grown; Richard P. Adams, Thomas Gullason, Albert E. Stone, and Philip S. Foner conclude that Huck has not.

19. Although Stone describes Huck's developing morality as a matter of his "growing awareness of social fact" (148), Stone concludes that Huck ultimately does not grow into maturity, which is an "ironic climax" to a novel about growth (158).

20. In *Tom Sawyer Abroad*, Jim identifies Moses as sharing his own religious faith: "He was a Presbyterian, and had a most deep respect for Moses which was a Presbyterian too, he said" (93–94). Later, Huck learns about religious diversity from Tom Sawyer: "When I asked [Tom] what a Moslem was, he said it was a person that wasn't a Presbyterian. So there is plenty of them in Missouri, though I didn't know it before" (105). Twain's ironic jokes about Presbyterianism in this 1896 novel demonstrate the author's understanding of how well he was indoctrinated in a provincial form of Presbyterianism as a child.

21. William Lloyd Garrison (1805–1879) was an abolitionist; Samuel Gridley Howe (1801–1876) founded the Perkins School for the Blind; Charles Sumner (1811–1874) was a U.S. senator from Massachusetts from 1851–1874; Abigail Hopper Gibbons (1801–1893) was a Quaker from Philadelphia whose commitment to reform included those interests that Alcott describes.

22. Stern provides examples of Alcott's reform writing that touch on domestic reform (food, drink, dress), health, education, abolition, and women's rights in *L.M. Alcott: Signature of Reform*. The section Stern includes on "communal society" as a reform includes Alcott's parodying the notion rather than her advancing it.

23. In 1950, Madeleine Stern described Alcott androgynously, long before it was fashionable to do so: "To her family she had been, and must be more than ever now, all things, fathering her father, mothering her mother, husbanding her sister, giving them the love she had given to no man" (*Louisa* 214). Nina Auerbach later praises Alcott for depicting a community of women in *Little Women*, but Ann B. Murphy points out how darkly competitive Jo and Amy's relationship is (562–85). Clark finds feminism in the novel's *künstlerroman* depiction of a successful female artist ("Portrait" 81–96), but Keyser perceives the gender roles that limit Jo's artistic potential (*Whispers* 61–81). Estes and Lant graphically depict how Jo dismembers herself, physically and metaphorically, to fit her society's notion of the feminine ("Dismembering" 113–19). Judith Fetterley criticizes Elizabeth Janeway for praising Jo's ultimate independence (40n5). Sarah Elbert traces how Alcott was socially linked to the social reformers and suffragists of the day, including Thomas Wentworth Higginson and Margaret Fuller, in writing a politically aware novel: "She made woman's rights integral to her stories, and above all to *Little Women*" (*Hunger* 193).

24. For a thorough analysis of how Huck Finn's "innocent eye" establishes him as a romantic child whose innocence enables him to make ironic and subversive social commentary without devolving to the level of the corruption that surrounds him, see Stone (134–58).

25. Jehlen cites Concord as the intellectual seat of American individualism, although she never actually connects the independence at work in *Little Women* to the tensions in *Huckleberry Finn*.

26. For example, Foster and Simons read the hair-cutting scene as a "reenactment of the experience of female castration" (96); Bedell calls it "a delicious father-daughter fantasy" ("Introduction" xxxiii); Griswold calls it "Amazonian" (160); Estes and Lant describe the act as part of Jo's ongoing process of "self-effacement" ("Dismembering" 118); Saxton calls the scene "redolent with significance" because it is an act of "active, male assertion" (10, 11); Crowley writes about readers possibly being "horrified . . . by the apparent masochism of Jo's mutilation" (390).

3. HISTORICAL INTERLUDE

1. For more on the relationship between *Little Women* and *Uncle Tom's Cabin*, see Estes and Lant, "Dismembering" (102–04); for more on the relationship between *Adventures of Huckleberry Finn* and *Uncle Tom's Cabin*, see Smiley (61–67).

2. Progressivism was one logical result of romantic evangelism: the many reforms of the Progressive era rely on a shared belief that materially blessed humans are responsible for improving the lot of those less fortunate.

3. This was a standard phrase that Ahlstrom attributes to the Congregationalist theologian Nathaniel William Taylor (420, 611).

4. See Clebsch (57–68, 112–24).

5. See chapter 2, note 21.

6. Clark describes an anonymous book review in a 1958 *New Yorker* that speculates that Alcott "may be the most widely read transcendentalist today" (qtd. in *Kiddie Lit* 105). See also Doyle, *Louisa* (88–107), in which Doyle comments fully on Theodore Parker's influence on Alcott, in addition to Alcott's relationship with transcendentalism through her father, Emerson, and Thoreau.

7. In his poem "Each and All" (1839), Emerson defines his belief in the interrelated spirituality of each and every living thing: "All are needed by each one; / Nothing is fair or good alone." The rest of the poem articulates his theism—that is, his sense that God exists within nature and all living things, which are most beautiful only within their original context:

Over me soared the eternal sky,
Full of light and of deity;
Again I saw, again I heard,
The rolling river, the morning bird;—

Beauty through my senses stole;
I yielded myself to the perfect whole.

8. Ahlstrom's source is "Remarks on the Rev. Dr. Worcester's Letter to Mr. Channing on the 'Review of American Unitarianism' in the Late Panoplist" (Boston, 1815, 38–39).

9. When Demi's father dies, the narrator asserts, "Slowly he came to feel that father was not lost, only invisible for a while. . . . To this belief Demi held fast, and in it found both help and comfort, because it led him unconsciously through a tender longing for the father whom he had seen to a childlike trust in the Father whom he had not seen. Both were in heaven, and he prayed to both, trying to be good for love of them" (329–30). John Brooke is saved without any apparent redemptive belief in Christ's divinity, and Demi is motivated to act charitably by his religious faith. Following Brooke's funeral, his charitable actions are held up to the pupils of Plumfield as an exemplar (327–29).

10. Alcott knew Conway through his relationship with the transcendentalists, who inspired him to become an active abolitionist. With Frank Sanborn, Conway was coeditor of the *Boston Commonwealth* and edited the *Dial* from 1860–61. Conway named his second son Emerson and wrote an early biography of Ralph Waldo Emerson, *Emerson at Home and Abroad* (1882). He also wrote a biography of Thomas Paine, *The Life of Thomas Paine* (1892). While living in England, he represented Clemens's publishing interests in Great Britain. For more on Clemens's relationship with Conway, see Chapter 6.

11. The only Americans Alcott listed among her favorite authors were Emerson and Thoreau: "My favorite authors are Shakespeare, Dante, . . . Emerson, Carlyle, Thoreau . . . Geo. Eliot and C. Bronte . . . I read no modern fiction. It seems poor stuff when one can have the best of the old writers" (*Selected Letters* 296, ellipses in original).

12. A passage in *An Old-Fashioned Girl* seems indicative of Alcott's critique of contemporary churches: "I like the plain, old-fashioned churches, built for use, not show, where people met for hearty praying and preaching, and where everybody made their own music instead of listening to opera singers, as we do now. I don't care if the old churches were bare and cold, and the seats hard, there was real piety in them, and the sincerity of it was felt in the lives of the people. I don't want a religion that I put away with my Sunday clothes, and don't take out till the day comes round again; I want something to see and feel and live by day by day" (200–01).

13. Walter Blair (343), Stanley Brodwin ("MT's Theology," 168–69), Louis J. Budd (*MT: Social Philosopher* 188), Harold K. Bush (55–94), John M. Ditsky (12–19), Hamlin Hill (*MT: God's Fool, passim*), Coleman O. Parsons (582–602), John S. Tuckey (532–42), and James D. Wilson (155–72) are among the dozens of scholars who have written about Clemens's vacillating faith. See also John Q. Hays's *Mark Twain and Religion*, William E. Phipps's *Mark Twain's Religion*, Allison Ensor's *Mark Twain and the Bible*, and Brodwin's "The Theology of Mark Twain" for full-length studies of the topic.

14. In *A Connecticut Yankee in King Arthur's Court*, Hank Morgan reorganizes feudal England. He says:

> I could have given my own sect the preference and made everybody a Presbyterian without any trouble, but that would have been to affront a law of human nature: spiritual wants and instincts are as various in the human family as are physical appetites, complexions and features, and a man is only at his best, morally, when he is equipped with the religious garment whose color and shape and size most nicely accommodate themselves to the spiritual complexion, angularities and stature of the individual who wears it. (127)

Hank's religious pluralism is commendable, but he establishes forty Protestant sects in medieval England and rails against the Catholic Church as being "only a political machine; it was invented for that it is nursed, cradled, preserved for that it is an enemy to human liberty, and does no good which it could not better do in a split-up and scattered condition" (207). Hank's anti-Catholicism echoes similar sentiments expressed in *The Innocents Abroad*, as when the narrator of that book notes that in the U.S., "Jews, there, are treated just like human beings, instead of dogs" because Americans live free of the tyranny of the Catholic Church (1.343). Twain also says in *The Innocents Abroad*: "I have been educated to enmity toward everything that is Catholic, and sometimes, in consequence of this, I find it much easier to discover Catholic faults than Catholic merits" (2.382). Twain's condemnation of Catholicism for not affording "freedom" is a notable extension of Clemens's Protestant belief in the priesthood of the believer, that is, the primacy of the individual's relationship with God.

15. Powers claims that Twain was the "American Poet" that Emerson called for in his lecture of the same name (66). As he frequently does, Powers may be overstating his case.

16. Stanley Brodwin refers to slavery as "the National Sin" ("Blackness" 314).

4. EDUCATION AND REFORM

1. Harriet Beecher Stowe's *Uncle Tom's Cabin* was published 1851–52; Susan Coolidge's *What Katy Did* was published in 1872.

2. Calling the pattern of pious cheerfulness "The Gospel of Optimism," Griswold identifies Mary Mapes Dodge's *Hans Brinker; or, The Silver Skates* as the first novel in this tradition (187).

3. John Howard (1726–1790) was the first major advocate of penal reform in England; Sylvester Graham (1794–1851) was a nutritionist and reformer whom Elbert compares to Bronson Alcott (Elbert 81); Horace Mann (1796–1859) advocated for public education in the U.S.

4. "The 'matter of Europe' furnished Mark Twain with culturally potent images of power, authority, and tradition" (Stahl xiii).

5. Wat Tyler and Jack Cade were both Kentish peasants who led revolts against kings. Tyler led a rebellion against Richard II in 1381; Cade led one against Henry VI in 1450.

6. Stone analyzes *Tom Sawyer* as a novel primarily about the "anatomy of social evil" (63). In the sense that rigid class structures are a social evil, I agree with him.

7. Those of us who teach writing might object to Twain's sexism, even while we are ourselves still working to eradicate the didactic endings from compositions written by students of both genders.

8. The conflicted racism found in *Adventures of Huckleberry Finn* continues, too. For example, Huck describes Jim: "He was only a nigger outside; inside he was as white as you be" (91).

9. Frederick J. Antzcak identifies Ralph Waldo Emerson and Mark Twain—along with William James—as the greatest proponents of the rhetoric of democratic education in the nineteenth-century United States (89–160).

10. Two passages in Alcott's journal reflect the literary genesis for the conversion that Dan experiences while he's in jail. In 1879, Alcott anxiously went to the state prison in West Concord to tell a story to the prisoners and felt proud because so many were visibly affected by her words (215). One of the men later came to thank her and told her that "my little story. . . kept him straight & reminded him that it is never too late to mend" (229). The man was a miner who had stolen from a doctor's office while drunk; his traveling companions were implicated in his crime, as are Dan's in *Jo's Boys*. While Dan is in prison, "a middle-aged woman in black, with a sympathetic face, eyes full of compassion, and a voice that seemed to warm the heart, because of certain motherly tones in it" comes to tell a story about two hospitalized soldiers (216). She reminds Dan of "Mrs. Jo," and the point she makes about a prison being "a hospital for soldiers wounded in life's battle" makes him "drop his eyes to hide the sudden dew that dimmed them" (217, 218) in much the same way that Alcott describes two prisoners: "One put his head down, & another winked hard" (*Journals* 215).

11. Perhaps the worst stereotyping of Native Americans in the March trilogy occurs in *Little Men*, when Nan has her doll painted "brick red, with staring black eyes" and transforms it into "an Indian chief" who tomahawks all the dolls in the nursery until it "run[s] red with imaginary gore" (123).

12. For more on Pestalozzi (1746–1827), see Good and Teller (335–38).

13. See also Doyle, "Transatlantic Translations" (267–68).

14. Roger Ascham was Queen Elizabeth's tutor in her youth. He records his intellectual admiration for Lady Jane Grey in his anti-corporal punishment pedagogical treatise, *The Schoolmaster* (1570).

15. To be fair, the little men have also been described as learning fewer academic subjects than boys at other schools (28).

16. Beverly Lyon Clark argues convincingly throughout *Kiddie Lit: The Cultural Construction of Children's Literature in America* that adults, as well as children, read both Alcott and Twain in nongendered ways in the nineteenth century; it was the twentieth-century literary academy that gendered the reading of their novels (48–127).

5. GENDER AND REFORM

1. Jean Matthews provides the standard definition of the New Woman: "As a type, the New Woman was young, well educated, probably a college graduate, independent of spirit, highly competent, and physically strong and fearless" (13). See also Patricia Marks for the image of the New Woman in the media (1–2) and Ellen Jordan's analysis of the genesis of the New Woman (19–21). Frances Cogan points toward the emergence of the New Woman when she identifies what she calls the "Ideal of Real Womanhood" that developed in opposition to the Cult of True Womanhood. The "Real Woman" in mid-nineteenth-century America exhibited "intelligence, physical fitness and health, self-sufficiency, economic self-reliance" and married intelligently (4). She would not have been as politically subversive as the New Woman, however, largely because New Women could emerge from the lower class, where "Real Womanhood" was a luxury of the middle and upper class.

2. For the standard definitional essay of True Womanhood, see Welter, "The Cult of True Womanhood" (151–74).

3. Doyle observes that Alcott depicts both marriage and spinsterhood respectfully; the context of Alcott's attitudes that Doyle describes are largely a function of Alcott's intuitive understanding of New Womanhood (*Louisa* 126–31).

4. Another girl comments, "Our brains may be smaller, but . . . the largest-headed man in our class is the dullest" (289).

5. Alcott wrote in 1883 about her desire to vote on matters pertaining to education, "Surely this will be as feminine and worthy an act as standing behind a stall at a charity fair, or dancing in a ball-room" (*Selected Letters* 269).

6. In 1884, only eight women turned up to vote (*Selected Letters* 281).

7. Doyle relies on the U.S. Census to document that, although the gender imbalance did not occur throughout the United States, it was a fact in New England, where women outnumbered men with a population of 7.3 million women and 7.1 million men (*Louisa* 184n7).

8. Frances Power Cobbe (1822–1904) was a British reformer and a scholar of religion and economics who edited Theodore Parker's works; Florence Nightingale (1820–1910) was internationally recognized for her work reforming nursing; Elizabeth Stuart Phelps (1844–1911) was a children's author who was as yet unmarried when *Jo's Boys* was published; Harriet Martineau (1802–1876) was a British writer and a reformer; Charlotte Cushman (1816–1876) was an actress and an acquaintance of Alcott's.

9. The subheading for this section is from a letter Alcott wrote to the *Woman's Journal*, which was edited by Lucy Stone and Henry Blackwell (*Selected Letters* 238).

10. Claudia Mills identifies *Eight Cousins* as a children's novel that advocates liberal education, especially in the way that Rose is allowed to choose between the various modes of education that her aunts and uncle offer her (71–75).

11. Aunt Jessie has already introduced this theme, saying, "Some women love to give more than they receive" (219).

12. Cardwell has a complementary interpretation that he refers to as Twain's "cult of Olivia" (121).

13. See Harris for an extended reflection on Twain's perception on Livy as the "Angel in the House," *MT's Escape* (118–19).

14. The original reference can be found in *Mark Twain's Notebooks*, ed. Albert Bigelow Paine, 256.

15. Harris writes that *Joan of Arc* was Clemens's attempt to return to the values of True Womanhood: "Twain portrays her as willingly subject to male authority of all kinds" ("MT and Gender" 186), and to Susan Gillman, Joan is just one more of the "child-women" that shows Clemens's inability to depict strong women (106). But for Fishkin, Joan "reinscribes conventional gender ideology in fresh ways" ("MT and Women" 61), while Stahl defines Joan as an "implicit critique of male character" (126).

16. Cooley believes that Twain "deconstructs assumptions about gender roles that dominate the thinking of his generation and his earlier fiction" with the "heroic maidens and inadequate males" in *Joan of Arc* (38), a pattern which Cooley ties to Twain's "awareness of a national debate over issues of gender and the place of women in his society" (39), but his reading ignores how deeply conventional Twain's reliance on tropes of True Womanhood actually are throughout the novel.

17. Cooley provides as his reference the Mark Twain Autobiographical Dictations, 1,034 in the Mark Twain Papers, University of California, Berkeley.

18. In "The Turning Point of My Life" (1910)—a point that Twain identifies as occurring for all of us with Adam's disobedience in the Garden of Eden—he wishes that Martin Luther and Joan of Arc had been the two people in Eden: "By neither sugary persuasions nor by hellfire could Satan have beguiled *them* to eat the apple" (937).

19. As Stahl puts it, "Twain feels the need to deny her sexuality and thus ultimately her humanity" (149).

20. Stone describes *Joan of Arc* as being as story about "a Roman Catholic girl couched in profoundly Protestant terms" (218).

21. For more on this issue, see Fishkin, "Mark Twain and Race" (145–46).

22. Stahl, Harris, and Fishkin offer sensitively nuanced readings of Twain's conflicted attitudes toward gender. Phipps, on the other hand, calls Twain a "profeminist" (183), which is something of an overstatement.

23. Twain praises Joan of Arc's work ethic: "Her motto was 'Work! stick to it; keep on working!' . . . And whoever will take that motto and live by it will be likely to succeed" (232).

6. HISTORICAL INTERLUDE

1. For a brief history of *Merry's Museum*, see Shealy, "Author-Publisher," Diss. (58–59). Shealy notes Alcott's prodigious number of contributions to the children's magazine, which included over thirty short stories and poems and a monthly column (58–59).

2. See Stern, *From Blood* (136–47).

3. For complete details of the publication of *The Innocents Abroad*, see Hill, *MT&EB* (1–4).

4. Alcott made a point of reassuring her readers that her profit "was not half so large a one as a generous world reported it to be" in *Jo's Boys*, however (46).

5. See Darling (246–47).

6. Mott reports that, although the preliminary sales of *The Luck of Roaring Camp and Other Stories* were slow, by the end of the 1870s, it had sold more than 375,000 copies (198–99, 309). Thus, Clemens's analysis of Harte's sales is to be taken with a grain of salt.

7. Alcott also complained about the time pressure involved in writing for serials, claiming in *Jo's Boys* that "serials can't wait" (54) and "serials wait for no man" (61).

8. Shealy provides a thorough historical account of Alcott's relationships with various publishers and editors, including James Redpath, A. K. Loring, and Horace B. Fuller of *Merry's Museum* ("Author-Publisher," Diss. 14–51). His dissertation also includes an extensive historical account of Alcott's relationship with Niles. Shealy concludes: "It is doubtful Alcott would have reached the pinnacle of her success had it not been for her various editors and publishers. From their help and advice, she had learned how to fit a tale to suit an audience, how to judge what the readers desired, and how to get the most profit from her work. Without question, Thomas Niles had been the most influential force in her literary career" ("Author-Publisher," Diss. 282).

9. Alcott engages in a dialogue with the readers who had written her about *Little Women* in chapter 19 of *An Old-Fashioned Girl*. The narrator opens the final chapter of the novel with this statement: "Intimidated by the threats, denunciations, and complaints showered upon me in consequence of taking the liberty to end a certain story as I liked, I now yield to the amiable desire of giving satisfaction, and, at the risk of outraging all the unities, intend to pair off everybody I can lay my hands on" (366).

10. Alcott told Niles in 1883, "You excel in names" (*Selected Letters* 271).

11. The reference is to a quotation in *Rose in Bloom* (346).

12. This is not to imply that Henry James ever gave Alcott constructive advice. In fact, quite the contrary. Nathaniel Hawthorne's son Julian reports that—even though James was eleven years younger than Alcott—he once told her, "Louisa—m-my dear girl—er—when you hear people—ah—telling you you're a genius you mustn't believe them; er—what I mean is, it isn't true!" (Shealy, *Alcott* 203). James also criticized Alcott for her "ignorance of human nature, and her self-confidence in spite of this ignorance," and he considered the "smart satirical tone" of *Eight Cousins* inappropriate for children's literature (James 194, 196).

13. Apparently, the utilities and railroad stock that Niles advised Alcott to buy provided the Alcott family with long-term profits. Evidence appears throughout the following Houghton Library archives: Pratt, Frederic Alcott (bMS Am 1130.17), and Roberts Brothers (bMS Am 1130.8).

14. For an extended depiction of the acrimonious relationship that developed between Clemens and Bliss, see Hamlin Hill's *Mark Twain and Elisha Bliss*.

15. The reference is from the 1802 preface to the *Lyrical Ballads*.

16. Hamlin Hill observes the ambiguity of this advice: "One possible interpretation of it is that Howells is urging Mark Twain to carry the adventures of Tom Sawyer into the hero's mature years, and to serialize the story in the *Atlantic*, though he may mean, 'Don't waste your story on a juvenile audience'" (Twain, *MT-Howells Letters* 91n2).

17. Hendler interprets Howells and Clemens's interactions in the planning of *Tom Sawyer* as making the ambiguity surrounding the novel's audience "no accident; it is typical of the bad-boy genre and was explicitly planned by Twain and Howells" (186). Hendler does not grapple with the implied stigma of publishing for youth in his argument, having conferred, instead, upon bad-boy stories a higher literary status than they perhaps actually held.

18. See Darling (40). *Publisher's Weekly*, as early as 1872, had begun to issue annually a list of holiday books for the Christmas trade market.

19. See *LthP* (313–15, 318–20).

20. C. S. Lewis, in 1952, expresses approximately the same attitude about writing for children: "writ[e] a children's story because a children's story is the best art-form for something you have to say" (208).

21. Edward George Bulwer-Lytton's 1830 *Paul Clifford* opens with this infamous sentence: "It was a dark and stormy night; the rain fell in torrents—except at occasional intervals, when it was checked by a violent gust of wind which swept up the streets (for it is in London that our scene lies), rattling along the housetops, and fiercely agitating the scanty flame of the lamps that struggled against the darkness."

22. See also Roberts Brothers, letters from Niles dated August 30, 1876; September 12, 1876; December 30, 1876; February 21, 1877.

23. Brodhead calls the *Atlantic* "the premier organ of literary high culture in America" (*Cultures* 79), indicating that Howells's influence on Clemens came from prominently placed quarters. The *Atlantic* was published by Ticknor and Fields, who also published works by Emerson, Hawthorne, Holmes, Longfellow, Lowell, Stowe, Thoreau, and Whittier; they were the publishing firm that established the royalty system as a method of creating binding commitments between authors and publishers. (See LeMaster and Wilson 44).

As I have noted in Chapter 1, Alcott published in the *Atlantic* long before Clemens did, publishing four stories with the *Atlantic* between 1860 and 1863 (Eiselein and Phillips 25). Clark includes a detailed analysis of how the three editors who edited the *Atlantic* between 1871 and 1898—Howells, Aldrich, and Horace Scudder—influenced the reception of children's literature during the Gilded Age, thus affecting Clemens's and Alcott's literary status profoundly (*Kiddie Lit* 55–59, 102–04, 109–14). She notes that two of these editors were themselves authors of children's literature: Aldrich's *Story of a Bad Boy* (1869) and Howells's *A Boy's Town* (1890) were influential children's books in their own right (55).

24. For a thorough review of British involvement in international copyright laws, see Nowell-Smith (1–21). For international copyright issues in the U.S., see Nowell-Smith (64–85).

25. Clemens himself was responsible for the delays in the American edition because he ordered the size of the American edition changed after he had already authorized an English edition. As a result, the American edition had to be reset and proofread a second time. Making the situation even worse was the premature release of Howells's review of *Tom Sawyer* in the *Atlantic Monthly*. He had read the book from galleys— the preliminary versions set in March 1876—rather than the final galleys issued the following fall. See Hill, *MT&EB* (113–15, 120); Twain, *LthP* (3–4, 95n1).

26. For more on Clemens and international copyright, see Welland (202–18).

27. The theme of popularity being a burden can be found as early as *An Old-Fashioned Girl* (1870), when one character warns another: "Beware of popularity; it is a delusion and a snare; it puffeth up the heart of man, and especially of woman" (268).

7. ADOLESCENT REFORM NOVELS

1. A character in *The Green Hills of Africa* (1935) claims that "all modern American literature comes from one book by Mark Twain called *Huckleberry Finn*. . . . [I]t's the best book we've had. All American writing comes from that" (22).

2. See Robert Small on standard literary aspects of this genre (277–85).

3. CliffsNotes sites Harvey Breit's August 1951 comparison of *The Catcher in the Rye* to *Huckleberry Finn* (Baldwin 22; Breit 82).

4. Ponyboy and Johnny self-identify as southerners, as is evidenced by their sympathies with the Confederates in *Gone with the Wind*: Johnny "was especially stuck on the Southern gentlemen—impressed with their manners and charm" (67).

5. Stein (1874–1946); Rich (1929–); Ozick (1928–); Oates (1938–), and de Beauvoir (1908–1986).

6. Addams (1860–1935); Gilman (1860–1935); Thomas (1857–1935).

7. Terrell (1863–1954); Wells (1862–1931); Petry (1908–1997).

8. Sicherman also notes Edith Wharton's (1862–1937) and Dorothy Richardson's (1873–1957) disapprobation of *Little Women*, indicating, if nothing else, that both of them had read it.

9. Barney (1876–1972) was a pioneering lesbian writer. Flanner (1892–1978) was an expatriate journalist who wrote primarily for the *New Yorker*. Toklas (1877–1967) was immortalized by her lover, Gertrude Stein, in her memoirs, *The Autobiography of Alice B. Toklas* (1933). Beach (1887–1962) was the first publisher of James Joyce's *Ulysses* (1922).

10. Unfortunately, Cheever's attempt at literary analysis in *American Bloomsbury* is riddled with error and sensationalism, one example of which has twenty-three-year-old Henry David Thoreau, broken-hearted by a frustrated romantic relationship in 1840, letting "the little girl Louisa May Alcott's adoration . . . soften the blows" (30). Although Cheever claims that Alcott was eight years old in 1840 (13), for all but the last month of the year, she would have been seven.

11. For a feminist reading of Wilder's independence and voice in the Little House books, see Romines's *Constructing the Little House*.

12. The original quotation reads: "Her voice was ever soft, / Gentle and low, an excellent thing in woman" (Act V, Scene iii).

13. See Trites, *Waking Sleeping Beauty* (65–70).

14. For more on the gender politics involved in Harriet's need to lie, see Paul, "The Feminist Writer in *Harriet the Spy*" (67–73).

15. See Trites, *Disturbing the Universe* (54–83). Few authors depict adolescence as a stage of life that it is desirable to remain in permanently. For example, Sylvia Engdahl's science fiction novel *Enchantress from the Stars* (1970) distinguishes immature civilizations from mature ones, placing value on technological advancements by labeling more advanced civilizations with that connotatively laden term "mature." The enchantress is an adolescent character from a mature civilization who works with two men while she is visiting a nascent society in which medieval customs hold sway. Ironically, she proves to be less mature (despite being from a supposedly more mature society) than either the scientist from an "adolescent" culture that is most like our own with whom she works or the peasant she meets from the emerging medieval culture. Engdahl implies that adolescence is temporary, and she implies that it is an undesirable stage of life. She problematizes the relative concept of maturation in this book in ways that expose the limitations of perpetual adolescence. The message to readers is a direct one: maturity is better than immaturity.

16. See Trites, *Disturbing the Universe* (41–43).

17. Bloom defines the "anxiety of influence" as the way in which poets misread one another "so as to clear imaginative spaces for themselves" (5). Donnelly relies on Alcott as a feminist author, but her protagonist misreads the novels as "sugary," ignoring the poverty in *Little Women*, the deaths of the Hummel child and Beth, and Jo's self-destructive repressed anger.

18. Abel, Hirsch, and Langland describe fictions of female development as entailing, "inner concentration" and a "value system . . . defined in terms of community and empathy rather than achievement and autonomy" (8, 10).

19. For more on novels of despair as they intersect with Twain and Alcott's legacy, see Trites, "Hope, Despair, and Reform" (3–16).

AFTERWORD

1. For example, J. D. Stahl has taught a course on Twain and Alcott at Virginia Tech; Gregory Eiselein has taught them together at Kansas State University; and Beverly Lyon Clark has taught them at Wheaton College, Massachusetts.

BIBLIOGRAPHY

Abel, Elizabeth, Marianne Hirsch, and Elizabeth Langland. *The Voyage In: Fictions of Female Development.* Hanover, NH: UP of New England, 1983.

Adams, Richard P. "The Unity and Coherence of *Huckleberry Finn.*" *Tulane Studies in English* 6 (1956): 87–103.

Ahlstrom, Sydney E. *A Religious History of the American People.* New Haven, CT: Yale UP, 1972.

Alcott Family. Additional papers, 1707–1904. bMS Am 1130.15. Houghton Library, Harvard University, Cambridge, MA.

———. Letters to Anna Ricketson. bMS Am 1130.2. Houghton Library, Harvard University, Cambridge, MA.

Alcott, Louisa May. *Eight Cousins; or, the Aunt-Hill.* Boston: Roberts, 1875.

———. *Jack and Jill: A Village Story.* Boston: Roberts, 1880.

———. *Jo's Boys, and How They Turned Out: A Sequel to "Little Men."* Boston: Roberts, 1886.

———. *The Journals of Louisa May Alcott.* Eds. Joel Myerson, Daniel Shealy, and Madeleine B. Stern. Boston: Little, 1989.

———. *L. M. Alcott: Signature of Reform.* Ed. Madeleine B. Stern. Boston: Northeastern UP, 2002.

———. *Little Men: Life at Plumfield with Jo's Boys.* Boston: Roberts, 1871.

———. *Little Women, or Meg, Jo, Beth and Amy.* 1868, 1869. Eds. Anne K. Phillips and Gregory Eiselein. New York: Norton, 2004.

———. *Louisa May Alcott: On Race, Sex, and Slavery.* Ed. Sarah Elbert. Boston: Northeastern UP, 1997.

———. "M. L." 1863. *Louisa May Alcott on Race, Sex, and Slavery.* Ed. Sarah Elbert. Boston: Northeastern UP, 1997. 3–28.

———. *An Old-Fashioned Girl.* Boston: Roberts, 1870.

———. *Rose in Bloom: A Sequel to "Eight Cousins."* Boston: Roberts, 1876.

———. *The Selected Letters of Louisa May Alcott.* Eds. Joel Myerson, Daniel Shealy, and Madeleine B. Stern. Boston: Little, 1987.

———. *Under the Lilacs.* Boston: Roberts, 1878.

———. *Work: A Story of Experience.* 1873. New York: Schocken, 1977.

Alcott, L[ouisa] M[ay], 1832–1888. Papers. bMS Am 800.23. Houghton Library, Harvard University, Cambridge, MA.

Alexander, Lloyd. *Taran, Wanderer*. New York: Holt, 1967.

Allingham, Philip V. "Nineteenth-Century British and American Copyright Law." Accessed 21 October 2005 http://www.victorianweb.org/authors/dickens/pva/pva74.html.

Alvarez, Julia. *Before We Were Free*. New York: Random, 2002.

Andrews, Kenneth. *Nook Farm: Mark Twain's Hartford Circle*. Cambridge, MA: Harvard UP, 1950.

Antczak, Frederick J. *Thought and Character: The Rhetoric of Democratic Education*. Ames: Iowa State UP, 1985.

Auerbach, Nina. *Communities of Women: An Idea in Fiction*. Cambridge, MA: Harvard UP, 1978.

Avi. *The True Confessions of Charlotte Doyle*. New York: Orchard, 1990.

Baldwin, Stanley P. *CliffsNotes: Salinger's* The Catcher in the Rye. Foster City, CA: IDG, 2000.

Banta, Martha. "Rebirth or Revenge: The Endings of *Huckleberry Finn* and *The American*." *Modern Fiction Studies* 15 (1969): 191–207.

Baym, Nina. *Woman's Fiction: A Guide to Novels by and about Women in America, 1820–1870*. Urbana: U of Illinois P, 1993.

Bedell, Madelon. *The Alcotts: Biography of a Family*. New York: Potter, 1980.

———. Introduction. *Little Women*. By Louisa May Alcott. New York: Modern, 1983.

Black, Linda. "Louisa May Alcott's *Huckleberry Finn*." *Mark Twain Journal* 21.2 (1982): 15–17.

Blair, Walter. *Mark Twain and Huck Finn*. Berkeley: U of California P, 1960.

Block, Francesca Lia. *Baby Be-Bop*. New York: Harper, 1995.

———. *Weetzie Bat*. New York: Harper, 1989.

Bloom, Harold. *The Anxiety of Influence: A Theory of Poetry*. 1973. New York: Oxford UP, 1997.

Branch, Edgar. "Mark Twain and J. D. Salinger: A Study in Literary Continuity." *American Quarterly* 9 (1957): 144–58.

Brashares, Ann. *The Sisterhood of the Traveling Pants*. New York: Delacorte, 2001.

Breit, Harvey. Rev. of *The Catcher in the Rye* by J. D. Salinger. *The Atlantic Bookshelf*. (Aug. 1951): 82.

Brewer, E. Cobham. *Dictionary of Phrase and Fable*. Philadelphia: Henry Altemus, 1898.

Bridgers, Sue Ellen. *Permanent Connections*. New York: Harper, 1987.

Brodhead, Richard H. *Cultures of Letters: Scenes of Reading and Writing in Nineteenth-Century America*. Chicago: U of Chicago P, 1993.

Brodwin, Stanley. "Blackness and the Adamic Myth in Mark Twain's *Pudd'nhead Wilson*." *Texas Studies in Literature and Language* 15 (1973–74): 167–76. Reprinted in *Pudd'nhead Wilson and Those Extraordinary Twins*. Ed. Sidney E. Berger. New York: Norton, 2005. 312–21.

———. "Mark Twain's Theology: The Gods of a Brevet Presbyterian." *The Cambridge Companion to Mark Twain*. Ed. Forrest G. Robinson. Cambridge: Cambridge UP, 1995. 220–48.

———. "The Theology of Mark Twain: Banished Adam and the Bible." *Mississippi Quarterly* 29 (1976): 167–89.

Budd, Louis J., ed. *Mark Twain: The Contemporary Reviews.* New York: Cambridge UP, 1999.

Budd, Louis J. *Mark Twain: Social Philosopher.* Bloomington: U of Indiana P, 1962.

Bulwer-Lytton, Edward. *Paul Clifford.* London: Routledge, 1830.

Bush, Harold K., Jr. "'A Moralist in Disguise': Mark Twain and American Religion." *A Historical Guide to Mark Twain.* Ed. Shelley Fisher Fishkin. New York: Oxford UP, 2002. 55–94.

Cadden, Mike. "The Irony of Narration in the Young Adult Novel." *Children's Literature Association Quarterly* 25 (2000): 146–54.

Cardwell, Guy. *The Man Who Was Mark Twain: Images and Ideologies.* New Haven, CT: Yale UP, 1991.

Carter, Paul A. *The Spiritual Crisis of the Gilded Age.* DeKalb: Northern Illinois UP, 1971.

Chbosky, Stephen. *The Perks of Being a Wallflower.* New York: MTV, 1999.

Cheever, Susan. *American Bloomsbury: Louisa May Alcott, Ralph Waldo Emerson, Margaret Fuller, Nathaniel Hawthorne, and Henry David Thoreau: Their Lives, Their Loves, Their Work.* New York: Simon, 2006.

Cheney, Ednah D., ed. *Louisa May Alcott: Her Life, Letters and Journals.* Boston: Little, 1928.

Clark, Beverly Lyon. *Kiddie Lit: The Cultural Construction of Children's Literature in America.* Baltimore: Johns Hopkins UP, 2003.

———. "A Portrait of the Artist as a Little Woman." *Children's Literature* 17 (1989): 81–97.

Clebsch, William A. *American Religious Thought: A History.* Chicago: U of Chicago P, 1973.

Cogan, Frances B. *All-American Girl: The Ideal of Real Womanhood in Mid-Nineteenth-Century America.* Athens, GA: U of Georgia P, 1989.

Cooley, John. Introduction. *Mark Twain's Aquarium: The Samuel Clemens Angelfish Correspondence, 1905–1910.* Athens, GA: U of Georgia P, 1991.

Covington, Dennis. *Lizard.* New York: Delacorte, 1991.

Crowley, John W. "*Little Women* and the Boy-Book." *New England Quarterly* 58 (1985): 384–99.

Crutcher, Chris. *Chinese Handcuffs.* New York: Greenwillow, 1989.

———. *The Crazy Horse Electric Game.* New York: Greenwillow, 1987.

———. *Staying Fat for Sarah Byrnes.* New York: Greenwillow, 1993.

Darling, Richard L. *The Rise of Children's Book Reviewing in America, 1865–1881.* New York: Bowker, 1968.

De Tocqueville, Alexis. *Democracy in America.* 1831. Trans. George Lawrence. Ed. J. P. Mayer. Garden City, NY: Anchor, 1969.

DeVoto, Bernard. *Mark Twain's America.* Moscow, ID: U of Idaho P, 1932.

Ditsky, John M. "Mark Twain and the Great Dark: Religion in *Letters from the Earth*." *Mark Twain Journal* 17.4 (1975): 12–19.

Donnelly, Jennifer. *A Northern Light*. New York: Harcourt, 2003.

Donovan, Ellen. "Reading for Profit and Pleasure: *Little Women* and *The Story of a Bad Boy*." *The Lion and the Unicorn* 18 (1994): 143–53.

Doyle, Christine. *Louisa May Alcott and Charlotte Brontë: Transatlantic Translations*. Knoxville: U of Tennessee P, 2000.

———. "Transatlantic Translations: Communities of Education in Alcott and Brontë." *Little Women and the Feminist Imagination: Criticism, Controversy, Personal Essays*. Eds. Janice M. Alberghene and Beverly Lyon Clark. New York: Garland, 1999. 261–83.

Edwards, Jonathan. *Jonathan Edwards: Basic Writings*. Ed. Ola Elizabeth Winslow. New York: Signet, 1966.

Eiselein, Gregory. *Literature and Humanitarian Reform in the Civil War Era*. Bloomington: Indiana UP, 1996.

———, and Anne K. Phillips. *The Louisa May Alcott Encyclopedia*. Westport, CT: Greenwood, 2001.

Elbert, Sarah. *A Hunger for Home: Louisa May Alcott's Place in American Culture*. New Brunswick: Rutgers UP, 1987.

———. Introduction. *Louisa May Alcott on Race, Sex, and Slavery*. By Louisa May Alcott. Ed. Sarah Elbert. Boston: Northeastern UP, 1997. ix–lx.

Eliot, T. S. [An Introduction to *Huckleberry Finn*]. *Adventures of Huckleberry Finn: A Norton Critical Edition*. 1st ed. Eds. Sculley Bradley, Richmond Croom Beatty, and E. Hudson Long. New York: Norton, 1962. 320–27. Rpt. from T. S. Eliot. Introduction. *Adventures of Huckleberry Finn*. London: Cresset, 1950. vii–xvi.

Ellis, Charles Mayo. "An Essay on Transcendentalism." 1842. *The American Transcendentalists: Their Prose and Poetry*. Ed. Perry Miller. Baltimore: Johns Hopkins UP, 1957. 21–35.

Ellison, Ralph. "Change the Joke and Slip the Yoke." *Shadow and Act*. Rpt. from *Partisan Review* (Spring 1958). New York: Vintage, 1972. 45–59.

Emerson, Ralph Waldo. *Selected Writings of Ralph Waldo Emerson*. Ed. William H. Gilman. New York: Signet, 1965.

Engdahl, Sylvia. *Enchantress from the Stars*. New York: Atheneum, 1970.

Ensor, Allison. *Mark Twain and the Bible*. Lexington: U of Kentucky P, 1969.

Estes, Angela M., and Kathleen M. Lant. "Dismembering the Text: The Horror of Louisa May Alcott's *Little Women*." *Children's Literature* 17 (1989): 98–123.

———. "The Feminist Redeemer: Louisa Alcott's Creation of the Female Christ in *Work*." *Christianity and Literature* 40 (1991): 223–53.

Feidelson, Charles N. Jr. *Symbolism and American Literature*. Chicago: U of Chicago P, 1953.

Fellman, Anita Clair. " 'Don't Expect to Depend on Anybody Else': The Frontier as Portrayed in the Little House Books." *Children's Literature* 24 (1996): 101–16.

Fetterley, Judith. "*Little Women*: Alcott's Civil War." Little Women *and the Feminist Imagination: Criticism, Controversy, Personal Essays*. Eds. Janice M. Alberghene and Beverly Lyon Clark. New York: Garland, 1999. 27–42.

Fiedler, Leslie A. "Come Back to the Raft Ag'in, Huck Honey." *Partisan Review* 15 (June 1948): 664–71. Rpt. in *Huck Finn among the Critics*. Ed. M. Thomas Inge. Frederick, MD: University Publications, 1985. 93–101.

Fishkin, Shelley Fisher. "Mark Twain and Race." *A Historical Guide to Mark Twain*. Ed. Shelley Fisher Fishkin. New York: Oxford UP, 2002. 127–62.

———. "Mark Twain and Women." *Cambridge Companion to Mark Twain*. Ed. Forrest G. Robinson. Cambridge: Cambridge UP, 1995. 52–73.

———. *Was Huck Black? Mark Twain and African American Voices*. New York: Oxford UP, 1993.

Fitzhugh, Louise. *Harriet the Spy*. 1964. New York: Dell, 1984.

Flake, Sharon. *The Skin I'm In*. New York: Hyperion, 1998.

Foner, Philip S. *Mark Twain: Social Critic*. New York: International, 1958.

Foster, Shirley, and Judy Simons. *What Katy Read: Feminist Re-Readings of "Classic" Stories for Girls*. Iowa City: U of Iowa P, 1995.

French, Marilyn. *The Women's Room*. 1977. New York: Jove, 1978.

"From *The Ladies Repository*." Rpt. in *Little Women: A Norton Critical Edition*. By Louisa May Alcott. Eds. Anne K. Phillips and Gregory Eiselein. New York: Norton, 2004. 549.

Garden, Nancy. *Annie on My Mind*. New York: Farrar, 1982.

———. *Good Moon Rising*. New York: Farrar, 1996.

Gerber, John C. "Mark Twain's Use of the Comic Pose." *PMLA* 77 (1962): 297–304.

Giles, Gail. *Shattering Glass*. Brookfield, CT: Roaring Brook, 2002.

Gillman, Susan. *Dark Twins: Imposture and Identity in Mark Twain's America*. Chicago: U of Chicago P, 1989.

Good, Harry G., and James D. Teller. *A History of American Education*, 3rd ed. New York: Macmillan, 1973.

Gribben, Alan. "'I Did Wish Tom Sawyer Was There': Boy-Book Elements in *Tom Sawyer* and *Huckleberry Finn*." *One Hundred Years of* Huckleberry Finn: *The Boy, His Book, and American Culture*. Eds. Robert Sattelmeyer and J. Donald Crowley. Columbia: U of Missouri P, 1985. 149–70.

———. *Mark Twain's Library: A Reconstruction*. 2 vols. Boston: Hall, 1980.

Griswold, Jerry. *Audacious Kids: Coming of Age in America's Classic Children's Books*. New York: Oxford UP, 1992.

Gullason, Thomas Arthur. "The 'Fatal' Ending of Huckleberry Finn." *American Literature* 29 (1957): 86–91.

Guy, Rosa. *Edith Jackson*. New York: Viking, 1978.

Hall, G. Stanley. *Adolescence: Its Psychology and Its Relations to Anthropology, Sociology, Sex, Crime, Religion, and Education*. 2 vols. New York: Appleton, 1905.

Hamilton, Virginia. *The Planet of Junior Brown*. 1971. New York: Collier, 1986.

Harris, Susan K. *The Courtship of Olivia Langdon and Mark Twain*. New York: Cambridge UP, 1996.

———. "Mark Twain and Gender." *A Historical Guide to Mark Twain*. Ed. Shelley Fisher Fishkin. New York: Oxford UP, 2002. 163–93.

———. *Mark Twain's Escape from Time: A Study of Patterns and Images*. Columbia: U of Missouri P, 1982.

Hays, John Q. *Mark Twain and Religion*. New York: Lang, 1989.

Heilbrun, Carolyn G. "Louisa May Alcott: The Influence of *Little Women*." *Women, the Arts, and the 1920s in Paris and New York*. Eds. Kenneth W. Wheeler and Virginia Lee Lussier. New Brunswick, NJ: Transaction, 1982. 20–26.

Hemingway, Ernest. *The Green Hills of Africa*. 1935. New York: Scribner, 1953.

Hendler, Glenn. *Public Sentiments: Structures of Feeling in Nineteenth-Century American Literature*. Chapel Hill: U of North Carolina P, 2001.

Henry, Peaches. "The Struggle for Tolerance: Race and Censorship in *Huckleberry Finn*." *Satire or Evasion? Black Perspectives on* Huckleberry Finn. Eds. James S. Leonard, Thomas A. Tenney, and Thadious M. Davis. Durham, NC: Duke UP, 1992. 25–48.

Herz, Sarah K., with Donald R. Gallo. *From Hinton to Hamlet: Building Bridges Between Young Adult Literature and the Classics*. Westport, CT: Greenwood, 1996.

Hill, Hamlin. *Mark Twain and Elisha Bliss*. Columbia: U of Missouri P, 1964.

———. *Mark Twain: God's Fool*. New York: Harper, 1973.

Hill, Hamlin, ed. and Introduction. *Mark Twain's Letters to his Publishers: 1867–1894*. Berkeley: U of California P, 1967.

Hinton, S. E. *The Outsiders*. 1967. New York: Dell, 1989.

Hoffman, Andrew. *Inventing Mark Twain: The Lives of Samuel Langhorne Clemens*. New York: Morrow, 1997.

Hunt, Peter. *An Introduction to Children's Literature*. New York: Oxford UP, 1994.

James, Henry. *Literary Criticism*. Vol. 1. New York: Viking, 1984.

Janeway, Elizabeth. *Between Myth and Morning: Women Awakening*. New York: Morrow, 1975.

Jehlen, Myra. "Banned in Concord: *Adventures of Huckleberry Finn* and Classic American Literature." *The Cambridge Companion to Mark Twain*. Ed. Forrest G. Robinson. Cambridge: Cambridge UP, 1995. 93–115.

Johnson, James L. *Mark Twain and the Limits of Power: Emerson's God in Ruins*. Knoxville: U of Tennessee P, 1982.

Jordan, Ellen. "The Christening of the New Woman: May 1894." *Victorian Newsletter* 63 (1983): 19–21.

Kaplan, Fred. *The Singular Mark Twain*. New York: Doubleday, 2003.

Kaplan, Justin. *Mr. Clemens and Mark Twain: A Biography*. New York: Simon, 1966.

Kesterson, David B. *Critics on Mark Twain*. Coral Gables, FL: U of Miami P, 1973.

Keyser, Elizabeth. *Whispers in the Dark: The Fiction of Louisa May Alcott*. Knoxville: U of Tennessee P, 1993.

Koistinen-Harris, Janice H. *Social Reform, Taste, and the Construction of Virtue in American Literature, 1870–1910*. Lewiston, NY: Mellen, 2002.

Korman, Gordon. *Jake, Reinvented.* New York: Hyperion, 2003.

Lacan, Jacques. "The Subject and the Other: Alienation." *The Four Fundamental Concepts of Psychoanalysis.* Ed. Jacques-Alain Miller. Trans. Alan Sheridan. New York: Norton, 1977. 209–15.

Lauber, John. *The Inventions of Mark Twain.* New York: Hill and Wang, 1990.

Leary, Lewis. "The Bankruptcy of Mark Twain." *Carrell* 9 (1968): 13–20.

Lee, Harper. *To Kill a Mockingbird.* 1960. New York: Warner, 1982.

Le Guin, Ursula K. *Tehanu.* New York: Macmillan, 1990.

LeMaster, J. R., and James D. Wilson. *The Mark Twain Encyclopedia.* New York: Garland, 1993.

Lewis, C. S. "On Three Ways of Writing for Children." *Only Connect: Readings on Children's Literature.* Eds. Sheila Egoff, G. T. Stubbs, and L. F. Ashley. New York: Oxford UP, 1969. 207–20.

MacLeod, Anne Scott. "The Common School." *Children's Literature Association Quarterly* 27 (2002–2003): 183–90.

Mailloux, Steven. "Reading *Huckleberry Finn*: The Rhetoric of Performed Ideology." *New Essays on* Adventures of Huckleberry Finn. Cambridge: Cambridge UP, 1985. 107–33.

Marks, Patricia. *Bicycles, Bangs, and Bloomers: The New Woman in the Popular Press.* Louisville: U of Kentucky P, 1990.

Marx, Leo. "Mr. Eliot, Mr. Trilling, and *Huckleberry Finn.*" *The American Scholar* 22 (1953): 423–40.

Matthews, Jean V. *The Rise of the New Woman: The Women's Movement in America, 1875–1930.* Chicago: Dee, 2003.

McCafferty, Megan. *Sloppy Firsts.* New York: Crown, 2001.

McCaffrey, Anne. *Dragonflight.* New York: Ballantine, 1968.

McKinley, Robin. *The Hero and the Crown.* New York: Greenwillow, 1985.

Mills, Claudia. "Choosing a Way of Life: *Eight Cousins* and *Six to Sixteen.*" *Children's Literature Association Quarterly* 14 (1989): 71–75.

Mintz, Steven. *Huck's Raft: A History of American Childhood.* Cambridge, MA: Belknap, 2004.

Moffitt, Cecil L. "The Historical Ending of *Adventures of Huckleberry Finn*: How Nigger Jim was Set Free." *American Literary Realism* 13 (1980): 280–83.

Morrison, Toni. *The Bluest Eye.* 1970. New York: Washington Square Press, 1972.

Mott, Frank Luther. *Golden Multitudes: The Story of Best Sellers in the United States.* New York: Macmillan, 1947.

Murphy, Ann B. "The Borders of Ethical, Erotic, and Artistic Possibilities in *Little Women.*" *Signs* 15 (1990): 562–85.

Nilon, Charles H. "The Ending of *Huckleberry Finn*: 'Freeing the Free Negro.'" *Satire or Evasion? Black Perspectives on* Huckleberry Finn. Ed. James S. Leonard, Thomas A. Tenney, and Thadious M. Davis. Durham, NC: Duke UP, 1992. 62–76.

Nimmo, Jenny. *Midnight for Charlie Bone.* New York: Orchard, 2002.

Nowell-Smith, Simon. *International Copyright Law and the Publisher in the Reign of Queen Victoria.* Oxford: Clarendon, 1968.

Oehlschlaeger, Fritz. "'Gwyne to Git Hung': the Conclusion of *Huckleberry Finn*." *One Hundred Years of* Huckleberry Finn: *The Boy, His Book, and American Culture.* Eds. Robert Sattelmeyer and J. Donald Crowley. Columbia: U of Missouri P, 1985. 117–27.

Paine, Albert Bigelow. *Mark Twain: A Biography.* New York: Harper, 1912.

Paolini, Christopher. *Eragon.* New York: Knopf, 2003.

Parker, Theodore. "A Discourse of the Transient and Permanent in Christianity." *The American Transcendentalists: Their Prose and Poetry.* Ed. Perry Miller. Baltimore: Johns Hopkins UP, 1957. 106–38.

Parsons, Coleman O. "The Devil and Samuel Clemens." *Virginia Quarterly Review* 23 (1947): 582–602.

Paterson, Katherine. *Jacob Have I Loved.* New York: Harper, 1980.

Paul, Lissa. "The Feminist Writer as Heroine in *Harriet the Spy*." *The Lion and the Unicorn* 13 (1989): 67–73.

Paulsen, Gary. *Hatchet.* New York: Simon, 1987.

———. *The Island.* New York: Orchard, 1988.

———. *The River.* New York: Dell, 1991.

Perkinson, Henry J. *The Imperfect Panacea: American Faith in Education, 1865–1990,* 3rd ed. New York: McGraw, 1991.

Phillips, Anne K. "The Prophets and the Martyrs: Pilgrims and Missionaries in *Little Women* and *Jack and Jill*." Little Women *and the Feminist Imagination: Criticism, Controversy, Personal Essays.* Eds. Janice M. Alberghene and Beverly Lyon Clark. New York: Garland, 1999. 213–37.

Phipps, William E. *Mark Twain's Religion.* Macon, GA: Mercer, 2003.

Powers, Ron. *Mark Twain: A Life.* New York: Free Press, 2005.

Pratt, Frederic Alcott, 1862–1910. Louisa May Alcott Literary Estate Papers. bMS Am 1130.17. Houghton Library, Harvard University, Cambridge, MA.

Reynolds, David S. *Beneath the American Renaissance: The Subversive Imagination in the Age of Emerson and Melville.* New York: Knopf, 1988.

Ricketson, Daniel. *Daniel Ricketson and His Friends.* Eds. Anna Ricketson and Walton Ricketson. 1902. New York: AMS, 1985.

Roberts Brothers. (Boston, Mass.). Letters to Louisa May Alcott. bMS Am 1130.8, folders 1–144. Houghton Library, Harvard University, Cambridge, MA.

Robinson, Forrest G. "Mark Twain, 1835–1910: A Brief Biography." *A Historical Guide to Mark Twain.* Ed. Shelley Fisher Fishkin. New York: Oxford UP, 2002. 13–51.

Romines, Ann. *Constructing the Little House: Gender, Culture, and Laura Ingalls Wilder.* Amherst: U of Massachusetts P, 1997.

Rowling, J. K. *Harry Potter and the Sorcerer's Stone.* New York: Scholastic, 1997.

Rubinstein, Gilbert M. "The Moral Structure of *Huckleberry Finn*." *College English* 18 (1956): 72–76.

Salinger, J. D. *The Catcher in the Rye.* Boston: Little, 1951.

Sanborn, Margaret. *Mark Twain: The Bachelor Years.* New York: Doubleday, 1990.

Saxton, Martha. *Louisa May: A Modern Biography of Louisa May Alcott.* Boston: Houghton, 1977.

Schmitz, Neil. "The Paradox of Liberation in *Huckleberry Finn*." *Texas Studies in Language and Literature* 13 (1971): 125–36.

Scott, Arthur L. *On the Poetry of Mark Twain: With Selections from His Verse*. Urbana: U of Illinois P, 1966.

Seelye, John. *Mark Twain in the Movies: A Meditation with Pictures*. New York: Viking, 1977.

Shealy, Daniel. "The Author-Publisher Relationships of Louisa May Alcott." *Book Research Quarterly* 3 (1987): 63–74.

———. "The Author-Publisher Relationships of Louisa May Alcott." Diss. U of South Carolina, 1985.

———. "Singing Mignon's Song: The Friendship of Ralph Waldo Emerson and Louisa May Alcott." *Emersonian Circles: Essays in Honor of Joel Myerson*. Eds. Wesley T. Mott and Robert E. Burkholder. Rochester, NY: U of Rochester P, 1997. 225–51.

———, ed. *Alcott in Her Own Time*. Iowa City: U of Iowa P, 2005.

Showalter, Elaine. *Sister's Choice: Tradition and Change in American Women's Writing*. Oxford: Clarendon, 1991.

Shulman, Robert. *Social Criticism and Nineteenth-Century American Fictions*. Columbia: U of Missouri P, 1987.

Sicherman, Barbara. "Reading *Little Women*: The Many Lives of a Text." *U.S. History as Women's History: New Feminist Essays*. Eds. Linda K. Kerber, Alice Kessler-Harris, and Kathryn Kish Sklar. Chapel Hill: U of North Carolina P, 1995. 245–66.

Small, Robert C., Jr. "The Literary Value of the Young Adult Novel." *Journal of Youth Services in Libraries* 6 (1992): 277–85.

Smiley, Jane. " 'Say It Ain't So, Huck': Second Thoughts on Mark Twain's 'Masterpiece.' " *Harper's* (Jan. 1996): 61–67.

Smith, Betty. *A Tree Grows in Brooklyn*. 1943. Cutchogue, NY: Buccaneer, 1976.

Smith, David Lionel. "Black Critics and Mark Twain." *The Cambridge Companion to Mark Twain*. Ed. Forrest G. Robinson. Cambridge: Cambridge UP, 1995. 116–28.

———. "Huck, Jim, and American Racial Discourse." *Satire or Evasion? Black Perspectives on* Huckleberry Finn. Eds. James S. Leonard, Thomas A. Tenney, and Thadious M. Davis. Durham, NC: Duke UP, 1992. 103–20.

Smith, Henry Nash. *Mark Twain: The Development of a Writer*. Cambridge, MA: Belknap, 1962.

Snicket, Lemony. *A Series of Unfortunate Events: The Bad Beginning*. New York: Harper, 1999.

Stahl, J. D. *Mark Twain, Culture and Gender: Envisioning America through Europe*. Athens, GA: U of Georgia P, 1994.

Steinbrink, Jeffrey. *Getting to be Mark Twain*. Berkeley: U of California P, 1991.

Stephens, John. *Language and Ideology in Children's Fiction*. New York: Longman, 1992.

Stern, Madeleine. Introduction. *The Feminist Alcott: Stories of a Woman's Power*. By Louisa May Alcott. Boston: Northeastern UP, 1996. vii–xxiii.

———. Introduction. *Louisa May Alcott: From Blood & Thunder to Hearth & Home*. Boston: Northeastern UP, 1998. 1–9.

————. Introduction. *Louisa May Alcott Unmasked: Collected Thrillers.* By Louisa May Alcott. Boston: Northeastern UP, 1995. xi–xxix.

————. *Louisa May Alcott.* Norman: U of Oklahoma P, 1950.

Stone, Albert E., Jr. *The Innocent Eye: Childhood in Mark Twain's Imagination.* New Haven, CT: Yale UP, 1961.

Stoneley, Peter. *Consumerism and American Girls' Literature, 1860–1940.* Cambridge: Cambridge UP, 2003.

————. *Mark Twain and the Feminine Aesthetic.* Cambridge: Cambridge UP, 1992.

Strickland, Charles. *Victorian Domesticity: Families in the Life and Art of Louisa May Alcott.* Tuscaloosa: U of Alabama P, 1985.

Tashjian, Janet. *The Gospel According to Larry.* New York: Dell, 2001.

Taylor, Mildred D. *Let the Circle Be Unbroken.* New York: Dial, 1981.

————. *The Road to Memphis.* New York: Dial, 1990.

————. *Roll of Thunder, Hear My Cry.* New York: Dial, 1976.

————. *Song of the Trees.* New York: Dial, 1975.

Tompkins, Jane. *Sensational Designs: The Cultural Work of American Fiction, 1790–1860.* New York: Oxford UP, 1985.

"Town Officers, 1884–85." Annual Reports of the Town Officers of Concord, Mass. for the Year Ending March 1, 1885. Boston: Thomas Todd, 1885.

Townsend, John Rowe. *Written for Children: An Outline of English Children's Literature.* London: Garnet Miller, 1965.

Trites, Roberta Seelinger. *Disturbing the Universe: Power and Repression in Adolescent Literature.* Iowa City: U of Iowa P, 2000.

————. "Hope, Despair, and Reform: Adolescent Novels of Social Hope." *Changing Concepts of Childhood and Children's Literature.* Eds. Vanessa Joosen and Katrien Vloeberghs. Newcastle, UK: Cambridge Scholars P, 2006. 3–16.

————. "'Queer Performances': Lesbian Politics in *Little Women.*" Little Women *and the Feminist Imagination: Criticism, Controversy, Personal Essays.* Eds. Janice M. Alberghene and Beverly Lyon Clark. New York: Garland, 1999. 139–60.

————. *Waking Sleeping Beauty: Feminist Voices in Children's Novels.* Iowa City: U of Iowa P, 1997.

Tuckey, John S. "Mark Twain's Later Dialogue: The 'Me' and the Machine." *American Literature* 41 (1970): 532–42.

Twain, Mark. *Adventures of Huckleberry Finn.* 1885. Intro. Justin Kaplan. New York: Random, 1996.

————. *The Adventures of Tom Sawyer.* 1876. Berkeley: U of California P, 1982.

————. *A Connecticut Yankee in King Arthur's Court.* 1889. Ed. Bernard L. Smith. Berkeley: U of California P, 1979.

————. "Corn-pone Opinions." 1923. *The Complete Essays of Mark Twain.* Ed. Charles Neider. Garden City, NY: Doubleday, 1963. 83–87.

————. "[Date, 1601.] Conversation, as it Was by the Social Fireside, in the Time of the Tudors." *Collected Tales, Sketches, Speeches, & Essays, 1852–1890.* [1876.] Ed. Louis J. Budd. New York: Library of America, 1992. 661–66.

————. "Disgraceful Persecution of a Boy." *Collected Tales, Sketches, Speeches, & Essays, 1852–1895*. Ed. Louis J. Budd. New York: Library Classics, 1992. 379–82.

————. "Eve's Diary." 1905. *Collected Tales, Sketches, Speeches, & Essays, 1891–1910*. Ed. Louis J. Budd. New York: Library of America, 1992. 695–709.

————. "Female Suffrage." *Mark Twain: Life as I Find It*. Ed. Charles Neider. Garden City, NY: Hanover, 1961. 10–21.

————. *The Innocents Abroad, or The New Pilgrim's Progress*. 1869. 2 vols. New York: Harper, 1904.

————. "Letters from the Earth." 1962. *Collected Tales, Sketches, Speeches, & Essays, 1891–1910*. Ed. Louis J. Budd. New York: Library of America, 1992. 880–928.

————. *Life on the Mississippi*. 1883. *Mississippi Writings*. Ed. Guy Cardwell. New York: Library of America, 1982. 217–616.

————. *Mark Twain at the Buffalo Express*. Eds. Joseph B. McCullough and Janice McIntire-Strasburg. DeKalb: Northern Illinois UP, 1999.

————. *Mark Twain-Howells Letters: The Correspondence of Samuel L. Clemens and William D. Howells, 1872–1910*. Eds. Henry Nash Smith and William M. Gibson. Cambridge, MA: Belknap, 1960.

————. *Mark Twain: Life as I Find It*. Ed. Charles Neider. Garden City, NY: Hanover, 1961.

————. *Mark Twain's Autobiography*. New York: Harper, 1924.

————. *Mark Twain's Letters*, 6 vols. Eds. Edgar Marquess Branch, Michael B. Frank, and Kenneth M. Sanderson. Berkeley: U of California P, 1987– .

————. *Mark Twain's Letters to his Publishers, 1867–1894*. Ed. Hamlin Hill. Berkeley: U of California P, 1967.

————. *Mark Twain's Notebooks*. Ed. Albert Bigelow Paine. New York: Harper, 1935.

————. *Mark Twain's Notebooks and Journals*. Ed. Frederick Anderson. Berkeley: U of California P, 1979.

————. "The Minstrel Show." *Mark Twain in Eruption*. Ed. Bernard DeVoto. 1922. New York: Harper, 1940. 110–18.

————. *The Mysterious Stranger. Mark Twain's Mysterious Stranger Manuscripts*. Ed. William H. Gibson. Berkeley: U of California P, 1969.

————. *Personal Recollections of Joan of Arc*. 1896. San Francisco: Ignatius, 1989.

————. *The Prince and the Pauper*. 1882. New York: Harper, 1909.

————. "The Private History of a Campaign That Failed." 1885. *Huck Finn; Pudd'nhead Wilson; No. 44, The Mysterious Stranger; and Other Writings*. New York: Library of America, 2000. 649–68.

————. *The Selected Letters of Mark Twain*. Ed. Charles Neider. New York: Harper, 1982.

————. "Some Thoughts on the Science of Onanism." [1879.] *Collected Tales, Sketches, Speeches, & Essays, 1852–1890*. Ed. Louis J. Budd. New York: Library of America, 1992. 722–24.

————. "The Story of the Bad Little Boy that Bore a Charmed Life." *Collected Tales, Sketches, Speeches, and Essays, 1852–1895*. Ed. Louis J. Budd. New York: Library Classics, 1992. 191–94.

————. "The Story of the Good Little Boy Who Did Not Prosper." *Collected Tales, Sketches, Speeches, and Essays, 1852–1895*. Ed. Louis J. Budd. New York: Library Classics, 1992. 374–78.

————. *Tom Sawyer Abroad*. 1896. *Tom Sawyer Abroad; Tom Sawyer, Detective; and Other Stories, Etc., Etc.* New York: Harper, 1902. 1–111.

————. *Tom Sawyer, Detective*. 1896. *Tom Sawyer Abroad; Tom Sawyer, Detective; and Other Stories, Etc., Etc.* New York: Harper, 1902. 112–90.

————. *[The Tragedy of] Pudd'nhead Wilson*. 1894. Ed. Sidney E. Berger. New York: Norton, 2005.

————. "A True Story, Repeated Word for Word as I Heard It." 1874. *Collected Tales, Sketches, Speeches, and Essays, 1852–1895*. Ed. Louis J. Budd. New York: Library Classics, 1992. 578–82.

————. "The Turning Point of My Life." *Collected Tales, Sketches, Speeches, and Essays, 1891–1910*. Ed. Louis J. Budd. New York: Library Classics, 1992. 929–38.

————. *Wapping Alice*. Ed. Hamlin Hill. Berkeley: Friends of the Bancroft Library, 1981.

————. *What Is Man? and Other Essays*. New York: Harper, 1917.

Vogelback, Arthur. *The Publication and Reception of* Huckleberry Finn *in America*. Chicago: U of Chicago Libraries, 1939.

Voigt, Cynthia. *Bad Girls*. New York: Scholastic, 1996.

————. *Come a Stranger*. New York: Atheneum, 1986.

————. *Dicey's Song*. New York: Atheneum, 1982.

————. *Homecoming*. 1981. New York: Atheneum, 1989.

————. *The Runner*. New York: Atheneum, 1985.

————. *Seventeen Against the Dealer*. New York: Atheneum, 1989.

————. *A Solitary Blue*. New York: Atheneum, 1983.

von Ziegesar, Cecily. *Gossip Girl*. Boston: Little, 2002.

Wallace, John H. "The Case Against *Huck Finn*." *Satire or Evasion? Black Perspectives on* Huckleberry Finn. Eds. James S. Leonard, Thomas A. Tenney, and Thadious M. Davis. Durham, NC: Duke UP, 1992. 16–24.

Washington, Booker T. *The Booker T. Washington Papers*, Vol. 10. Eds. Louis R. Harlan and Raymond W. Smock. Urbana: U of Illinois P, 1981.

Webster, Jean. *Daddy-Long-Legs*. 1912. New York: Puffin, 1995.

Webster, Samuel Charles. *Mark Twain: Business Man*. Boston: Little, 1946.

Weir, Robert E. "Mark Twain and Social Class." *A Historical Guide to Mark Twain*. Ed. Shelley Fisher Fishkin. New York: Oxford UP, 2002. 195–225.

Welland, Dennis. *Mark Twain in England*. London: Chatto, 1978.

Wells, David F. "Hodge, Taylor and Bushnell." *Eerdman's Handbook to Christianity in America*. Mark A. Noll, et al., eds. Grand Rapids, MI: Eerdman, 1983. 232–33.

Welter, Barbara. "The Cult of True Womanhood: 1820–1860." *American Quarterly* 18 (1966): 151–64.

Wilder, Laura Ingalls. *Little House on the Prairie.* 1935. New York: Harper, 1971.

———. *Little Town on the Prairie.* 1941. New York: Harper, 1981.

Willis, Resa. *Mark and Livy: The Love Story of Mark Twain and the Woman Who Almost Tamed Him.* New York: Atheneum, 1992.

Wilson, James D. "Religious and Esthetic Vision in Mark Twain's Early Career." *Canadian Review of American Studies* 17 (1986): 155–72.

Wolff, Virginia Euwer. *Make Lemonade.* New York: Holt, 1993.

Woodard, Frederick, and Donnarae MacCann. "Minstrel Shackles and Nineteenth-Century 'Liberality' in *Huckleberry Finn.*" *Satire or Evasion? Black Perspectives on Huckleberry Finn.* Eds. James S. Leonard, Thomas A. Tenney, and Thadious M. Davis. Durham, NC: Duke UP, 1992. 141–53.

Woodson, Jacqueline. *From the Notebooks of Melanin Sun.* New York: Scholastic, 1995.

———. *If You Come Softly.* New York: Putnam's, 1998.

Yep, Laurence. *Dragonwings.* New York: Harper, 1975.

Zehr, Janet S. "The Responses of Nineteenth-Century Audiences to Louisa May Alcott's Fiction." *American Transcendental Quarterly: New Series* 1 (1987): 323–42.

Zwinger, Lynda. *Daughters, Fathers, and the Novel: The Sentimental Romance of Heterosexuality.* Madison: U of Wisconsin P, 1991.

INDEX

Abelard, 23

abjection, 75, 154

abolitionism, 9, 12, 15, 19, 32, 38, 44–45, 55, 57, 60, 96

Adams, Charles Francis, 131

Adams, William T., 133–34

Addams, Jane, 147

adolescence, 18–19, 28, 29–30, 33–34, 42, 50–53, 68, 71, 79–80, 92–93, 161–62, 164; defined, 33. *See also* youth

adolescent literature, 1, 39, 52–53, 54, 71, 76, 112–13, 114–15, 143–64. *See also* young adult novels

adolescent readers, 31, 70, 76, 92–93, 97, 105, 112, 113, 141, 163. *See also* audience

adolescent reform: characters, 1, 2, 30, 32, 34–35, 50–53, 54–55, 68, 69, 71, 75–76, 79–80, 82, 92–93, 97, 99–100, 104, 105, 112–13, 141–42, 143–44, 149–50, 161–64; defined, 143–44; novels, 38, 113, 143–64

African Americans, 9, 34–44, 52, 110, 147, 150–51, 152, 153, 156, 161; literature, 162

Ahlstrom, Sydney, 57, 58, 61, 62

Alcott, Abigail May "Abba," 6, 9, 10, 17, 21, 44, 98

Alcott, Anna, 6, 9, 10, 17–18

Alcott, Bronson, 6, 9, 10, 14, 17, 29, 61, 64, 88, 90, 103; *Conversations with Children on the Gospels,* 9

Alcott, Elizabeth "Lizzie," 9, 10, 17, 60

Alcott, Louisa May: and abolitionism, 12, 44–45, 60, 96; as author, 1, 11, 18–19, 28–30, 31, 50–53, 54, 58–59, 61–63, 69, 71, 72, 90–91, 92–93, 112–13, 127–28, 132, 140–41, 149, 154, 155–56, 159, 160, 163–64; autobiographical impulse, 24–25, 124, 148; biography, 1–30, 32, 35, 44–45, 60–64, 88, 95, 114–16, 118–28, 132–37, 139–42, 163; childhood of, 1, 7–11, 15, 29, 60; on childhood/youth, 7, 50–53, 54–55, 58–59, 61–63, 68–69, 71, 91, 104, 114–15, 130–31, 134–35, 163; and Civil War, 1, 12–14, 29, 47, 51, 163; and Clemens, 1–5, 22–30, 51–53, 54–55, 64–65, 66, 68–69, 70, 85–86, 90–91, 92, 105, 111–13, 114–16, 118, 120–21, 127–29, 131, 132, 134–37, 139–42, 160–64; death of, 14; depression, 17; drug use, 14; and education, 70–73, 85–91, 93–95, 97, 100, 102–04, 111; European travels, 25; family, 1, 5–8, 17–18, 20, 29, 123, 141, 163–64; finances, 1, 6, 7–8, 9, 14, 16–17, 29, 30, 123–24, 126–28, 132–35, 140, 141–42, 164; and gender, 20–23, 35, 44–50, 59, 69, 90–91, 92–104, 105, 112–13, 114, 123; health, 6, 14, 17, 29; humor, 24, 25, 86, 87, 90, 99; ideologies, 28, 31, 48, 52, 69, 70–71, 73, 77, 85–91; legacy, 1–2, 53, 103,

197

16, 29, 31–32, 33–44, 46, 50–53, 54,
59–60, 67, 68, 79, 83, 84, 86, 87, 91,
104, 111, 112, 114, 117, 132, 136, 144–
46, 150–51, 153, 155, 158, 159, 161; *The
Adventures of Tom Sawyer*, 3, 5, 8, 15,
18, 36, 67, 69, 80–83, 84, 85, 86, 91,
111, 112, 113, 114, 117, 128–32, 134, 136–
37, 159; *The Celebrated Jumping Frog
of Calaveras County*, 24, 138;
Christian Science, 64; *A Connecticut
Yankee in King Arthur's Court*, 16, 66,
67, 71, 76–80, 84, 85, 113, 117, 132;
"Corn-pone Opinions," 36; "The
Dandy Frightening the Squatter,"
115; "Date, 1601," 22; "Disgraceful
Persecution of a Boy," 170n; "An
Encounter with an Interviewer," 139;
"Eve's Diary," 16; "Female Suffrage,"
166n; *The Gilded Age*, 15, 25, 117, 141,
168n; *The Innocents Abroad*, 6, 15, 23–
29, 36, 43, 116–17, 127, 138, 169n,
179n; "Last Words of Great Men," 2;
"Letters from the Earth," 22, 104,
169n; *Life on the Mississippi*, 8, 15, 25,
65, 93, 129; *Mark Twain's
Autobiography*, 36, 37; *Mark Twain's
Notebooks*, 37, 178n; *Mark Twain's
Sketches, New and Old*, 117; "The
Minstrel Show," 37; *The Mysterious
Stranger*, 6, 64, 161; *Personal
Recollections of Joan of Arc*, 16, 23, 69,
92, 104–13, 116, 171n, 178n; *The
Prince and the Pauper*, 15, 16, 18, 69,
70, 71, 72, 73–76, 77, 79, 80, 84, 91,
104, 106, 112, 113, 116, 117, 138, 143;
"The Private History of a Campaign
That Failed," 11–12; "Reflections on
Religion," 64; *Roughing It*, 15, 117,
140; *Selected Letters*, 17, 36, 65, 66,
67; "Some Thoughts on the Science
of Onanism," 22, "The Story of the
Bad Little Boy That Bore a Charmed
Life," 120; "The Story of the Good

Little Boy Who Did Not Prosper,"
120; "To the Person Sitting in
Darkness," 64; *Tom Sawyer Abroad*,
71, 83–84, 85, 113, 116, 132; *Tom
Sawyer, Detective*, 71, 84–85, 113, 116;
The Tragedy of Pudd'nhead Wilson, 6,
16, 110, 161; *A Tramp Abroad*, 117; "A
True Story," 36; "The Turning Point
in My Life," 178n; *Wapping Alice*, 22;
What Is Man?, 6, 54, 64, 66
Clemens, Susy, 15, 16, 17, 20, 105
Cobbe, Frances Power, 98
Coleridge, Samuel Taylor: *Aids to
Reflection*, 58
colonialism, 84
commercialism, 29, 63. *See also*
consumerism
commodification, 20, 25, 115, 123, 141–
42, 159
community, 1, 18–19, 30, 51, 52, 59, 146,
147, 150–51
Concord, 3, 7, 9, 10, 13, 19, 73, 95
Concord Free Trade Club, 3
Concord Public Library, 3, 59–60
Confederacy, 11–12
Congregationalism, 32, 55–59
consumerism, 25, 32, 145, 157, 158–59.
See also commercialism
Conway, Moncure Daniel, 62, 67, 123,
131–32, 136, 137
Cooley, John, 16, 19–20, 105
Coolidge, Susan: *What Katy Did*, 72
Cormier, Robert, 158; *I Am the Cheese*,
158
Covington, Dennis, 145; *Lizard*, 145
Crutcher, Chris, 144; *Chinese Handcuffs*,
145; *Crazy Horse Electric Game*, 144–
45; *Staying Fat for Sarah Byrnes*, 145
Cushman, Charlotte, 20, 98

Daily Alta California, 15, 116, 138
Darling, Richard L., 115, 120, 133–34
de Beauvoir, Simone, 146

McCaffrey, Anne, 160; *Dragonflight*, 160
McCullers, Carson: *The Member of the Wedding*, 161
McKinley, Robin, 160; *The Hero and the Crown*, 160
Merry's Museum, 72, 115
Methodism, 32, 57
Middle East, 24, 29, 65, 83–84, 116
Mintz, Steven, 70
Mississippi River, 8, 11, 18, 20, 155
Mitchell, Margaret: *Gone With the Wind*, 181n
Montessori, Maria, 88
Montgomery, L. M.: *Anne of Green Gables*, 146
moral development, 32, 38–44, 46–50, 71, 94, 103, 149
morphine, 14
More, Hannah, 47
Morrison, Toni: *The Bluest Eye*, 161
Mott, Frank Luther, 3, 112
Moulton, Louise Chandler, 22; *Our Famous Women*, 169n

Name-of-the-Father, 106, 107, 110
Napoleon Bonaparte, 67, 110
Napoleon III, 26
Native Americans, 36, 78–79, 80, 86–87, 98, 146
nature, 9, 41, 58, 59, 60–61, 64, 65, 69, 88, 89, 110, 111, 158, 163
Nevada Territory, 12
New Criticism, 162
New England, 3, 9, 35, 51, 57, 98
New Woman, 92–113, 178n; defined, 92
New York City, 8, 36, 145, 149, 150–51, 155, 156, 161
New York World, 3
The New Yorker, 181n
Nieriker, Louise Marie "Lulu," 17, 126
Nightingale, Florence, 98

Niles, Thomas, 17, 19, 23, 95–96, 118, 119–20, 121, 122–23, 124–27, 129, 135, 140. *See also* Roberts Brothers
nonconformity, 48, 68
Nook Farm, 18, 67

Oates, Joyce Carol, 146
Olive Branch, 10, 115
Oliver Optic's Magazine, 134
opium, 14
oral tradition, 36
Osgood, James, 138
Othello, 87
other(ness), 14, 41, 46
Ozick, Cynthia, 146

Paige Typesetting Machine, 16
Paine, Albert Bigelow, 36, 37, 66, 67, 116
Pantheism, 63
Parker, Theodore, 55–59, 60, 61, 62, 63, 68, 73
Paterson, Katherine, 145, 156; *Lyddie*, 145
Patmore, Coventry, 104; "The Angel in the House," 104
Paulsen, Gary, 145; *Hatchet*, 145; *The Island*, 145; *The River*, 145
pedophilia, 20, 22–23
penal reform, 71, 74, 75
Père la Chaise, 26
Perkinson, Henry J., 70
Pestalozzi, Johann, 88, 90
Peterson's Magazine, 115
Petry, Ann, 147
Phelps, Elizabeth Stuart, 98
Phillips, Anne K., 25, 112
Phillips, Wendell, 45
Phipps, William E., 15, 23, 58, 65, 66, 68
picaresque, 144, 145, 146
plasmon, 16
Porter, Eleanor H.; *Pollyanna*, 73, 146